Debates in Economic History

Edited by Peter Mathias

British Agriculture
1875–1914

GW00568769

British Agriculture
1875–1914

edited with an introduction by
P. J. PERRY

METHUEN & CO LTD
11 NEW FETTER LANE LONDON EC4

First published 1973 by Methuen & Co Ltd
Introduction © by P. J. Perry
Printed in Great Britain by
Richard Clay (The Chaucer Press), Ltd,
Bungay, Suffolk

SBN 416 75940 8 hardback
SBN 416 75950 5 paperback

Distributed in the USA by
HARPER & ROW PUBLISHERS, INC.
BARNES & NOBLE IMPORT DIVISION

Contents

Preface

The first volume to be published in this series was concerned with the relations between agriculture and economic growth during the initial phases of industrialization in England. The agricultural transformation experienced in Britain during the last quarter of the nineteenth century, the topic of the present book, provides a complementary theme. In most general textbooks the chapter covering this episode has been billed as 'agricultural depression' but, as Dr Perry's introduction and the succeeding articles make clear, this blanket term is a misnomer for rapid and complex changes in agriculture, which greatly enhanced the economic efficiency of British farming under circumstances of intense social and economic pressure.

The wider implications which this process had for the efficiency of the British economy as a whole have not been stressed as much as the social benefits brought by a fall of over 40 per cent in the price of food during these years. The labour force in farming had been growing until 1851 (despite the relative fall in its share of the total labour force). But, between 1861 and 1901, while the redeployment of activities in agriculture away from cereal production maintained and increased the value of total agricultural production, over half a million people left the farms. This has been the most dramatic, and the most sustained, change in economic structure experienced by the British economy: when the nineteenth century opened almost a third of the national income and over a third of the labour force were sustained by agriculture; by its close a mere 6 per cent of the national income came from agriculture, produced by 9 per cent of the labour force. At this date a third of the labour force in the United States, France and Germany, and over 40 per cent of the labour force in Denmark, Sweden and Italy, were still on the farm. We have heard much of the economic advantages enjoyed since 1945 by continental countries transferring labour from low-productivity agricultural pursuits to industry, as their farm sectors have run down towards British levels. The contribution of agriculture in the process of advancing productivity in the British economy in the later nineteenth century needs equivalent recognition (as does the rise in productivity of British agriculture itself through mechanization and science, which brought it to be the most efficient in Europe in these same years).

The redeployment of resources in British agriculture, and the contraction of the labour force, were so sustained because there was no significant legislative interference to counter the effects of international competition and world prices upon British farmers and landowners. This was so in generations when tariff barriers were rising across the world; and where most European nations were seeking to protect themselves from the flood of agricultural produce released from the new world. In longer perspective we can see exactly how unique this was in British history: a short interlude, it might be argued, between the long centuries before the mid-nineteenth century when landowners had sufficient political power to ensure legislation controlling the trade in agricultural products in their favour and that extraordinary worldwide political phenomenon of the mid-twentieth century – in the most advanced industrial nations no less than in the developing world – of the renaissance in the political influence of the farmer.

All Souls College, Oxford   PETER MATHIAS
14 July 1972

Acknowledgements

The editor wishes to thank the following for their help:

The Erskine Fund of the University of Canterbury; Dr R. G. Cant; Dr I. J. Catanach; Mr A. T. G. McArthur; the late Mr T. W. Fletcher; Mrs J. Robertson; the library staff of the University of Canterbury, Lincoln College, the Canterbury Public Library and the Dorset County Museum.

Editor's Introduction

THE BACKGROUND

The last quarter of the nineteenth century was a turning-point and climacteric in British economic history. The period was and is often referred to as the 'great depression'; it is perhaps more accurately epitomized as a period of economic change and reorientation, when new industries and new regions challenged the pre-eminence, at least in terms of growth and expansion, of the industrial pacemakers of the middle decades of the century. Such a view of the depression appears in the writings of Beales[1] and Wilson[2] to mention but two scholars whose work in this field has been widely influential and of a generally revisionist character. The received view of general and widespread agricultural depression, particularly associated with the writings of Lord Ernle,[3] has been similarly challenged by several economic historians, notably Fletcher, who, together with geographers such as Coppock, have emphasized the regionally variable character of the depression and the fact that during this period the collapse of some sectors of the agricultural economy was paralleled by the expansion of others.[4] It is however indisputable that the last quarter of the nineteenth century was a period of agricultural crisis; whether or not the period was one of general economic depression, it was certainly one of agricultural depression, of

---

[1] H. L. Beales, ' "The Great Depression" in industry and trade', *Economic History Review*, V (1934), pp. 65–75.

[2] C. Wilson, 'Economy and society in late Victorian Britain', *Economic History Review*, XVIII (1965), pp. 183–98.

[3] Lord Ernle (R. E. Prothero), *English Farming Past and Present*, 6th ed. (London, Heinemann, 1961), especially chapter 18 (reprinted in this volume). (Ernle's position as an historian of the depression is aptly summarized in O. R. McGregor's introduction to this edition, pp. lxxxi–xc.)

[4] T. W. Fletcher, 'The Great Depression of English agriculture 1873–96', *Economic History Review*, XIII (1960–1), pp. 417–32; 'Lancashire livestock farming during the Great Depression', *Agricultural History Review*, IX (1961), pp. 17–42; J. T. Coppock, 'Agricultural changes in the Chilterns 1875–1900', *Agricultural History Review*, IX (1961), pp. 1–16. (Reprinted in this volume.)

falling prices, more numerous bankruptcies, lower rents and untenanted farms. These were the facts which left contemporary farmers, landowners and agricultural pundits in no doubt as to the reality of their problems – problems which were to continue with only one brief respite until the 1940s. By contrast the first three-quarters of the nineteenth century had been characterized by agricultural prosperity and technical progress save for a period of general depression after 1815, and a much shorter crisis after the repeal of the Corn Laws in 1846. In particular the 1850s and 1860s had been very prosperous, a 'golden age' for 'high farming', with high investment and high returns for both landlord and tenant.

The historical context is of great importance in the understanding and interpretation of the agricultural depression – particularly in its early phase. While it is possible to agree with Jones[1] that agricultural developments in the 1850s and 1860s foreshadowed some of the salient features of the depression, the transition from prosperity to misfortune was generally unexpected and bewildering to most of those directly concerned. Many assumed that it was just a temporary state of affairs caused by bad seasons and would correct itself in no more than a few years, a view which persisted in some quarters into the 1880s.[2] The evident transition from success to failure, from prosperity to poverty, was however no more than the basic phenomenon common to any depression. Other changes originating in the depression may be regarded as of greater long-term importance because they became the normal circumstances and characteristics of British farming in the twentieth century. Farming ceased to be either Britain's major industry, in terms of employment of labour and capital and of social and political influence, or the source of the greater part of the nation's food supply. Its contribution to the gross national product fell from 20 per cent in the late 1850s to 6 per cent in the late 1890s; in 1880 one-sixth of Britain's supply of meat was imported; imported meat made

[1] E. L. Jones, 'The changing basis of English agricultural prosperity 1853–1873', *Agricultural History Review*, X (1962), pp. 102–10.

[2] Thus, for example, Sir Matthew Ridley, M.P., a Northumberland landowner, ascribed the depression almost entirely to bad seasons in his evidence before the Royal Commission on Agriculture in May 1881 (Question 45821).

up more than half of a considerably larger total in 1914.[1] International consequences were also important. British food prices began to diverge from those of continental Europe where the experience of depression in the last decades of the century generated a revived protectionism.[2] A special commercial (as well as sentimental) relationship developed between Britain and its food suppliers, New Zealand for example. Both of these circumstances have now become significant in the context of Britain's relationship with the European Common Market.

Paradoxically this decline in the importance of agriculture was accompanied by an increasingly commercial outlook among agriculturalists, a greater rather than a lesser interest in the business side of farming. Only as better businessmen as well as technically more efficient farmers and landowners was it possible to survive the strains and stresses of depression. Not all the spectacular innovations and practices of mid-century high farming – the lavish application of artificial fertilizers, ambitious building programmes – remained economically viable during the depression. Economy became the prime objective, with the result that many accepted practices became irrelevant luxuries which had to be given up. However the depression was also a period of innovations, often of long-lasting significance; dairy farming and horticulture expanded to supply an increasingly numerous and prosperous urban population; cereal production yielded preeminence to grassland farming; many farmers and labourers abandoned agriculture, the former to be replaced by new men with new ideas who in many cases had travelled the length or breadth of Britain to take up vacant farms.

The agricultural depression was then a phenomenon as much of change as of decay – 'not a uniform tendency to move in one direction but a marked proclivity to move in several different directions at once'.[3] It was made up of the experience

[1] S. B. Saul, *The Myth of the Great Depression* (London, Macmillan, 1969), pp. 35–6; J. Burnett, *Plenty and Want: A Social History of Diet in England from 1815 to the Present Day* (London, Nelson, 1966), p. 100.

[2] For example in France the Mèline tariff of 1892, although some historians would also stress the industrial element in these developments.

[3] C. Wilson, op. cit., p. 198.

and response of thousands of individuals, facing – and commonly failing to understand in their own particular circumstances – the novel experience of financial misfortune and changing status in economy and society.

THE CAUSES OF THE DEPRESSION

The collapse of cereal prices from the late 1870s onwards has always been regarded as the quintessence of the depression and as such has attracted the attention of numerous economists;[1] wheat sold at an average price of 55s. a quarter in the period 1870–4, at 28s. in the period 1895–9. There were similar, albeit lesser, falls in other cereal prices. To most farmers such a fall in the value of their produce, matched only belatedly and in part by a reduction in costs, was potentially or actually disastrous. The fall in prices followed increased grain imports – 30 million cwt in 1870, almost 70 million by 1900 – mainly from the newly opened-up wheat lands of the North American prairies and Argentina. These two regions exported 15 million cwt of grain to Britain in 1870, almost 60 million in 1900. This fall in prices generated considerable agricultural depression in the old-established farming regions of the eastern United States as well as in Britain. It was however not only a matter of new railways giving access to virgin arable lands – and in the case of the USA the return to political stability after the Civil War – but of improvements in the technology of railway and marine transportation. The over-all result was lower costs. In the late 1860s it had cost 15s. 11d. to move a quarter of wheat from Chicago to Liverpool; in the early 1900s it cost 3s. 11d. The difference in cost between the two dates represents almost half the fall in British wheat prices during this period.[2] Technology, political circumstances

---

[1] Two examples are reprinted in this volume: H. M. Conacher, 'Causes of the fall in agricultural prices between 1875 and 1895', *Scottish Journal of Agriculture,* XIX (1936), pp. 239–47; M. Olson and C. C. Harris, 'Free trade in "corn": a statistical study of the prices and production of wheat in Great Britain from 1873 to 1914', *Quarterly Journal of Economics,* LXXIII (1959), pp. 145–68.

[2] P. Besse, *La Crise et l'évolution de l'agriculture en Angleterre de 1875 à nos jours. Essai d'histoire économique* (Paris, 1910), p. 32. This useful study of the depression appears to be little known among English historians; likewise Albert Dulac,

and perhaps indirectly a succession of gold discoveries in the middle of the nineteenth century, had at last brought about the situation feared by the proponents of protection in the 1840s.

The livestock producer was confronted with a collapse of prices apparently of a lesser magnitude than that which faced the cereal grower, and one which occurred later in the depression. At one extreme the price of dairy products fell by no more than 20 to 25 per cent at the most during the depression, somewhat less than the overall fall in prices during this period.[1] At the other extreme Lincoln wool which fetched more than 20d. per lb during three consecutive years early in the 1870s fetched less than 10d. per lb between 1897 and 1903.[2] In general, however, it is much more difficult to generalize about the livestock producer's experience of the depression than the cereal grower's, and this is particularly true with respect to store and fat cattle and sheep. Whereas an official record of cereal prices was kept, and published in the *London Gazette* (although it is a far from perfect indication of prices paid and received), those quoted by scholars for livestock products are local and unofficial approximations, or single cases used as examples. Not only is less known about prices fetched by livestock products but more factors are involved than a mere fall in prices. In the first place there was a considerable symbiosis of cereal husbandry and livestock production, the high farming of the mid-century having emphasized, at best perfected, a mixed and intensive farming system. Jones[3] has suggested that the traditional farmer's view of such systems – a view which died very hard – that the livestock element paid its way not directly but through muck and

---

Agriculture et libre-échange dans le Royaume–Uni (Paris, 1903) and P. Flavigny, *La Régime agraire en Angleterre au XIXme siècle et la concentration de l'exploitation agricole* (thèse-lettres, Paris, 1932).

[1] For a discussion of dairy farming see G. E. Fussell, *The English Dairy Farmer 1500–1900* (London, Cass, 1966). The sale of fresh milk proved more remunerative and better protected from overseas competition than butter and cheese making.

[2] P. Besse, op. cit., pp. 343–4.

[3] E. L. Jones, 'The changing basis of English agricultural prosperity 1853–1873'.

thus grain, was erroneous. However, as successful a depression farmer and experimenter as Edward Strutt found that his cost accounts, themselves an innovation, showed that feeding cattle on traditional lines – mixed high farming – did not pay, and he gave up this activity.[1] Falling grain prices might as effectively jeopardize the grazier's economy, as increase his prosperity by reducing the price of a major input.

Feed and fertilizer prices were, however, but one of the livestock fattener's concerns. His most important margin was much less certain and predictable, the difference between the price of lean store stock purchased from breeders, and the market value of the same beasts as fatstock at a later date.[2] The major uncertainty lay in the time interval; the price fetched by fat beasts would almost certainly change, likewise the cost of imported feeding stuffs; and utterly unpredictable was the availability of grass and other farm-produced feeding stuffs during this period.[3] These uncertainties affected not only the price the feeder and fattener might obtain for fatstock, but also, in the light of his judgement as to the likely course of future events, the price he was ready to pay the rearer and breeder of lean store stock. The skill of the feeder and fattener lay in buying in store cattle, necessarily of variable quality, fattening them as quickly and cheaply as possible and selling them fat at the best time and price. A notoriously risky, hazardous and capital-demanding enterprise – as one contemporary writer aptly expressed the position, 'if a man can live by grazing he can live without it'[4] – the grazier's business demanded less time and constant attention, but more skill and

---

[1] Sir William Gavin, *Ninety Years of Family Farming: the Story of Lord Rayleigh's and Strutt and Parker Farms* (London, Hutchinson, 1967), pp. 85–6. Chapters 5, 6 and 7 cover the period 1871–1914 with particular reference to the Terling estate in north Essex.

[2] Almost every writer and speaker on the topic tries to stress this point; e.g. H. Overman, a Norfolk tenant-farmer, in evidence before the Royal Commission on Agriculture in June 1881 (questions 51870–1).

[3] A useful brief survey, with respect to cattle, appears in J. Wrightson, *Livestock* (London, Cassell, 1892), p. 48.

[4] Quoted by S. B. L. Druce, an assistant commissioner appointed by the Royal Commission on Agriculture to report on eastern England, in his final report (*British Parliamentary Papers*, 1882, XV, pp. 247–362) on Leicestershire.

judgement than cereal cultivation or dairying. The aim of the rearer of lean store cattle, usually a farmer in the hills, was to produce robust and healthy stock which would fatten quickly and to sell them at the opportune moment; his fixed costs were low, but his opportunities for flexibility of practice were limited, and he was largely at the mercy of the seasons both in his own district and in his market.

Two further changing circumstances have been suggested as exacerbating the livestock producer's problems during this period. For much of this period foreign store cattle (save from Canada) were not allowed to enter Britain, but frozen meat, and live fat cattle for slaughter at the port of entry, could be imported.[1] To the grazier this represented an embargo on cheap raw materials coupled with competition from the finished product. Secondly the grassing-down of arable land – a characteristic response to falling grain prices – was thought to have upset the established regional and seasonal balance of the livestock industry. More stock were needed to feed off an increased spring and summer supply of grass than could be fed through autumn and winter in the hill country, thus disrupting markets and prices.[2]

The livestock producer was undoubtedly affected by the depression, the upland breeder as well as the lowland feeder, but the complex economy of this branch of farming, at least in comparison with cereal production and even allowing for some degree of symbiosis, makes generalization difficult. These problems, as much as the realities of the situation, may well be why most writers on the depression have placed more emphasis on the cereal producer's difficulties. Few scholars

[1] A. Hutcheson, 'The past and future of Scottish agriculture', *Transactions of the Highland and Agricultural Society of Scotland*, 5th series, XI (1899), pp. 121–35. The transatlantic live cattle trade was investigated, because of allegations of cruelty, by an interdepartmental committee in 1890 and 1891 (*British Parliamentary Papers*, 1890–1, LXXVIII, 269–568); cattle from the USA had to be slaughtered at the port of entry, but not so Canadian cattle until 1893. By 1890 some 400,000 cattle from the USA and over 100,000 from Canada were imported. The livestock trade was in turn affected by the import of frozen meat and by the imposition of much more severe disease-control regulations in 1900. The first cargo of frozen mutton left New Zealand in 1882; by 1889 more than a million carcasses a year were exported.

[2] A. Hutcheson, op. cit.

have been able to match their assertions – that the livestock producer was less severely affected than the grain grower – with a reasoned support of this position in depth and detail sufficient to counter the contemporary complaint of the pastoralist.

Adverse seasons were a third cause of depression, of concern to both cultivator and pastoralist. 1875, 1877, 1878 and above all 1879[1] were wet summers; the quality of the grain harvested was poor, quantity was below average and costs above. However the massive growth of imports inhibited the rise in prices which would formerly have compensated farmers in such circumstances. Difficult years later in the depression were more characteristically summer droughts – 1892, 1893, 1895 and 1896 – and as such more of a problem to the livestock producer.[2] And by this date the rather marginal role of adverse seasons as a cause of depression was well understood. The severe problem to rearer and fattener earlier in the depression was disease, associated with unusually cool and wet summers. As rinderpest and pleuro-pneumonia had decimated the cattle population in the 1860s, so liver-rot cut back the sheep population a decade later. Some estimates suggest that 10 per cent of Britain's sheep population perished, and at a time when overseas competition was severely affecting wool prices. In some localities a much larger proportion of the sheep population died, but the grazier's and shepherd's skills counted for a great deal in this context as in any other. Some degree of prevention was possible, and if this

[1] This notoriously cold and wet summer was commented upon by Tennyson in his 'Prefatory poem to my brother's sonnets – midnight June 30th, 1879':

> *Midnight – and joyless June gone by,*
> *And from the deluged park*
> *The cuckoo of a worse July*
> *Is calling thro' the dark.*

Several farmers and landowers from the north and west later recalled, however, that for their district 1879 had been quite a good year, e.g. R. S. Olver of Bodmin, a witness before the Royal Commission on Agricultural Depression in December 1894 (question 37432).

[2] Again some areas benefited. R. H. Pringle, one of the best-known assistant commissioners of the Royal Commission on Agricultural Depression, was able in 1895 to describe the very dry summer of 1893 as splendid for the cleaning of clay land, much of which had become foul with weeds as a result of labour economies (question 47550).

failed, 'rotted' sheep could profitably be fattened if their condition were noted in good time.[1] Nevertheless the evidence suggests that in some Welsh and West-of-England counties livestock disease was as much of a disaster as falling grain prices in the eastern counties during the first period of acute depression.

The depressed condition of British farming from the 1870s must then be related to several circumstances. It was part of a general deflation, a widespread fall in prices and slowing-down of economic activity related to such matters as the relative scarcity of gold. More directly depression was brought about by the opening up of new land in the Americas and Australasia in a new political, technological and not least demographic environment. The adverse seasons of the later 1870s were important not so much as basic causes of the sustained depression, but because they misled almost everyone concerned with the fortunes of agriculture as to the reality of the new situation, and because they drained farmers' and landowners' reserves of cash and courage at the very start of a difficult period.

THE COURSE OF THE DEPRESSION

Discussion of causes of the depression has necessarily involved presenting an outline of its main chronological features. Its antecedents can be traced back at least as far as 1846 – some extreme radicals might prefer to cite the misty origins of the landlord and tenant system which reached its apogee in the middle of the century. In all probability the political circumstances of the mid-century, the Crimean War, the American Civil War, were all that prevented the short-lived depression which followed Corn Law repeal from growing into a major crisis.

By 1873 quite characteristic depression problems had appeared on the heavy Essex clays. The papers of John Oxley

---

[1] E. L. Jones, *Seasons and Prices. The Role of the Weather in English Agricultural History* (London, Allen and Unwin, 1964), pp. 87–8. Liver-rot is caused by the flatworm, *fasciola hepatica*, ingested by sheep grazing on damp pastures. Since the life cycle of the worm involves a period in the liver of a water snail, liver-rot (or fluke) prevails only on low-lying and poorly drained pastures or in unusually wet and cold seasons such as 1879 when its occurrence may be widespread.

Parker, an Essex land-agent, record that in that year farms were in hand (i.e. unlet) on Lord Rayleigh's Terling estate; by 1874 tenant farmers were asking for rent reductions, and by 1877 Parker was advising that almost any action necessary to keep a tenant on his farm – rent remission or reduction, drainage for example – should be taken. Already tenants were expressing apprehension as to the future prospects for the heavy clays; in one case in the 1870s Oxley Parker quotes a tenant who arrived at a farm with his goods and chattels, but turned back with the words 'I'm not going to stop here; I shall be ruined if I do'.[1] 1874 was widely regarded as the last of the good years in southern and eastern England and recalled as such by several Royal Commission witnesses twenty years later.[2] 1879 was more often remembered as the beginning of hard times in the north and west[3] although there in fact farmers were less disastrously affected by bad seasons than in the southern and eastern lowlands. As the climax and culmination of a series of bad years 1879 was the apparent nadir of the first acute phase of depression, but in many instances its effects became apparent in bankruptcy, liquidation or departure only in the early 1880s.

The better seasons of the 1880s, a revival in the price of some livestock products – notably cheese – and a lessening of the ravages of liver-rot engendered some degree of optimism, some lessening of distress. Farmer bankruptcies, one index of the extent of depression, dropped quite markedly at the end of this decade.[4] Again this generalization is more true of southern and eastern Britain than of the highland north and west where 1885 witnessed something of an intensification of the depres-

[1] J. Oxley Parker (ed.), *The Oxley Parker Papers* (Colchester, Benham, 1964), especially chapters 6, 8 and 9.

[2] For example C. S. Read, a well-known Norfolk farmer, in his evidence before the Royal Commission on Agricultural Depression in April 1894 (question 16330).

[3] For example the evidence given to the Royal Commission in May 1895 by H. R. Hughes, a North Wales land-agent (question 50324).

[4] According to the *Annual Reports of the Board of Trade under section 131 of the Bankruptcy Act of 1883* (published annually in the *British Parliamentary Papers* from 1885) receiving orders against farmers were at their highest in 1886 (332) and 1895 (313); 1890 and 1891 (172 and 187) were good years, and between 1898 and 1914 the number of receiving orders exceeded 200 in only three years.

sion.[1] It is also likely that by the end of this decade reduced rents were providing some relief, and as a consequence there were fewer unlet farms and fewer farm sales (of live and dead stock and farming equipment) during this period than in the crises which preceded and followed it. As late as 1888 one writer could speak of a more cheerful prospect and, while recognizing that pasture was to an increasing extent the profitable part of any farm, recommended that a wheat crop should be grown as often as possible.[2] The same writer also spoke of home dominance of the meat market, but this was shortly to be ended by the full effects of the advent of marine refrigeration, pioneered during the 1880s.

The second acute phase of depression which developed in the 1890s was much more evidently related to low prices than to adverse seasons, although these latter were, as has been mentioned, a secondary problem. Imported frozen meat and butter poured on to the market and wheat reached its lowest official price, 22s. 10d. a quarter being the average price for 1894. In fact farmers often received less; writing in 1913 W. J. Malden recalled that he sold top grade wheat for 18s. a quarter in 1893.[3] The depression worsened such problems and fluctuations, forcing financially embarrassed farmers to sell as soon as possible after harvest – in some cases before the crop was harvested – and thus over-supplying the market. The depletion of the financial reserves of farmers and landowners, the result of twenty years of misfortune, also limited their ability to make further economies and changes or even to leave farming.[4] Once more, numerous farms were unlet, and a few – how many remains a matter of controversy – were completely abandoned.

---

[1] See note 3, p. xx.

[2] J. Walker, *Farming to Profit in Modern Times* (London, T. C. Jack, 1888), pp. vi–vii. Walker specifically excludes heavy clay land from this comment.

[3] W. J. Malden, 'The greater agriculture', *The Nineteenth Century and After*, LXXIV (1913), pp. 92–108. Farming diaries of the period commonly record that farmers sold their wheat only at a second or third visit to the market, holding on for but not always succeeding in getting a higher price; see for example the Stanton diaries, Bedfordshire Record Office, CRT 160/54D.

[4] Sir John Lawes commented on these lines before the Royal Commission in February 1895 (question 41182) – 'his capital is gone and that is why he hangs on, because if he goes out he is lost'.

The subsequent recovery from acute depression to perhaps a very modest prosperity has received much less attention than its onset. A prolific agricultural writer, P. A. Graham, published a book entitled *The Revival of Agriculture* in 1899[1] after no more than two or three better seasons, but in fact the early 1900s were far from prosperous and profitable for most farmers.[2] After 1903 wheat prices stayed above 28s. a quarter although livestock prices rose only slightly. A. G. Street wrote of his boyhood on a Wiltshire sheep and chalk farm in the early years of this century under the title *Farmer's Glory* but he was writing nostalgically from the depths of the inter-war depression. There seems little doubt, however, that for many farmers who went in at exceptionally low rentals in the worst depression years this period must have been relatively prosperous.[3] Revival like depression was uneven in its incidence, and at best uncertain and ephemeral until the 1940s; cereal acreages and prices remained low, marginal land derelict and moderate land under-used, but the innovation and expedients of the depression became normal practice. It is probable that marginal areas within southern and eastern England, heavy clays and bleak uplands, were slowest to recover, their capital depleted and livestock prices slow to rise. Graham singled out the Cotswolds in this respect on account of this region's unsuitability for dairying, and the fact that the Cotswold breed of sheep produced neither carcass nor fleece in line with contemporary requirements.[4] It must however be admitted that this topic has been little explored.

[1] P. A. Graham, *The Revival of English Agriculture* (London, Jarrold, 1899). Considerable emphasis was given by Graham to the rise of dairying, poultry farming and market-gardening.

[2] Wheat fetched an average price of less than 27s. a quarter in 1899, 1900 and 1901 after exceeding 30s. in 1897 and 1898. In Dorset there was a marked and renewed increase in farm sales in 1900 and 1901.

[3] A. G. Street, *Farmer's Glory* (London, Faber, 1932). 'But that large tenant farmers were doing well then there is no question.' (Penguin edition, 1951, p. 28.) Also J. Wrightson, 'The Agricultural Lessons of "the eighties" ', *Journal of the Royal Agricultural Society of England* (series 3), I (1890), pp. 275–88.

[4] P. Graham, op. cit., pp. 91–100.

CONTEMPORARY UNDERSTANDING OF THE
DEPRESSION

It is scarcely a matter for surprise that those most directly caught up in the events and changes of the depression, tenant farmers in particular, were ready to adopt explanations of their misfortune which were imperfect, subjective, individual and almost invariably neglectful of their own shortcomings. Men generally of limited and narrow education and experience who had rarely had the opportunity to travel or read extensively, they were not well equipped to make objective assessments of their experience. It was, however, from their own experience and understanding that the tenant farmers' and landowners' response and their attempted solutions to their problems were derived.

Three more specific obstacles to contemporary comprehension of the depression require more detailed consideration. The onset of the depression was for the most part gradual; there was no such evident watershed as the repeal of the Corn Laws in 1846, and such cataclysms as the summer of 1879 and the outbreaks of liver-rot were calculated to mislead rather than to enlighten those who were seeking to understand the causes of the depression. These events were so conspicuous that it is hardly surprising that the first acute phase of depression was commonly explained in meteorological terms. As expert a witness as Sir James Caird could place unprecedentedly bad seasons first among his list of causes of the depression in his evidence to the Royal Commission in 1881, adding, 'until we have had a succession of good years we cannot contemplate anything but a period of low farming'.[1] Bad seasons being so widely ascribed a dominant role, farmers not unreasonably assumed that the seasons would eventually return to normal, and were disinclined to change their methods.

The considerable prosperity enjoyed by farmers in the 1850s and 1860s was a second obstacle to understanding. A hundred years later the circumstances of this prosperity appear necessarily exceptional and ephemeral; but to perhaps the majority of farmers in the 1870s and 1880s such good fortune tended to

[1] Question 62674.

appear as the normal condition of farming. For at least twenty years it had been possible to make a good living in farming, despite rising rents.[1] A rising standard of living, a more polished way of life where most farmers' wives no longer worked, and their daughters devoted their time to the piano and water-colours[2] – much mocked by later agricultural commentators – rather than the dairy and the poultry yard, came to be taken for granted. It was by no means self-evident that the methods which had worked so well for mid-century farming would not continue to be profitable.

A third obstacle to understanding was unsophisticated management and inadequate accounting; farmers were not yet essentially businessmen. Characteristically a farmer witness before the Royal Commission in 1881 – and thus presumably of above-average energy and enthusiasm – when asked what profit he made on a cow in the course of the year admitted that he had no idea.[3] In 1894 a farmer witness before the second Royal Commission gave as his main purpose 'to call farmers' attention to the need to keep accounts'.[4] Most farmers appear to have done no more than keep an eye on their bank balance, an adequate enough procedure in the prosperous fifties and sixties but not in the difficult eighties and nineties. And even Strutt had to admit that no man could keep cost accounts and yarded cattle except a dealer;[5] the problem was as much technical as personal.

The incidence of depression was uneven in space and time, yet the merest browsing through contemporary sources indicates a widespread – and by no means irrational – belief in its reality. Not only the unhappy tenants of the Essex clays around Maldon, commonly regarded as the heartland of the depression, but also Scottish, Welsh and West-of-England

---

[1] 'They did not have to make money, it was brought home and shot down at their doors.' J. G. Cornish, *Reminiscences of Country Life* (London, Country Life, 1939). (Writing of Berkshire in the 1860s.)

[2] For example Richard Jefferies in two essays in *Hodge and his Masters* (London, Smith Elder, 1880): 'The fine lady farmer – country girls', and more acidly 'Mademoiselle, the governess'.

[3] H. Overman, a Norfolk tenant farmer, question 51731.

[4] W. Richards, a Rutland gentleman farmer, question 33724.

[5] W. Gavin, op. cit., chapter 6.

farmers, who suffered comparatively little, complained bitterly about their financial difficulties.[1] Most commentators on the depression, even Lord Ernle, compared and commented upon relative western prosperity and eastern adversity – essentially a pastoral-arable contrast; but it seems doubtful that this is how landowners and tenant farmers viewed matters. Farming tends to tie its practitioners to one locality – few farmers have been great travellers – and deprives them of the opportunity to make broad regional comparisons. In the last resort the depression was a matter of bank balances, of present insolvency compared with past prosperity, a comparison which could be made by most farmers. As Olson and Harris have pointed out it was in fact trends in cereal prices over several years rather than absolute levels which appear to have affected farmers' decisions as to how much wheat to grow.[2] In such circumstances it is easy to see how widespread belief in the reality of the depression could exist alongside seemingly self-evident variations in regional levels of prosperity.

RESPONSES TO THE DEPRESSION

In many respects the depression belongs to that unusual class of historical phenomena of which the causes are better under-stood than the immediate and long-term consequences. This is perhaps a reflection of the technical character of most of these changes generated by twenty-five or so difficult years; but agricultural history is necessarily technical history, and because of the importance of environmental factors – climate, soil, location – in agriculture it is necessarily historical geography as much as economic history.

Landowners and farmers – tenants and the less numerous owner-occupiers – both suffered in the depression. Impover-ished tenants sought relief in permanent rent reductions, or

---

[1] For example in 1881, A. S. George, a Banffshire tenant farmer, question 44240; in 1895 T. Jones, a Merionethshire farmer, question 56926–7. These are but two random examples chosen from among many more.

[2] M. Olson and C. C. Harris, 'Free trade in "corn": a statistical study of the prices and production of wheat in Great Britain from 1873 to 1914', *Quarterly Journal of Economics*, LXXIII (1959), pp. 145–68. (Reprinted in this volume.)

temporary abatements – in some cases they merely refused or were unable to pay, and arrears accumulated.[1] Neither reduction nor abatement was invariably granted – Welsh landlords, always on rather bad terms with their Nonconformist tenants, were particularly prone to refuse this kind of relief[2] – either because other means of assistance were preferred or because the landlord did not think any help was needed. Most landlords gave some financial support of this kind, but nevertheless many tenants gave up their farms – even at reduced rentals – during the depression. The threat of leaving was often used by tenants as a means of obtaining rent reduction,[3] most landowners being well aware that there would be little profit, if any, in farming their own land. Many would have agreed with Lord Wantage, an energetic landowner of considerable property in three counties, who in 1893 enunciated as one of his principal aims 'to keep tenants on their legs'.[4]

In the most depressed eastern counties rent reductions, over twenty years of depression, sometimes exceeded 50 per cent; in some northern and western counties they scarcely reached 10 per cent. Overall and nationwide generalization on this point is of dubious value, but one analysis made in 1907[5] suggested a figure of 25 per cent between the early seventies and the mid-nineties. In other words the depression wrote off

---

[1] For example on the Duke of Bedford's Thorney estate rents were reduced by 10 per cent in 1881, and 25 per cent in 1895; remissions ranging from 10 per cent to 50 per cent were given in fifteen out of seventeen years between 1879 and 1895. In this latter year only £17,568 of a nominal rental of £26,196, the bulk of this being farm rents, was paid. Duke of Bedford, *A Great Agricultural Estate* (London, Murray, 1897), pp. 116–22.

[2] This unhappy situation is very fully explored in the minutes of evidence of the Royal Commission on Land in Wales (*British Parliamentary Papers*; 1894, XXXVI and XXXVII; 1895, XL and XLI; and 1896, XXXV).

[3] On the Weld estate in south Dorset eight out of thirty-one tenants gave notice to quit on 31 March 1880. The agent gave as his opinion that three of these were unlikely to stay in any event, and reported that negotiations on a rent reduction were in progress for the other five. Dorset Record Office, Weld papers, rent accounts etc. D10AE89/139.

[4] *Royal Commission on the Agricultural Depression*, question 4405. The Crown shared this view (question 151).

[5] R. J. Thomson, 'An enquiry into the rent of agricultural land in England and Wales in the nineteenth century', *Journal of the Royal Statistical Society*, LXX, (1907), pp. 587–616.

the rent increases of the prosperous mid-century decades, bringing rents back to the level of the 1840s.[1]

Rent reductions were always welcomed although often criticized as too little and too late. It is not surprising that abatements – temporary and sometimes selective reductions – were less popular among tenant farmers. Their selective character – sometimes intentionally in favour of good tenants, sometimes unintentionally in favour of bad ones – was disliked; because they were temporary they were regarded as inimical to long-term planning, and unlike permanent reductions they were not followed by lower rating assessments; rates, often referred to as 'the burden on the land', naturally enough came in for plenty of discussion during the depression. Though rent reductions might be inadequate and abatements inequitable, the freeholder who could benefit from neither was far worse off in this respect than the tenant. Many had purchased their properties at high prices and with heavy mortgages in the early 1870s, in the Isle of Axholme for example; in these circumstances the depression was characterized by foreclosure, not always to the mortgagee's advantage.[2]

Keeping old tenants and finding new ones was a major problem encountered by landlords during the depression. At some periods individual estates had thousands of acres 'in hand' (i.e. unlet); one landlord described his position to the Royal Commission in 1894 as 'a sort of residual legatee of all the worst land on my estate'.[3] A few landlords farmed such land expertly, imaginatively and successfully – Lord Wantage on the Berkshire Downs for example; most could not make a profit in such circumstances. In some areas, notably Essex,

[1] The view expressed by Sir Robert Giffen, a leading economist and member of the Royal Commission on the Agricultural Depression in 1894 (question 18163).

[2] Discussed by James Martin, a Lincolnshire land-agent in his evidence to the Royal Commission on 20 May 1880 (especially questions 7003 and 7012 to 7015). In 1882 Doyle, one of the assistant commissioners, if not always a particularly perceptive one, quoted a previous witness: 'at Axholme labouring men have saved £50 or £60 or £100 by the age of twenty-three or twenty-four'. This is interesting evidence of the extent to which the farm worker was able to save, given the right incentives. Axholme was one of the areas selected for special attention by an assistant commissioner, R. H. Pringle, in 1894. (*British Parliamentary Papers*, 1894, XVI, part 1, pp. 671–96.)

[3] W. Hall, a Cambridgeshire landowner (question 34592).

unlet farms were completely abandoned; these were few, but more common was the practice of running a few cattle or sheep in summer on the 'tumbledown' (i.e. self-sown) grass of farms in hand or let at a nominal rent. In most cases however farms to let were widely and persistently advertised, and many in the south and east were taken up by Scots, West-countrymen, Lancastrians and Cumbrians, usually small farmers or their sons, able by energy, skill, family labour, reduced rents and the temporary acceptance of a lower standard of living[1] to survive where others had failed. This movement began very early in the depression and may well be no more than a sharp and conspicuous acceleration of an established pattern.[2] The best-known such migration was of dairy farmers from Ayrshire to Essex and Hertfordshire.[3] Perhaps for the last time in British agricultural history the 'farming ladder' was a working reality on a large scale; it was an ideal time for an energetic young man of limited means to enter farming, low rents and low capital requirements compensating for low prices.

How many farmers moved? The question cannot be answered since as well as long-distance movements there were very many more short-distance moves as the number of failures and departures from farming increased. In 1932 Smith estimated that about one-fifth of Essex farmers, and one-fifth of the graziers of the Rugby district, had come into the locality from the north and west, in the latter case from Wales.[4] At first they were by no means invariably popular – or even successful – but in the long run assimilation and adaptation proved no problem.[5]

---

[1] C. Matthews, a Chelmsford tenant farmer, wryly commented to the Royal Commission in 1895, 'You cannot starve a Scotchman' (question 61636).

[2] My colleague Dr R. G. Cant comments that his farming forebears migrated from Scotland to Essex in the seventeenth century.

[3] The topic as a whole is explored in: E. L. Smith, *Go East for a Farm: a Study of Rural Migration* (Oxford, Agricultural Economics Research Institute, 1932).

[4] E. L. Smith, op. cit., chapter 2.

[5] In his report to the Royal Commission on the Agricultural Depression in 1894 on the Ongar, Chelmsford, Maldon and Braintree district (*British Parliamentary Papers*, 1894, XVI, Part 1, pp. 697–801), R. H. Pringle suggested that in this area the majority of Scots succeeded, but that some might be described as 'robber farmers'. A useful contemporary account is Primrose McConnell, 'Experiences of a Scotsman on the Essex clays', *Journal of the Royal Agricultural Society of England* (Series 3), II (1891), pp. 311–25.

Not only the landowner's tenants but also his pattern of expenditure changed during the depression. Moreover, as Perren has pointed out,[1] the level of investment in earlier more prosperous years was also of importance in hard times. Expenditure usually followed income downwards, although usually by no means as rapidly, and the frills of farming – well-kept hedges for example – and some essentials – in many cases drainage – were given up. This was not, however, invariably the case; some landlords preferred to support their tenants by continuing investment rather than by reduced rents; many of the most substantial had other sources of income, urban rents, mining royalties, railways shares, with which they supported their rural properties. In general the largest landowners were better placed, and thus more popular with tenant farmers, than the lesser gentry and squires in this respect. When the landowner was most hard-pressed the house might be let to a shooting or hunting tenant, more interested in game and foxes than sympathetic to the tenant farmer. Herein was another minor exacerbation of distress. A generation later Robertson Scott blamed this proliferation of non-resident owners for the poor condition of much rural housing.[2] The landowner was then a key figure in the depression, albeit less likely to receive public sympathy and support than his tenants.

From the farmer's point of view, tenant or freeholder, the most important feature of the depression was the increased likelihood that he would be unable to carry on. A shrewd minority chose to leave while there remained some capital left for them to take with them. Some farmers moved down the ladder, to smaller farms, making way for the more successful; others left farming, making room for new entrants and inter-regional movement. Farms changed hands more often; farm sales increased by about 20 per cent in Dorset and 30 per cent

[1] Among studies of this topic of some importance are: R. Perren, 'The landlord and agricultural transformation, 1870–1900', *Agricultural History Review*, XVIII (1), (1970), pp. 36–51 (reprinted in this volume); J. T. Ward, *East Yorkshire Landed Estates in the Nineteenth Century* (East Yorkshire Local History Series No. 23, York, 1967); T. W. Beastall, 'A south Yorkshire estate in the late nineteenth century', *Agricultural History Review*, XIV (1), (1966), pp. 40–4.

[2] J. W. Robertson Scott, *England's Green and Pleasant Land* (London, Cape, 1925, and Pelican, 1947), p. 23.

in Huntingdonshire during the period 1875–1902 in comparison with the preceding years of prosperity.[1] Again this phenomenon was more marked in the south and east than the north and west.

Incompetence and misfortune were no doubt as much prime causes of individuals' problems during the depression as before and since. Most farmers acted with no great alacrity to adjust their methods to changed circumstances, being misled by the weather and more inclined to pursue traditional paths than to perceive the underlying trend and react accordingly; as early as 1878 Richard Jefferies, a shrewd agricultural journalist, castigated this conservatism – 'an obstinate and traditionary rule requires that under any and every circumstance such and such farms shall grow nothing but corn . . . let the result be what it may'.[2] And yet, as Olson and Harris have observed, the equipment and layout of farms at this date was still such as to allow considerable potential flexibility of operation.[3] Some farmers were locked into unsatisfactory rotations by leases and covenants or by their own indebtedness, but the ability of a number of farmers, not obviously advantaged otherwise, to succeed through making simple and inexpensive changes is evidence of the sluggish response of the majority.

Change and experimentation took place in several directions. The cereal acreage rapidly diminished, fields were laid down to grass, the labour force was reduced and personal expenditure limited, livestock were managed on less intensive lines. In many cases this meant that farmers were living – or at least surviving – on their capital, although not all were aware of it. This was one among several factors in the sustained demand for small farms; and for primarily political reasons smallholdings were widely advocated as a solution to a wide range of rural problems. 'Three acres and a cow' would bring in the millennium. But another trend was equally important, the aggregation of very large holdings by men of ability and good

---

[1] These figures are based on the advertisement columns of the *Dorset County Chronicle* and the *Peterborough Advertiser*.

[2] Richard Jefferies, 'Minute cultivation – a silver mine', *Chronicles of the Hedges and other Essays*, edited by S. J. Looker (London, Phoenix House, 1948).

[3] See note 2, p. 25.

fortune. In 1894 C. S. Read, an agricultural expert of wide experience, noted that half a dozen farmers in his part of Norfolk had built up holdings of 2,000 or 3,000 acres.[1]

New methods were characteristic of no more than a minority of farmers and landowners, newcomers rather than old timers, and of the lowland rather than the highland districts. In the hill country the harsh environment left little room for manœuvre, and retrenchment was the rule. Pressure of population was such in these areas that the demand for farms (and thus rents) remained high despite substantial migrations. Those rural farmers and their offspring who moved, into Essex for example, were better known for their acceptance of a low standard of living than for daring innovations. They were not the only farmers to move into dairying, which was in fact already well established in such regions as south-west Scotland, Devon and Cornwall; and despite its lowly social status dairy farming for the urban market was basic to the success of the Strutt and Parker enterprise in northern Essex, and to similar enterprises on the heavy clays of the Vale of Pewsey.[2] The basis of the more successful of these systems was not summer grass on former arable, rather it was root cultivation to provide winter feed and a flush of milk at the most remunerative winter season. But even dairying had its problems – the supply of skilled labour, the railway monopoly, the far from ideal climate of eastern England.

The second major area of successful innovation was market-gardening. Rhubarb forcing in the West Riding, fruit and vegetables around Wisbech, Evesham and Sandy, the Spalding bulb industry, all grew up or expanded in response to the absence of profit in traditional methods, the availability of cheap land and the provision of access to urban markets by the railways. Spalding had only one bulb grower in 1885, twenty-two seven years later, a result of falling land values and an injection

---

[1] Royal Commission on Agricultural Depression, question 16052. A little later (question 16315) he noted that in this district two out of three country gentlemen no longer lived at home.

[2] F. M. L. Thompson, 'Agriculture since 1870', *Victoria History of the County of Wiltshire*, IV (1959), pp. 92–114. A. G. Street, op. cit., comments on its lowly status in the 1920s.

of outside capital from small cultivators and businessmen.[1] The rhubarb industry developed on farms given up during the first period of acute depression in the early 1880s.[2]

A third group developed new farming systems closer to, but more profitable than, the traditional framework. Since the price of barley and oats fell less than the price of wheat some farmers concentrated on these cereals. Traditional livestock breeds were in many areas replaced by varieties more appropriate to contemporary needs, the Leicester in its native county by the Shropshire Down and the crossbred,[3] the mongrel cow by the pedigree, and in some dairies already the Friesian.[4] In fact most of the pedigree sheep herd books and societies, although not the breeds themselves, date from this period – the Oxford Down from 1888, the Dorset Horn from 1891, for example – rather than from the preceding high farming period. Most commonly farmers were willing to disrupt rotations either by leaving temporary pasture in existence for several years longer than intended or by inserting a profitable cash crop – commonly potatoes – at an appropriate point.

The labourer is generally regarded as having suffered less than any other group from the impact of depression. Labourers were moving off the land before the depression began, and continued to do so during this period while farmers tried to economize on labour. As a result farm workers were able largely, if not completely, to maintain the higher money wages attained by their militancy early in the 1870s; as prices fell this meant higher real wages. The perennial complaint of farmers that the quality of labour had declined, that it was too expensive, should not be taken too seriously. But without doubt the most able and most energetic working men were leaving the

[1] E. C. Eagle, 'Some light on the beginnings of the Lincolnshire bulb industry', *Lincolnshire Historian*, VI (1950), pp. 220–9.

[2] E. A. Pratt, *The Transition in Agriculture* (London, John Murray, 1906), chapters 9–11. (Developments in west Middlesex, Bedfordshire and Worcestershire are also discussed.)

[3] G. E. Fussell, 'Four centuries of Leicestershire farming', in W. G. Hoskins (ed.), *Essays in Leicestershire History* (Liverpool, University Press, 1950), pp. 154–76.

[4] W. Gavin, op. cit., chapter 10, discusses the advent of the Friesian in an Essex context. He suggests that during the last quarter of the nineteenth century no more than thirty or forty British cowkeepers specialized in Dutch cattle.

countryside – for the railways and police force, the city and the colonies.[1] The labourer's success and good fortune was, however, no more than relative; rural housing was generally of low quality, the social standing of the labourer at best uncertain and at worst degrading. High real wages, shorter hours, the advent of universal literacy, and above all the coming of the bicycle, gave the labourer – the young man in particular – a new freedom and mobility;[2] but he remained impoverished by comparison with the averagely embarrassed farmer and landowner, and was often destined to end his days in the union workhouse. One eminent and sympathetic authority of the early depression period commented, 'labourers did not live in the proper sense of the word, they merely didn't die',[3] and as late as 1914 there is good reason to believe that most labourers were still underfed.[4]

Diversification of farming methods and reduction of the farmer's capital was accompanied by a decline in the value and saleability of land. Farm sales increased as the depression intensified; land sales were fewer, and often proved abortive.[5] It is only too easy to cite spectacular examples; a Suffolk landowner and tenant quoted to the Royal Commission in 1894 cases of farms which sold for £13,000 and £3,000 in the early seventies and £1,800 and £450 in 1893.[6] But in the widely prevailing circumstances of an inactive and uncertain market, these, and similar, examples are not neccessarily an indication of changing values. No one wanted to sell and there was no

[1] 'From the parish in which I write thirty-one sons of the soil have been enrolled as London policemen in thirty years.' Augustus Jessopp, *Arcady: for Better for Worse* (London, T. Fisher Unwin, 1897), p. 117. Jessopp, who had been a reforming headmaster in the Arnold tradition, was vicar of Scarning, Norfolk, from 1879.

[2] P. J. Perry, 'Working class isolation and mobility in rural Dorset, 1837–1936: a study of marriage distances', *Transactions of the Institute of British Geographers*, XLVI (1969), pp. 121–42.

[3] Canon Girdlestone, the radical vicar of Halberton, Devon, from 1862–72, and organizer of schemes to foster surplus rural labour to move to industrial work. Not surprisingly he was unpopular with local farmers. Quoted in Burnett, op. cit., p. 115.

[4] Burnett, op. cit., p. 135.

[5] An excellent discussion is F. M. L. Thompson, 'The land market in the nineteenth century', *Oxford Economic Papers* (New Series), IX (1957), pp. 285–308.

[6] Questions 7648 and 7654.

B

incentive to buy; so an exceptionally large proportion of sales were forced by such an event as death or bankruptcy.[1] The landed interest not only wished but was also able in many cases to retain its land through hard times, in sharp contrast to the situation a generation or so later. Many landowners however were forced into non-residence. Corporate landowners were in a particularly difficult position, and in at least one case the fellows of a Cambridge college had to forgo their dividend.[2]

The effects of the depression on the rural landscape were evident as early as the 1870s, and the most conspicuous response of grassing-down had begun in better times twenty years earlier. Much marginal land was abandoned during the depression, and labour economies were reflected in a general deterioration of traditional standards – overgrown hedges, dilapidated gates, unweeded crops. In the short run these developments could prove to be a false economy; in the wet years of the 1870s weeds proliferated to the detriment of yields, quality and income. On the other hand game flourished under conditions of less careful and intensive husbandry.[3]

The official and parliamentary response to the depression took several forms, but never extended to the reimposition of protection as a means of raising prices to an acceptable level. Two Royal Commissions investigated the state of agriculture, in the early 1880s and the mid-1890s; commissioners of a variety of political opinion – so much so that the second commission functioned by no means smoothly[4] – and agri-

---

[1] The failure of the Weymouth bank of Eliot, Pearce and Co. in 1897 led to the sale of the Plush Manor estate in mid-Dorset. According to the Official Receiver the fall in value of the estate was one reason for the bank's failure. Purchased for £28,000, it was reckoned to be worth about £40,000 in 1879 after some £12,500 had been spent on repairs and improvements; in 1896 it was worth only £18,000. (See *Dorset County Chronicle* 13 May 1897.)

[2] Downing College, Cambridge, in 1894, according to L. L. Price, Fellow and Treasurer of Oriel College, Oxford, in evidence to the Royal Commission on Agricultural Depression, (question 47433).

[3] An interesting early comment on these topics is 'Midsummer' in Jefferies, *Hodge and His Masters* (London, Smith Elder, 1880), written in 1879. See also 'Nutty autumn' in Jefferies, *Nature Near London* (London, Chatto and Windus, 1883).

[4] Minority reports and dissenting opinions occupied as much space as the report proper. Disagreement between two commissioners, Chaplin, the farmers' champion, and G. J. Shaw-Lefevre, chairman until he resigned, engendered an acrimonious correspondence in *The Times* in April and May 1896.

cultural experience examined a large body of witnesses. Until
recently most writing on the agriculture of the period derived
primarily from their work. It was widely recognized that
protection, the only short cut to rural prosperity, was impossible; attention was therefore concentrated on secondary issues
– rates and railways, for example – and in the case of the first
commission on the role of the weather, as much misunderstood
by the commissioners as by almost everyone else.[1] This
concentration, and the resultant legislation, was by no means
entirely irrelevant. The Small-holdings Act of 1892 facilitated
the entry of the small man, *par excellence* the labourer, into the
farming community; the several Agricultural Holdings Acts,
from 1875 onwards, gave the tenant farmer better security –
particularly after the amendment of 1883 – and compensation
for improvements carried out during the tenancy with his own
resources. These and other legislative measures have sometimes been regarded as epitomizing on the one hand Parliament's refusal to face realities and on the other the power of
radical politicians determined to attack the landed interest at
every opportunity. But real agricultural problems, albeit not
the agricultural problem, were alleviated by such measures. The
depression was characterized by an increase in the number of
farmers leaving the land, many of whom had invested considerable sums in improvement in the preceding period of prosperity; to this group 'compensation for unexhausted improvements' was very important. Likewise such innovations as
horticulture, and to some extent dairying, often involved
tenant investment legally unprotected under many traditional
agreements.

Parliament itself contained representatives of both the landed
and agricultural interest and of those generally hostile to landowners and farmers and their reputed privileges. Among the
former the last chairman of the Protection Society of the 1840s,
Newdegate, was still an M.P. in 1881 when protection was
discussed in the Commons for the first time in thirty years; but
the best-known agricultural spokesman in Parliament at this

[1] Even Voelcker, a professor of the Royal Agricultural College, commented
'bad weather had done more mischief than anything else to the agricultural
community' (question 57060).

date was Henry Chaplin, a Lincolnshire landowner and member of both Royal Commissions. At the other extreme Joseph Chamberlain and the radicals advocated, in their election programme of 1884–5, cheaper transfer of land, higher rates, the abolition of primogeniture and the taxation of sporting, uncultivated and unoccupied lands. Some went so far as to advocate land nationalization; others like Chamberlain himself retained a belief in private enterprise and property but wished to end what they saw as abuses of this system. It is also possible to follow back the ideas of limited protection and imperial preference into the early years of the depression.[1]

Surprise is sometimes expressed that a parliament in which the landed interest remained strongly represented did so little to assist agriculture. It is perhaps as much of a mistake to identify the landed interest with agriculture alone as to join the radicals in assuming that improving the tenant farmer's position constituted an attack on the landlord. In Kitson Clark's words, 'the interests of neither the aristocracy nor the gentry were wholly identified with the fortunes of agriculture; and it probably made a very great difference to the social history of the country that when the fortunes of agriculture collapsed many of the great estates had other reasonably solid support.'[2] It was horse-racing and high living not the depression which ruined Chaplin. During the first part of the depression rural support for the Conservatives, traditionally a party concerned to support the landed and farming interest, waned; at the 1880 election only 116 Conservatives were returned in counties where formerly there had been 143. The rural vote tended to return to the Conservatives after 1885, perhaps because the Liberals showed no more inclination than their rivals to bail out the farmers, perhaps because of some minor revival of rural fortunes; but the Conservative governments of this period nevertheless implemented several measures of a moderately anti-landlord character, notably in establishing county councils in 1888. Most historians would agree how-

---

[1] Useful discussions are: R. B. McDowell, *British Conservatism: 1832–1914* (London, Faber, 1969); P. Fraser, *Joseph Chamberlain* (London, Cassell, 1966).

[2] G. S. R. Kitson Clark, *The Making of Victorian England* (London, Methuen, 1962), p. 216.

ever that the collapse of agriculture was one factor in the diminution of the political power of the landed interest.

A GEOGRAPHY OF THE DEPRESSION

The first serious historian of the depression, Lord Ernle, subsequently much criticized as an exaggerator of the extent and intensity of farmers' and landowners' problems, nevertheless acknowledged that the problems appeared greater, in the earlier acute phase of depression in particular, in the south and east than in the north and west. The broad divisions, often referred to by geographers and archaeologists as the 'highland zone' and the 'lowland zone', are created by a line from the mouth of the Tees to the mouth of the Exe; cereal cultivation, albeit often in the guise of mixed farming, is generally more important in the drier and sunnier lowland zone, pastoral farming in the cooler, moister highland zone. The boundary is neither precise nor exclusive – the depression of cereal prices tended as on other such occasions to generate extension of the pastoral domain further into midland England and consequently contraction of the arable district – but such a division would be regarded by most geographers as basic and persistent in the geography of Britain, and not merely its agricultural geography. As livestock were kept in the lowland zone generally for fattening, so cereals were grown in the highland zone, but more often for feed on the farm than for the market. Changes in cereal prices were thus relatively unimportant to the farmer in the highland zone.

The basis of this regional division is essentially environmental, a matter of climate, soils, topography.[1] In the depression context the highland zone was favoured in this respect. The cereal cultivator of the lowland zone feared above all other environmental hazards cool, wet summers, so common in the later seventies, when crops ripened late and unsatisfactorily, the yield was light[2] and quality low, the harvest pro-

---

[1] It was first formally enunciated by a geographer, Sir Halford Mackinder in *Britain and the British Seas* (London, Heinemann, 1902).

[2] For example in Aberdeenshire one farm recorded a yield of oats of 3·75 quarters per acre; by comparison the yield in 1898, a good year, was 6·5 bushels [a quarter is equal to 8 bushels]. J. A. Symon, 'Cairnhill, Turriff, 1861–1926', *Scottish Agriculture*, XXIX (1951), pp. 199–202 and XXX, pp. 24–9.

tracted and expensive. As prices declined the seasonal hazard became more serious, even though the run of bad years in the seventies did not repeat itself. Diversification within arable husbandry did little to ease this problem; malting barley, for example, commonly fetched about 20s. a quarter more than feeding barley in the early nineties,[1] an incentive to the farmer to aim for a malting sample, although in this too his success depended as much on the weather as on his own skill. On the other hand low rainfall and the risk of summer drought, of which there were several in the early nineties, made it difficult to establish and maintain good permanent pasture in most of the lowland zone, inhibiting the development of systems of livestock husbandry better suited than cereal cultivation to the economic circumstances of the depression.

The livestock producer faced environmental hazards which were perhaps more expected and more accepted than those of the arable farmer. To many such farmers wet seasons were advantageous, ensuring an abundance of feed, and even such general exceptions as 1879 were not the universal or over-whelming disaster to the pastoralist that they were to the cultivator. A few men and districts even remembered the 1870s as reasonably good years, notably in the Scottish Highlands.[2] In general these adverse seasons were more markedly so in the lowland zone where most of the heavy clays, suitable only for cereal growing but a hopeless and heartbreaking proposition in wet seasons, were located. Environmental circumstances in the lowland zone did, however, affect the highland zone; a shortage of feed, a late spring or a dry summer, depressed the prices received for lean stock by hill farmers, an abundance of feed in good seasons raised these same prices.

The farming systems of the lowland zone – intensive arable-livestock husbandry in particular – were high-cost systems in which high levels of investment were the basis for high returns. Such systems are particularly vulnerable to any downward turn in prices; economies in the use of fertilizers, in cultivation, in labour, tend to be quickly reflected in diminished output. Of

[1] J. Wrightson, *Farm Crops* (London, Cassell, 1892), pp. 134–5.

[2] For example Cameron of Lochiel, an M.P. and Highland landowner, in his evidence to the Royal Commission in May 1881 (question 43444).

these major fixed costs only rent and maintenance can, where the landlord is willing, be reduced without adversely affecting production. No doubt the social aspirations and attitudes of lowland zone farmers exacerbated this problem. By comparison the highland zone farming systems contained a greater momentum enabling production to be sustained for some years in spite of much-reduced investment. Family labour was more important than wage labour, artificial feeds and fertilizers much less of an essential input than in arable farms. Moreover highland zone farmers, the Scots and Welsh in particular, were almost proverbially frugal, as willing as they were able to pull in their horns in bad times.[1] In this respect the lesser social aspiration, perhaps replaced by educational ambitions, of the highland zone farmer were significant.

Two other factors also favoured the north and west. Nearby industrial markets, Lancashire and South Wales for example, were buoyant and remunerative and the industrial worker was eating more pastoral produce, meat and cheese for example; London alone provided a comparable, in some cases remote, opportunity for much of the lowland zone. In some parts of the highland zone small farmers were comparatively numerous; this group had not only their landlord to look to for help in hard times but their own willingness to carry on at a very low standard of living made them less willing to leave than the tenant farmer of the lowland zone, unless they reached the extreme of bankruptcy or liquidation. In some localities they were reduced to near-subsistence, in others most of their stock was owned by dealers, but generally these farmers showed considerable tenacity in clinging to their holdings.

The favourable position of the highland zone in these respects was not merely a depression phenomenon; such long-standing differences were probably the main reason why

---

[1] A. Jessopp, op. cit., p. 11, held this view of the small farm dependent on family labour in general, recording one discussion on its economics thus: ' "How do you manage to pay all your outgoings in these bad times?" I said to one good woman whose husband farms some 50 acres at a ruinous rent. "Why you see, sir, the corn about pays the landlord and such, and then we reckon to live, and there's seven of us and we all help. I don't know how we do, but we keep going." ' The Royal Commission on Land in Wales and Monmouthshire abounds with examples of this kind of near-subsistence farming.

financial failure among farmers was less common in the high-land than the lowland zone even before the depression. About one farmer in 150 was forced into bankruptcy in Huntingdon-shire, the heartland of depression in the early 1880s, only about one in 500 in Lancashire;[1] but from past experience this difference might well have been regarded as predictable. Bankruptcy and failure were more part and parcel of the farming system of the lowland zone than of the highland zone, perhaps because in some instances relatively low capital requirements tempted the inexperienced and the ill-equipped.

The geography of depression is also a question of levels of generalization. Scholars have usually considered either Britain as a whole, or the county, or the landed estate; at the national and the county level spatial generalization is evidently worth-while. For example a model of the incidence of the depression in Dorset has been constructed[2] which explains about 40 per cent of the variation in the intensity of depression within the county in spatial terms; in other words 60 per cent of the variation in intensity from parish to parish appears to have been random, probably relating for the most part to such spatially irregular variables as landlord attitudes and abilities, and the skill and fortune of the individual farmer. No doubt these latter factors were responsible for the substantial variation in the intensity of depression in adjacent parishes within the same broad agricultural region and even the same landlord's estate. In a few such cases other than personal explanations are possible, disease for example; in others, perhaps particularly in Wales, religious and social antipathies exacerbated the feeling if not necessarily the actuality of depression in some localities. These are a salutary caution against too largely a spatial or environmental interpretation of the depression, too high a level of generalization, and a reminder that in the last resort

---

[1] The comparisons are based on material in the *London Gazette*: see P. J. Perry 'Where was the "great agricultural depression"? A geography of agricultural bankruptcy in late Victorian England', *Agricultural History Review*, XX (1972), pp. 30–45. (Reprinted in this volume.)

[2] P. J. Perry and R. J. Johnston, 'The temporal and spatial incidence of agricultural depression in Dorset, 1868–1902', *Journal of Interdisciplinary History*, III (1972) pp. 297–311.

the depression was a matter of the individual farmer or landowner, his success or failure.

PROBLEMS AND DEBATES

The agricultural depression, although the progenitor of Ernle's
pioneering classic,[1] has in recent years received much less
attention from agricultural historians than such topics as the
origins and antecedents of the 'agricultural revolution' and the
developments of the first three-quarters of the nineteenth
century. The role of the depression as a significant link rather
than a purposeless vacuum between an old and a new agricultural world, and as the developmental era of many present-day
practices, has been little noticed by scholars.[2]

The most significant recent work on the depression has given
due emphasis to its regional character; the writings of Fletcher
on Lancashire and Coppock on the Chilterns are of this kind,
although the latter is considering a less extreme example than
the former. But in many cases re-evaluation of late nineteenth-
century economic experience has, in rejecting the general idea
of depression, also disregarded the reality of agricultural
distress. The process of historical winnowing has sometimes
failed to separate grain and chaff. What is needed is a re-
examination of the agricultural economy in terms broadly
similar to Wilson's scrutiny of the period as a whole. Some
recent work has looked at new and spatially comprehensive
sources, measuring as well as describing the impact and
incidence of depression, building spatial and economic models
and examining contemporary perception and understanding.
These approaches are more characteristic of the work of
economists and geographers than of historians; they are more
likely to add new perspectives to our view of the depression
through a broader and eventually complete geographical

---

[1] *English Farming Past and Present* grew out of an earlier and much shorter
book *The Pioneers and Progress of English Farming* (London, Longmans, 1888). In
turn that book grew out of an article of the same name in the *Quarterly Review*,
CLIX (April 1885), pp. 323–59.

[2] The most obvious exception is Viscount Astor and B. Seebohm Rowntree,
British Agriculture: the Principles of Future Policy (London, 1939, as a Pelican
Special).

coverage than continuation of traditional methods, or exploitation of well-known sources.

Foremost among continuing problems open for examination is that of the position of the livestock producer in both highland and lowland zones. The problem is that of the greater functional complexity of this kind of farming, compared to cereal cultivation, and of the more limited source materials. Likewise the landowner has received more attention than the farmer; the former's family and estate papers are often, if by no means invariably, gathered and catalogued in a record office; the latter remains by comparison an unknown and shadowy figure. The second principal area requiring and meriting further study is that of the movement of farmers into, out of and within the industry during this period of unprecedented change. Movement into farming and within farming was thoroughly examined by Smith as long ago as 1932; his work, and that of others, has given the hard-working Scot or Devonian, the successful labourer and the urban businessman, an established place in the received view of the depression. More uncertain is what proportion of movements within and into farming belonged to these groups; were they a substantial majority or a small, albeit influential, minority? And what was the impact of former experience, of new ideas, of personal dynamism on their own and their neighbours' farming practice? To what extent was their sometimes meagre capital augmented by country solicitors and bankers, and by suppliers of feeding stuffs and fertilizers? What happened to those who left the land is much less well known. Vanishing from the agricultural scene they have left little mark on agricultural history. Some went overseas – for example in the late 1880s farmers and labourers from the Banbury district to the USA[1] – while financial failure reduced some farmers to the level of bailiff or labourer.[2] Others who extracted their reduced capital, not always without difficulty, set up as shopkeepers

[1] A. M. Taylor, *Gillett's, Bankers at Banbury and Oxford* (Oxford, Clarendon, 1964), pp. 163–84. The profits of this rural bank fell by two-thirds between 1878 and 1884.

[2] Discussed with moving pathos by Richard Jefferies in such essays as 'Leaving his farm', *Hodge and His Masters* (London, Smith Elder, 1880), and 'Going downhill', ibid.

and seaside hoteliers.[1] Some of the most perceptive, who got out at an early stage, came back a decade or so later at lower rents and with the real capital value of their resources enhanced.[2] By 1879 the ex-farmer living off his capital was a sufficiently well-known figure to appear in *Punch*;[3] almost a century later he is worthy of serious scholarly consideration.

Finally there is the question of the social impact of the depression. At the one extreme Lady Bracknell epitomized it thus: 'land has ceased to be either a profit or a pleasure. It gives one position and prevents one from keeping it up.'[4] At an intermediate level the farmer's social life was inhibited; to quote the *Banbury Guardian* as early as 1880, 'farming will not, to use a common phrase, "run to hunting"'.[5] On the other hand some shrewd contemporary commentators scarcely mention that the depression existed; among such interesting correctives are the assertion in *Lark Rise to Candleford* that 'everybody in those days [the early 1890s] seemed to do well on the land, except the farm labourer',[6] and Wingfield-Stratford's comment that 'it was possible to be born and come to maturity in the countryside of these last two decades of the century without ever having one's attention called to its [the depression's] existence'.[7] Some writers of the period and some historians appear to regard this period as the nadir of the social life of rural Britain, basing this analysis particularly on the extent of rural depopulation. The newspapers of the period and grandparents' reminiscences, notoriously unreliable as are the latter, do not seem to confirm this view. Against the forced non-residence and reduced expenditure of some landowners

[1] Question 50390, Royal Commission on Agriculture, 1881.

[2] E. Riley, a retired East Riding farmer, made this point to the Royal Commission in 1894 (question 36508). The suggested reason for their return was that they were tired of being idle.

[3] The cartoon appeared on 30 August 1879. Other interesting comment of this kind on the farming scene appeared in *Punch* on 13 March 1880 and 7 September 1895.

[4] *The Importance of Being Earnest* (Act 1). I am grateful to the late Mr T. W. Fletcher for making this point to me.

[5] Taylor, op. cit.

[6] F. Thompson, *Lark Rise to Candleford* (London, O.U.P., 1939 and World's Classics, 1945), p. 41.

[7] E. Wingfield-Stratford, *The Squire and His Relations* (London, Cassell, 1956), pp. 404–5.

must be set the improved financial position and shorter working week of the labourer. There are here two topics worthy of further research, the effects of the depression on the labourer, and the changing character of rural society. In each case the news columns of county papers appear likely to be the most valuable source.

The depression remains a promising field for continuing scholarship, opened-up, exploited, but by no means worked out. An abundance of accessible sources awaits attention, from the social scientist with his new concepts and methods, in particular. This introductory essay attempts not only to introduce the topic through a selection of research papers but also to indicate where its future lies, and what sort of super-structure should be erected on the sure foundation of established work.

1 The Great Depression and Recovery, 1874–1914

LORD ERNLE

This article was first published as Chapter 18 of *English Farming Past and Present*, 6th edition, Heinemann, 1961.

Since 1862 the tide of agricultural prosperity had ceased to flow; after 1874 it turned, and rapidly ebbed. A period of depression began which, with some fluctuations in severity, continued throughout the rest of the reign of Queen Victoria, and beyond.

Depression is a word which is often loosely used. It is generally understood to mean a reduction, in some cases an absence, of profit, accompanied by a consequent diminution of employment. To some extent the condition has probably become chronic. A decline of interest on capital lent or invested, a rise in wages of labour, an increased competition for the earnings of management, caused by the spread of education and resulting in the reduction or stationary character of those earnings, are permanent not temporary tendencies of civilization. So far as these symptoms indicate a more general distribution of wealth, they are not disquieting. But, from time to time, circumstances combine to produce acute conditions of industrial collapse which may be accurately called depression. Such a crisis occurred in agriculture from 1875–84, and again from 1891–9.

Industrial undertakings are so inextricably interlaced that agricultural depression cannot be entirely dissevered from commercial depression. Exceptional periods of commercial difficulty had for the last seventy years recurred with such regularity as to give support to a theory of decennial cycles.[1] In previous years, each recurring period had resulted in a genuine panic, due as much to defective information as to any

[1] e.g. 1825–6, 1836–7, 1847, 1857, 1866, 1877–8.

real scarcity of loanable capital. The historic failure of Overend and Gurney in 1866 and the famous 'Black Friday' afford the last example of this acute form of crisis. Better means of obtaining accurate intelligence, more accessible supplies of capital, the greater stability of the Bank of England have combined with other causes to minimize the risk of financial stampedes. But, though periods of depression cease to produce the old-fashioned panic, they are not less exhausting. Their approach is more gradual; so also is the recovery. Disaster and revival are no longer concentrated in a few months. Years pass before improvement is apparent; the magnitude of the distress is concealed by its diffusion over a longer period. The agricultural depressions of 1875–84 and of 1891–9 had all the characteristics of the modern type of financial crisis.

In 1870 had begun an inflation of prices. The outbreak of the Franco-German War and the withdrawal of France and Germany from commercial competition enabled England to increase her exports; the opening of the Suez Canal (1869) stimulated the ship-building trade; the railway development in Germany and America created an exceptional demand for coal and iron. Expanding trade increased the consuming power of the population, and maintained the prices of agricultural produce. The wisest or wealthiest landowners refused the temptation to advance rents on sitting tenants. But in many cases rents were raised, or farms were tendered for competition. Farmers became infected with the same spirit of gambling which in trade caused the scramble for the investment of money in hazardous enterprises. In their eagerness for land they were led into reckless biddings, which raised rentals beyond reasonable limits. In 1874 the reaction began. Demand had returned to normal limits; but the abnormal supply continued. Over-production was the result. The decline of the coal and iron trade, the stoppage, partial or absolute, of cotton mills, disputes between masters and men, complications arising out of the Eastern question, the default on the Turkish debt, disturbances of prices owing to fluctuations in the purchasing power of gold and silver, combined to depress every industry. In 1878 the extent to which trade had been undermined was revealed by the failure of the Glasgow, Caledonian and West

of England Banks. One remarkable feature of the crisis was
that it was not local but universal. New means of communica-
tion had so broken down the barriers of nations that the
civilized world suffered together. Everywhere prices fell,
trade shrank, insolvencies multiplied. In the United States the
indirect consequences of the industrial collapse of 1873–4
proved to be of disastrous importance to English farming. A
railway panic, a fall in the price of manufactured articles, a
decline in wages drove thousands out of the towns to settle
as agriculturists on the virgin soils of the West.

English farming suffered from the same causes as every other
home industry. In addition, it had its own special difficulties.
The collapse of British trade checked the growth of the consuming power at home at the same time that a series of inclement seasons, followed by an overwhelming increase of
foreign competition, paralysed the efforts of farmers. For three
years in succession, bleak springs and rainy summers produced
short cereal crops of inferior quality, mildew in wheat, mould
in hops, blight in other crops, disease in cattle, rot in sheep,
throwing heavy lands into foul condition, deteriorating the
finer grasses of pastures. In 1875–6 the increasing volume of
imports[1] prevented prices from rising to compensate deficiencies in the yield of corn. The telegraph, steam carriage
by sea and land, and low freights, consequent on declining
trade, annihilated time and distance, destroyed the natural
monopoly of proximity, and enabled the world to compete
with English producers in the home markets on equal, if not
more favourable, terms. Instead of there being one harvest
every year, there was now a harvest in every month of each
year. In 1877 prices advanced, owing to the progress of the
Russo-Turkish War. But the potato crops failed, and a renewed outbreak of the cattle-plague, though speedily sup-
pressed, hit stockowners hard. The tithe rent-charge was
nearly £12 above its par value. Rates were rising rapidly. Land-
agents began to complain of the scarcity of eligible tenants
for vacant corn-land. During the sunless ungenial summer of
1879, with its icy rains, the series of adverse seasons culmina-
ted in one of the worst harvests of the century, in an outbreak

---

[1] For the growth of foreign imports of food, see Appendix VII.

of pleuro-pneumonia and foot-and-mouth disease among cattle, and among sheep a disastrous attack of the liver-rot, which inflicted an enormous loss on flockmasters. The English wheat crop scarcely averaged 15½ bushels to the acre. In similar circumstances, farmers might have been compensated for the shortness of yield by an advance in price. This was no longer the case in 1879. America, which had enjoyed abundant harvests, poured such quantities of wheat into the country as to bring down prices below the level of the favourable season of the preceding year. At the same time, American cheese so glutted the market as to create a record for cheapness. Thus, at the moment when English farmers were already enfeebled by their loss of capital, they were met by a staggering blow from foreign competition. They were fighting against low prices as well as adverse seasons.

English farmers were, in fact, confronted with a new problem. How were they to hold their own in a treacherous climate on highly rented land, whose fertility required constant renewal, against produce raised under more genial skies on cheaply rented soils, whose virgin richness needed no fertilizers? To a generation familiar with years of a prosperity which had enabled English farmers to extract more from the soil than any of their foreign rivals, the changed conditions were unintelligible. The new position was at first less readily understood, because the depression was mainly attributed to the accident of adverse seasons, and because the grazing and dairying districts had as yet escaped. Thousands of tenants on corn-growing lands were unable to pay their rents. In many instances they were kept afloat by the help of wealthy landlords. But every landowner is not a Dives; the majority sit at the rich man's gate. In most cases there was no reduction of rents. Remissions, sometimes generous, sometimes inadequate, were made and renewed from time to time. Where the extreme urgency of the case was imperfectly realized, many old tenants were ruined. It was not till farms were re-let that the necessary reductions were made, and then the men who profited were new occupiers.

If any doubt still existed as to the reality of the depression, especially in corn-growing districts, it was removed by the evidence laid before the Duke of Richmond's Commission, which sat from 1879–82. The Report of the Commission established, beyond possibility of question, the existence of severe and acute distress, and attributed its prevalence, primarily to inclement seasons, secondarily to foreign competition. It was generally realized that the shrinkage in the margin of profit on the staple produce of agriculture was a more or less permanent condition, and that rents must be readjusted. Large reductions were made between 1880 and 1884, and it was calculated that in England and Wales alone the annual letting value of agricultural land was thus decreased by 5¾ millions. Yet in many cases the rent nominally remained at the old figure. Only remissions were granted, which were uncertain in amount, and therefore disheartening in effect. According to Sir James Caird's evidence given in 1886, before the Royal Commission on Depression of Trade, the yearly income of landlords, tenants and labourers had diminished since 1876 by £42,800,000.

The worst was by no means over. On the contrary, the pressure of foreign competition gradually extended to other branches of agriculture. The momentum of a great industry in any given direction cannot be arrested in a day; still less can it be diverted towards another goal without a considerable expenditure of time and money. Unreasonable complaints were made against the obstinate conservatism of agriculturists, because they were unable to effect a costly change of front as easily as a man turns in his bed. The aims and methods of farming were gradually adapted to meet the changed conditions. As wheat, barley and oats declined towards the lowest prices of the century, increased attention was paid to grazing, dairying and such minor products as vegetables, fruit and poultry. The corn area of England and Wales shrank from 8,244,392 acres in 1871 to 5,886,052 acres in 1901.[1] Between the same years the area of permanent pasture increased from 11,367,298 acres to 15,399,025 acres. Yet before the change was complete farmers once more found themselves checkmated. The old adage 'Down horn, up corn' had once held true. Now both were down together. Till 1885 the prices of fat cattle had been

[1] For statistics of agriculture, see Appendix VIII.

well maintained, and those of sheep till 1890. Both were now beginning to decline before the pressure of foreign competition. Up till 1877 both cattle and sheep had been chiefly sent in alive from European countries. Now America and Canada joined in the trade, and the importation of dead meat rapidly increased. Consignments were no longer confined to beef and pig meat. New Zealand and the Republic of Argentina entered the lists. The imports of mutton, which in 1882 did not exceed 181,000 cwts, and chiefly consisted of meat boiled and tinned, rose in 1899 to 3½ million cwts, of frozen carcasses. The importation of cheese rose by more than a third; that of butter was doubled; that of wool increased more than twofold. Meanwhile the outgoings of the farmer were steadily mounting upwards. Machinery cost more; labour rose in price and deteriorated in efficiency. The expenses of production rose as the profits fell.

Some attempt was made by Parliament to relieve the industry. The recommendations of the Richmond Commission were gradually carried into effect. Grants were made in aid of local taxation. Measures were adopted to stamp out disease among livestock, and to protect farmers against the adulteration of feeding-stuffs, and against the sale of spurious butter and cheese. The primary liability for tithe rent-charge was transferred from occupiers to owners (1891). The law affecting limited estates in land was modified by the Settled Lands Act (1882). A Railway and Canal Traffic Act was passed, which attempted to equalize rates on the carriage of home and foreign produce. The permissive Agricultural Holdings Act of 1875, which was not incorrectly described as a 'homily to landlords' on the subject of unexhausted improvements, was superseded by a more stringent measure and a modification of the law of distress (1883). A Minister of Agriculture was appointed (1889), and an Agricultural Department established.

But the legislature was powerless to provide any substantial help. Food was, so to speak, the currency in which foreign nations paid for English manufactured goods, and its cheapness was an undoubted blessing to the wage-earning community. Thrown on their own resources, agriculturists fought the unequal contest with courage and tenacity. But, as time went on, the stress told more and more heavily. Manufacturing populations seemed to seek food markets everywhere except at home. Enterprise gradually weakened; landlords lost their ability to help, farmers their recuperative power. Prolonged depression checked costly improvements. Drainage was practically discontinued. Both owners and occupiers were engaged in the task of making both ends meet on vanishing incomes. Land deteriorated in condition; less labour was employed; less stock was kept; bills for cake and fertilizers were reduced. The counties which suffered most were the corn-growing districts, in which high farming had won its most signal triumphs. On the heavy clays of Essex, for example, thousands of acres, which had formerly yielded great crops and paid high rents, had passed out of cultivation into ranches for cattle or temporary sheep-runs. On the light soils of Norfolk, where skill and capital had wrested large profits from the reluctant hand of Nature, there were widespread ruin and bankruptcy. Throughout the eastern, midland and southern counties – wherever the land was so heavy or so light that its cultivation was naturally unremunerative – the same conditions prevailed. The west on the whole, suffered less severely. Though milk and butter had fallen in price, dairy farmers were profiting by the cheapness of grain, which was ruining their corn-growing neighbours. Almost everywhere retrenchment, not development, was the enforced policy of agriculturists. The expense of laying land down to grass was shirked, and arable areas which were costly to work were allowed to tumble down to rough pasture. Economy ruled in farm management; labour bills were reduced, and the number of men employed on the land dwindled as the arable area contracted.[1]

During the years 1883–90, better seasons, remissions of rent, the fall in tithes, relief from some portion of the burden of rates, had arrested the process of impoverishment. To some extent the heavy land, whether arable or pasture, which wet seasons had deteriorated, recovered its tone and condition. But otherwise there was no recovery. Landlords and tenants still stood on the verge of ruin. Only a slight impulse was needed to thrust them over the border line. Two cold summers (1891–2), the drought in 1893, the unpropitious harvest of

[1] See Census Returns of Occupations, Appendix VII.

1894, coupled with the great fall in prices of corn, cattle, sheep, wool, butter and milk produced a second crisis, scarcely, if at all, less acute than that of 1879. In this later period of severe depression, unseasonable weather played a less important part than before. But in all other respects the position of agriculturists was more disadvantageous than at the earlier period. Foreign competition had relaxed none of its pressure; on the contrary, it had increased in range and in intensity. Nothing now escaped its influence. But the great difference lay in the comparative resources of agriculturists. In 1879 the high condition of the land had supplied farmers with reserves of fertility on which to draw; now, they had been drawn upon to exhaustion. In 1879, again, both landlords and tenants were still possessed of capital; now, neither had any money to spend in attempting to adapt their land to new conditions.

In September, 1893, a Royal Commission was appointed to inquire into the depression of agriculture. The evidence made a startling revelation of the extent to which owners and occupiers of land, and the land itself, had been impoverished since the Report of the Duke of Richmond's Commission. It showed that the value of produce had diminished by nearly one-half, while the cost of production had rather increased than diminished; that quantities of corn-land had passed out of cultivation; that its restoration, while the present prices prevailed, was economically impossible; that its adaptation to other uses required an immediate outlay which few owners could afford to make. Scarcely one bright feature relieved the gloom of the outlook. Foreign competition had falsified all predictions. No patent was possible for the improved processes of agriculture; they could be appropriated by all the world. The skill which British farmers had acquired by half a century of costly experiments was turned against them by foreign agriculturists working under more favourable conditions. Even distance ceased to afford its natural protection either of time or cost of conveyance, for not even the perishable products of foreign countries were excluded from English markets. Yet the evidence collected by the Commission established some important facts. It proved that many men, possessed of ample capital and energy, who occupied the best-equipped farms, enjoyed the greatest liberty in cropping, kept the best stock and were able to continue high farming, had weathered the storm even on heavy land; that small occupiers employing no labour but their own had managed to pull through; that, on suitable soils, market-gardening and fruit-farming had proved profitable; that, even on the derelict clays of Essex, Scottish milk farmers had made a living. At no previous period, it may be added, in the history of farming were the advantages and disadvantages of English land-ownership more strongly illustrated. Many tenants renting land on encumbered estates were ruined, because their hard-pressed landlords were unable to give them financial help. At least as many were nursed through the bad times by the assistance of landowners whose wealth was derived from other sources than agricultural land.

When the extent of the agricultural loss and suffering is considered, the remedies adopted by the legislature seem trivial. Yet some useful changes were made. Farmers were still further protected against adulteration of cake, fertilizers and dairy produce by the provision of the Fertilizers and Feeding-Stuffs Act (1893) and the Sale of Food and Drugs Act (1899). The Market-Gardeners Compensation Act (1895) enabled a tenant, where land was specifically let for market-garden purposes, to claim compensation for all improvements suitable to the business, even though they had been effected without the consent of the landlord. The Improvement of Land Act (1899) gave landowners increased facilities for carrying out improvements on borrowed money. The amendment of the Contagious Diseases of Animals Act (1896), requiring all foreign animals to be slaughtered at the port of landing, was a valuable step towards preventing the spread of infection. The Agricultural Rates Act (1896) and the subsequent Continuation Acts (1901, etc.), though they were only palliatives which did not settle the many questions involved in the increasing burden of rates, rendered the load of local taxation for the moment less oppressive. After all, agriculturists received little assistance from Parliament. They had to help themselves. Conditions slowly mended. More favourable seasons, rigid economy in expenses, attention to neglected branches of the industry have combined to lessen the financial strain. But the greatest relief has been afforded by the substantial reduction in the rents of agricultural land, which has resulted in a fairer adjustment of the economic pressure of low prices as between owners and occupiers.

The nadir of the great depression came in 1894–5, when the price of wheat per imperial quarter fell to 22s. 10d. and 23s. 1d., the lowest figures recorded for 150 years. From that time began a slow but steady rise in prices, sufficient to counterbalance the definite increase in wages which became manifest between 1895 and the end of the century and indeed continued, though more gradually, until the outbreak of war in 1914. After 1907 the price of wheat never fell below 30s.; but wheat had become a commodity of less importance to farmers at large, for the acreage had declined to about 1¾ millions. More than anything else milk had become the most money-making product, for the demand was continuously increasing with the growth of population and the industrial prosperity of the period. Changes in the farming population were marked as the old-time arable farmers of the south and east of England, who had persisted in their traditional but now too expensive methods of cultivation, had to retire. About 1895, rents had really adjusted themselves to the times, indeed on the heavy lands of Essex, where the reductions of rent had not been rapid or large enough to save the old tenants, farms could be had on payment of the tithe, and many large estates took the greater part of their farms in hand rather than let to the sort of men who offered themselves. Tempted by these conditions, Scotsmen migrated in numbers from a country where rents were still competitive and brought their knowledge of milk production and their more economical methods into Essex and Hertfordshire, and to a lesser degree into Kent and Surrey. Similarly, the dairy farmers of the west drifted into the south and Midlands, from Devonshire and Wales, men who had been bred to live harder and do their work more economically, if more roughly.

For this was the great lesson that was being learned, how to get the work done on the arable land with less labour. What with the turning over of arable land to grass (2½ million acres between 1872 and 1900) and economy in methods, something like a third of the labouring population left the land in the last quarter of the nineteenth century. There were other occupations to absorb the men, but none the less this forced exodus left a bitterness against farmers and landlords among the working classes that has not yet wholly disappeared.

The cheapness of land during this last decade of the nineteenth century gave to many shrewd men who had broken with tradition and learnt how to farm cheaply an opportunity of putting together exceptionally large farming businesses. S. W. Farmer of Little Bedwyn was reputed to be farming 20,000 acres at the outbreak of war, at the same time George Baylis of Wyfield Manor near Newbury was farming over 12,000 acres in Berkshire and Hampshire, growing corn and hay without any stock,[1] and in Lincolnshire men like Dennis and the Worths built up great estates on potato-growing out of little farms whose owners had been broken in the depression. These were examples of the success of better farming, but there were many instances where some sort of a paying return was got out of the land by turning it down to grass and reducing expenses to a minimum. Such was an estate put together near Ramsbury in Wiltshire, where about 4,000 acres of light arable land on the chalk were turned into a sheep ranch. In the early eighties, there was a hamlet called Snape on one part of the estate, containing a chapel, fourteen cottages, and a school attended by forty-four children. In 1921 the street was grass-grown and almost obliterated, the buildings were in ruins. The working population had been reduced to a shepherd and his dog, like the owner, living elsewhere.[2]

Though the accomplishment was irregularly distributed, considerable progress in the technique of farming was taking place. It was no longer possible for landowners and their agents to insist on particular methods of farming; covenants remained in the agreements, but were ignored as long as the tenant could pay his rent, so the diffusion of better methods came about by example, not by pressure from above. Indeed, in the main, landlords had accepted the position that there was little future for farming, that the development of their estates did not offer an outlet for their energies or capital comparable

[1] See Orwin, *Progress in English Farming Systems*, III (1930).
[2] See Orwin, *Journal of the Royal Agricultural Society*, LXXXIII (1922), p. 10.

to those available elsewhere, and that their function was to be easy with their tenants in return for the sport and the social status that the ownership of land conferred. Their direct interest in agriculture was often confined to the breeding and showing of pedigree stock, the practical value of which began to be obscured almost in proportion to it becoming a rich man's plaything and a form of social competition. Of course, a generalization of this kind about any of the classes engaged in agriculture, landlords, tenants or labourers, is contradicted by a number of individuals, who worked hard at farming and managed their estates with knowledge and judgement, but none the less this period did witness the continued disappearance of the landowner as *entrepreneur*. In general the land was not sold, the possibilities of its monopoly values were too evident in a country of growing population and increasing industrial prosperity. It is true that towards the end of the first decade of the twentieth century there arose a number of land speculators who bought up embarrassed and under-rented estates and offered the farms to the selling tenants at greatly enhanced prices. The speculators had realized better than the landlords that farming was again a remunerative business and were not afraid of the odium of making the tenants pay its full value. Moreover, this was a time when considerable political attacks were being directed against the landlords, without much discrimination between the owners of agricultural land and those who were reaping 'unearned increment' from ground rents in the growing urban areas. Some landowners took alarm and disembarrassed themselves of an investment which at the time was yielding an inferior rate of interest, yet carried with it heavy social obligations. Thus the Duke of Bedford sold both his Thorney and Tavistock Estates on terms favourable to the selling tenants.

It was at the very depth of the depression that a beginning was made with state-aided agricultural education, in the train of which research soon followed. But this will be dealt with elsewhere – results had hardly begun to accrue before the new century; the first improvements in technique came from the farmers themselves. Machinery was becoming more general upon the farm, the greatest single improvement having been the self-acting binder, the use of which began to be general about the end of the eighties; after the introduction of the knotting mechanism and twine. But haymaking machinery and springtined cultivators were also doing their share in reducing the costs of cultivation and the amount of labour required upon the arable land. In the more specialized industries change was at work: in hop-growing, for example, the eighties and early nineties saw the general replacement of the old poles by string and wire erections on which the bines could be trained so as to get proper exposure to sun and air, and spraying methods were evolved to deal with blight and mould. Until these improvements began, the methods of hop-growing had not altered in any substantial respect from those described by Reynolde Scot in 1574. While the use of artificial fertilizers was not growing as rapidly as in countries like Holland and Germany, that was because the acreage under arable cultivation continued to decline and the farmers who were winning through were mostly those who relied on keeping their expenses down, yet the knowledge of how to apply them appropriately was spreading. In the latter years of the nineteenth century one might still meet the landlord who forbade his tenants to put any artificials on their land or the farmer who had substituted Kainit for nitrate of soda because it was cheaper, but such instances disappeared as the new century opened out. One new fertilizer, indeed, was beginning to prove itself of immense value to the grassland which was becoming the mainstay of English farming. Basic slag was invented in 1879, but it only reached agriculture after 1885, when Wrightson and Munro demonstrated that its phosphate required no treatment with acid if only the slag was finely ground. It soon showed itself as possessing a marvellous regenerative value on old pastures, especially on the clay soils on which its application induced a speedy growth of white clover whereby not only the stock gained but the pasture continued to acquire fertility. While farmers have always been immediately appreciative of improved strains of seed, it can be said that during the years 1890–1910 their interest in the value of pure seed and good strains was being continually stimulated, though the history of actual introductions may best be dealt with under research.

In matters of livestock the impulse towards the selection and standardization of a pure breeding strain under the care of a Breed Society, which had been one of the chief achievements of English farming in the nineteenth century, was still active, as witness the formation of the following Societies – The Guernsey Cattle Society in 1885, the Dexter and Kerry Handbook in 1890, the Welsh Black Cattle Society in 1904, the British Holstein (now Friesian) Cattle Society in 1909. Flock Books began for Shropshires in 1883, Oxfords in 1889, Hampshires in 1890, Lincolnshires in 1892, Romney Marsh in 1895 and many others. Though from some points of view it might be questioned whether all these new breeds were wanted, the formation of a Society did tune up the general standard in the district occupied by the breed. The chief development during the period was concerned with milk, the demand for which was continuously increasing with the growing population and industrial prosperity. The milking capacity of the various breeds received more attention; for example, during this period the Dairy Shorthorns began to be differentiated and in 1905 an Association was formed in its interests, and herds like those of Hobbs and Evens obtained a repute to rival the northern beef herds. The necessity for care and cleanliness in the preparation and dispatch of milk to the public was being continually forced upon the farmers by the Health Authorities of the large towns, who had from time to time experience of milk-distributed epidemics. Regulations were enforced concerning such matters as water supply and air space in cowsheds, and if at times they were uninformed and dictatorial about the unessentials, they did arouse in the dairy world the sense that success in this growing business depended upon the purity of the product. It was indeed in the eighties that the process of butter and cheese-making, hitherto a matter of traditional and personal farm practice, were studied and standardized. At the same time the correct temperatures and acidities were determined so that the desired result could be obtained with certainty. 'Creameries' and cheese factories began to be established in order to handle milk more efficiently and economically. The importation of butter from Denmark and the Baltic countries was growing rapidly and setting a standard of quality and uniformity that neither the English nor the Irish market butter could equal, however much a dairymaid here and there could turn out a 'gilt-edged' product such as can never be obtained by factory methods.

However, there is little or no market in England for fine butter at an adequate price; the English dairy farmers could get a better return by selling raw milk and abandoned the butter market to their foreign and colonial competitors. Only a few farmers in the west and south-west, Wales and its borders, continued to make butter because the rail communications precluded them from getting whole milk to market, while they could also turn the separated milk to account by calf-rearing. The Irish butter-making was transformed on Danish lines, their farmers, like the Danish, being content with returns per gallon well below that expected by the English farmer. The machinery of the dairy was undergoing revolution; barrel churns replaced the old upright churns in which a dasher worked up and down in the whole milk, the only reminder of the old shape being the metal churns in which, for a few years longer perhaps, milk will travel by rail. Rail transport again brought the necessity of milk coolers, though the customers of the small farmers, each with their own milk round, still demanded 'milk warm from the cow'. But the most important of these machines for the dairyman was the centrifugal separator of which really efficient types began to be available about 1890, though, as indicated above, the perfecting of this exquisite machine coincided with the decline and practical extinction of commercial butter-making in England. Among other labour-saving machines that began to appear on the farms towards the close of the nineteenth century were the small oil engines to run the grinding and food preparation plant, and sheep-shearing machines, the use of which grew but slowly because there were still men enough about to clip the comparatively small flocks running on the usual farm.

The commercial development of poultry rather belongs to the post-war period. Even down to the end of the century poultry-keeping still halted between the methods of the fancier and of the farmer who had a mongrel flock picking about his stack-yard. W. B. Tegetmeier, in his day an authority, was said to have an offer open of £50 for anyone who could produce an accredited balance sheet showing a year's profit on a poultry farm, excluding those dealing in stock birds or eggs. About Heathfield in Sussex there was a successful cramming industry producing birds for the table, though the crammers did no breeding, but bought young birds for fattening from as far afield as Ireland.

The period we are considering, 1890–1914, was also one of expansion and improved technique in market-gardening and fruit-growing, industries that were prospering in response not only to the growing population but to a change in the general dietary. Potato-growing, which had proved but a treacherous foundation for the Lincolnshire Yeomen in the seventies and eighties, became one of the money-making crops for certain selected districts, like the Lothians and Ayrshire in Scotland, the silt and the warp soils of Lincoln and Yorkshire, the light soils of West Lancashire and Cheshire. Even on the gravels of Hertfordshire, where Arthur Young had found himself 'living in the jaws of a wolf', potato-growing brought wealth to some of the migrants from Scotland. Nothing revolutionary had happened to make the industry so profitable; it was a good instance of the accumulation of a number of small improvements, each of which could be pooh-poohed as not worth while by the old-time farmer. New varieties were being introduced, 'Up-to-date' had a long run about the turn of the century; the virtue of Scotch seed was recognized, though the reason for its success was yet undiscovered. Boxing the seed and planting sprouted sets became standard practice; the fertilizers to procure large crops became understood, for the growers were substantial men willing to spend money and open to advice. Spraying with Bordeaux mixture was standardized, but did not become general in all districts because many growers preferred to gamble on intermittent appearance of blight.

Market-gardening was increasing and improving its methods, though it was still dependent upon the lavish supplies of stable manure that could be obtained from the great towns. Naturally it was segregating into selected areas – the brick earths of the Thames Valley and North Kent, Bedfordshire,

Huntingdon, Wisbech and the Fens, and the Vale of Evesham, where it was found that asparagus would flourish on stiffish clays, while selected areas in Cornwall could follow the earliest potato crops with a second crop of autumn and winter broccoli.

Lastly, this period saw the great development of the glass-house cultivation in districts like Worthing, Swanley Junction and above all the Lea Valley. Fifty years ago the tomato was as great a rarity in England as an avocado pear is today; a few were imported, a few were grown in private conservatories. In the late eighties market cultivation under glass began and early in the nineties Worthing tomatoes had established their position as superior to any importations. From that time until the outbreak of war there was no pause in the extension of the industry. Cucumbers went with the tomatoes, grapes and chrysanthemums completed the old cycle; forced bulbs – tulips, narcissus and iris, were later additions, as again has been the perpetual-flowering carnation, for flowers have become as much a matter of general household expenditure as tomatoes or eggs.

Looking at the state of agriculture generally the early years of the century may be recalled as a time of quiet but growing prosperity for farmers. One may read in *Farmer's Glory*, that singularly faithful presentation of farming life in Wiltshire, how Mr A. G. Street, who settled down on his father's farm in 1907, looks back to those years before the war as 'the spacious days', just as the man of an older generation recalled the sixties and early seventies as the good old times. 'But that large tenant farmers were doing pretty well then, there is no question. I suppose the business side of farming had its worries in those days, but it is difficult to recall any. There were good seasons and bad seasons, doubtless. I can remember wet weather in harvest time and good weather. Good luck at lambing time and bad I can also call to mind, but nothing ever seemed to make any difference in our home life. It all seemed such a settled prosperous thing.'

Again I may quote my own contemporary opinion, written after a series of farming tours round the United Kingdom in 1910–12. 'In the first place we must recognize that the industry is at present sound and prosperous.'

2 Causes of the Fall of Agricultural Prices between 1875 and 1895

H. M. CONACHER

This article was first published in the *Scottish Journal of Agriculture*, XIX (1936).

The recent depression in agriculture from time to time recalls to the minds of students of economics the previous depression, which set in after 1875 and lasted for twenty years. Towards the end of the time a Royal Commission inquired into its causes and found that it was expressed in a steady fall in the prices of such important products as grain (especially wheat), wool, meat and dairy produce, and that the fall was due mostly to increased heavy imports thereof. There were some authorities, however, at the time who attributed the depression at least in part to currency movements. It was easier to bring out the effect of such movements at a later date, when prices had risen again, for the rise was thought to be capable of explanation on these lines. Thus it was said that the fall was due to the stocks of gold in the world being insufficient to carry on exchange at the level required by international trade, and that relief had come through the great quantities of new gold yielded by the South African mines.

The situation was supposed to have been aggravated by the movement usually described as the demonetization of silver. Now the two sets of forces (monetary and other) are usually put in the foreground by persons with different points of view, and as a rule little attempt is made to co-ordinate them.

1 It is indeed difficult to do so, because the demonstration of the connection between supplies of money and price levels usually takes the form of a graph, which shows a 'correlation' between them. The two sets of phenomena are set out as if between them they made a closed system and there were not room for other agencies to come in.

2 Again increases in the supplies of 'money' tend to be treated as if they were windfalls and just dependent on the chance discovery of new supplies of the precious metals – or in recent times simply gold. Besides such cases, however, many changes in the quantity of 'money' are due to the deliberate action of governments and communities in expanding and contracting the supply of legal tender money and credit or in discarding one kind of money, as when various countries left bimetallism for a gold standard.

Thus it was the low price of wheat which stimulated the demand for the restoration of silver in the American currency in the seventies and eighties. Hence simply to say that an increase in the supplies of money causes a rise in prices does not tell the whole truth.

3 Those who recognize that in tracing such a connection we are isolating certain groups of phenomena have often put the position in this way – that changes in the prices of certain classes of goods for a time may be due to non-monetary causes, but that a general rise and fall of most commodities over a fairly long period is due to changes in the supplies of money. It is recognized, of course, that within such a long period there may be more than one full term of a trade cycle with its special movements of prices.

4 Attempts too are sometimes made to allocate the effect of the different factors at work causing price movements, as when Cassel suggests that of the general rise in prices of 30 per cent in the sixties perhaps 18 per cent might be attributed to the increase in the supplies of gold; and again 'the much discussed scarcity of gold in the nineties' is responsible for a fall of 8 per cent in the general price level below the normal.

If without further analysis of all the data we try to make any such allocation in the case of the fall in prices after 1875 some such consideration as the following presents itself. We might ask 'If there had been smaller imports of grain, wool, etc., from abroad, would there have been a fall in prices all the same as a result of the *relatively* smaller supplies of money?'

Now it would have been very hard to convince the farmer or the plain man that anything like the same fall in the prices of grain, meat and wool would have taken place.

It will then occur to us, no doubt, that the new supplies of grain and other things from overseas, apart from their intrinsic effect in lowering prices, also constituted a large element in the additional amount of international trade, with which, in the view of the currency experts, existing supplies of money were less and less able to cope – and so they helped to lower prices twice over. Such a suggestion implies, of course, that it was only as adding to the total amount of *exchange* of goods to be undertaken that these new supplies were helping to throw more work on existing stocks of money and not that their original production depended so much on 'money' or 'credit'. For the production of agricultural goods is managed without the appeal to credit that would be necessary to produce comparable amounts of manufactured goods. Anyhow, the suggestion made above does connect the two sets of influences tending to lower prices in a very close fashion. The inference seems to be that the greater demands made by various countries on gold for currency, in the seventies at least, did not seriously retard the great increase in international trade then going on.

Apart from the foregoing there seems reason to suppose that the calculus by which the statisticians were led to see a connection between stocks of gold and price movements is in some ways faulty. Thus the prices were usually taken from an index number, which included about 100 commodities of different kinds. Now recent experience shows us that the prices of agricultural products and vegetable raw materials usually fall faster and lower than those of manufactured articles – separate index numbers for different groups should therefore be prepared. Again, the time with which we are dealing was one in which great changes were taking place in the currencies of important countries. The leading states were changing from bimetallism to the gold standard, and the silver-using countries were thus left confronting the rest of the world with depreciated currencies through the discarded silver and an increase in stocks of silver. Under these circumstances, and in view of the fact that we are dealing very much with commodities which were sent from bimetallist or silver money countries to gold monometallist or bimetallist countries, to confine oneself to the supplies of gold in dealing with prices seems inadequate. Cassel, noting that prices in 1905 were back at the 1850 level, said that if the new supplies of gold had been made available uniformly at the rate of 2·8 per cent a year, prices might have been kept level. But this is to read back the situation when gold has become the main standard into a bimetallist world. Even accepting the recognized calculus one is free to contend that the rise and fall in prices between 1850 and 1880 is too steep and too jagged on the graphs (there being a high peak about 1872) to be accounted for by variations in the supplies of gold. We cannot expect to find the whole truth about the fall in prices after 1873 or 1875 without also considering the rise in the previous twenty years, keeping in view abnormal increases in the gold supply in the earlier period, and demonetization of silver in the latter, as well as the great political and economic movements of the generation.

The experts, of course, are always seeking to find a pattern in these things – hence the eagerness with which they settle on the trade cycle, a promising material. In the economic, financial, and monetary processes of the time under consideration it is difficult to find one pattern. No doubt looking back from the present time one can see certain resemblances with our own experience. It was a time of wars in Europe and North America, of much borrowing, inflated currencies, feverish production to make up the losses of war, followed by crises; further, just as we have been through all the troubles of exchange between countries with depreciated currencies and those still on gold, so the belligerents of that time passed through a period of inconvertible paper and in the end usually discarded bimetallism for the gold standard.

There is no doubt that, after the series of wars, there was a great increase in the production of grain, meat, wool and dairy produce in North America, eastern Europe, Australia, India and later Argentina, and that we took more of them than the other European countries, though in France and Germany there were complaints in the seventies of the low prices of wheat through the new foreign supplies. These increased supplies were due partly to great new tracts of land being

C

made available for cultivation and partly through the great 'boom' in railway construction in the sixties and early seventies. In fact various European and American countries which were not at war were borrowing as feverishly as the belligerents in order to execute public works, principally railways. Thus the public debts of many countries were doubled between 1862 and 1872. Perhaps the most conspicuous cases of more land being made available were in the United States and later Canada. The US Congress passed the Homestead Act in 1862 providing for the final settlement of the public domains by grants of land not less than 160 acres with a nominal charge, on the understanding that the settler reclaimed and cultivated the land and built a house. Under this law a great part of the Middle West was settled. In 1872 Canada followed with a similar law, under which the prairie provinces in turn were settled. In the United States the land was given partly to ex-soldiers and other American citizens and also to the great number of European immigrants who came in after the war. Immigrants also helped to settle the new Canadian provinces. All this new production of grain then was due to a union of land and labour, for which credit was not necessary as it would have been in industrial production. A further development happened in Rumania, another grain-growing country opened up by railways and steamers, in which the great landowners owned most of the land and exploited it by the more or less forced labour of recently emancipated serfs. One may put it in this way as regards North America that the United States and Canada made great amounts of 'credit' available in the form of free land. Marshall said something to the same effect in a memorandum on Currency Differences and International Trade – 'Wheat is in many new countries practically a by-product, the main product is often cultivated land; people are willing to grow wheat at a loss if meanwhile they get a good title to the fertile land which they have been bringing into cultivation.' This was said primarily with reference to the Indian wheat, which was being imported in growing quantities a little later, but it applies to North America.

Land and labour, however, do not account for the great extension of railways in North America and central and eastern

Europe which went on in the late sixties and seventies. And this appears to have been the other great development leading to an increase in the production of grains by making the transport of them to remote markets easier. To quote Marshall again (giving evidence): 'I quite admit that the fall in the price of wheat has been very great. I say it has been due exclusively or almost exclusively to the fall in the price of iron; that silver has had no effect on it whatever; but that the fall in the price of iron and steel has effected it.' (The building of steamships as well as railways would of course be made cheaper thereby.) He was speaking in 1886 after prices had fallen generally. We had a big share in the extension of railways; for in the sixties our later rivals the Germans and Americans were taken up with fighting or recovering from their wars. So we were busy in turning out the products of the heavy industries. Further, we seem to have made so much money during the disturbed period, being neutrals after the Crimean war, that we could lend great sums abroad. The borrowers took the loans out in the form of capital goods for railways and other undertakings. Generally there was at this time such an increase in wealth that Marshall looked forward to the possibility of a general fall in the rate of interest to 2 per cent, a thing which, it was said, John Bull would never stand. It is generally recognized now that borrowing countries are entitled to repay their loans and pay the interest on them by sending goods to their creditors. We made the unwillingness of the United States, as shown in their high tariffs, to accept goods from other countries (except those raw materials and foodstuffs which they want but cannot produce for themselves) a plea for suspending payment of our debt to them. It was inevitable then, as we were in the latter part of the nineteenth century admitting most imports free, that we should receive in great quantities the exports of the new countries which we had helped to develop by loans. This series of events then seems to account for the great increase in the imports of foodstuffs after 1870. The case of wool stands by itself in one way—for it was the gradual building up of flocks by the Australian pastoralists, which went on until the heavy droughts at the end of the century, that made the export possible. It was equally inevitable that great quantities should come here because Australia was nearly always borrowing from us when we had capital to export.

The chilled meat from Argentina comes a little later, just as our well-known investments in Argentine railways are later. North American cheese, which came first from the United States, then from Canada, seems due to a cross-over to dairying in some states, because the growing of wheat had passed over to the Middle West. Certainly Ontario became a dairying province when the prairie provinces checked grain-growing therein.

To turn to the currency influences with which the movement of prices is often associated. In the old days only 'England' and Portugal were on gold, as Bagehot reminds us. The United Kingdom obtained its share of the new gold from California and Australia. The greater part apparently came to the London market to be distributed; between 1858 and 1875 this country itself absorbed £79¾ millions worth, and in the more recent years of the period the world's annual production was about £20 millions worth, of which, taking the average, we had between a quarter and one-fifth every year. It is probable then that with the earlier supplies, which of course we had to pay for, we helped to increase the volume of credit needed to stimulate the extra production of our industries, which was all helping in turn to increase the supplies of grain and foodstuffs from the new countries. Further, we did not apparently have to send great quantities of gold away in connection with our export of capital, because so much of it was 'in kind'. Again the rise in prices in the United States, Germany and France in the sixties and seventies was not due to the new supplies of gold, because while these countries were at war, and in the case of the United States for fourteen years afterwards, they were not on gold or on gold and silver, but on paper; in fact going through inflation, which is the common expedient of countries at war. Prices rose so high in the United States after the war that even European countries could not afford to buy their products, partly no doubt because in many cases they were also using depreciated currencies. Equally the sudden break in prices in the United States and Germany, and in Great Britain in 1873, was rather due to a kind of trade cycle collapse

– the feverish activity of the war period having been continued for a time after the end of the last of the wars. In Germany the payment of the French indemnity is also supposed to
have had a demoralizing effect. It should be added that Germany used £50 millions worth of the sum to buy the gold
reserve needed for its new gold currency.

Under the Resumption Act, 1875, the United States, which
had formerly been bimetallist, went back to specie payments
in 1879, adopting gold as the basis of the currency. It would
be difficult to say whether this adoption of the 'gold standard'
forced down prices in the United States during the next fifteen
years through failure to secure enough gold. It might have
done if it had been worked on the lines of Peel's Bank Act; but
it was not. Thus there was in circulation a great mass of 'legal
tender' paper, issued since 1861. Under the act of 1875 it
should have been redeemed, but this process went on slowly,
so the gold reserve was supporting a greater mass of currency
than it should have done. Naturally, while the excess of legal
tender notes was in circulation, the reserve was always in
jeopardy. The agrarian states from time to time complained
that lack of currency was keeping down the prices of grain.
So they backed the cry of the silver-producing states for some
reinstatement of silver (though the American public did not
care much for silver dollars, preferring dollar bills), and in 1886
the Silver Purchase Act was passed requiring the Treasury to
buy so much silver, just as President Roosevelt has been doing
for the past year or two. Certain elements in the Republican
Party objected, and after a few years the act was repealed after
it had done endless mischief, helped to cause an inflation of the
currency, which in turn stimulated a boom and led to another
collapse in 1893, when desperate efforts had to be made to
save the country from going off gold. The Republican Party
in the east and north were generally in favour of sound money,
as suiting finance and industry. Industrial prices, too, were
kept up by the tariff so that the north-eastern states did not
want more currency to achieve this result. It was, however, on
the agrarian states that the business of providing exports to
help to pay interest and dividends on the European holdings
of the United States securities fell. Hence the prices of their

products rose and fell according to whether European harvests were good or bad, or, in the case of cotton, according to the Indian harvest. It is difficult to speak of long-term trends in this period, for there were recoveries and depressions of trade every few years; and if we are inclined to be superior about the aberrations of American big business and finance, an American writer could point to the Baring collapse in 1890 after excessive British investments in Argentina and the Kaffir market a few years later.

It is curious to see that, faced with the present division of the world into the 'gold block', the 'Sterling area' and the rest, the 'City' should look back wistfully to a time when the general adoption of gold had provided an international currency. This, however, was achieved only at the end of the nineteenth century. Before then traders and bankers knew something of our perplexities. They were not so much worried about whether there would be enough gold to go round when Germany, the United States and the Latin Union had gone on to gold, but (at least in this country) with the difficulty of trading with India or Russia or the Far East, when silver had depreciated so conspicuously in terms of gold. It was complained on one side that the depreciation of the rupee had given a bonus to the export of wheat from India to this country, thus adding one more to the competitors of the British farmer in his home market. It was also true that the inevitable railways had made it easier to bring the grain to Karachi. At that time some authorities like Marshall (unlike most of our contemporaries) looked a little further below the surface and saw that it was not really good for the producers in a country with a depreciated currency to be selling their goods cheap to buyers in a country that was on gold. In our case it meant that if Indian grain was cheaper, Manchester goods had to be cheaper if the ryot was to buy them. That was one way of bringing gold prices down. In due time the rupee, rouble and yen went on to gold; but, in the meantime, the gold monometallists in their controversy with the bimetallists were inclined to make light of the troubles caused by the depreciation of silver in terms of gold. The German and French farmers complained of the fall of prices of agricultural produce; but this was not due to a fall in internal prices in the country caused by the fact that there was not enough gold to act as cover for their currencies. Germany started with the equivalent of £50 millions worth, which should have been enough.

On the whole, the fall of agricultural prices was due to the overseas supplies of grain and wool (especially in Germany). In Germany, too, the grievance was a curious one. The powerful landowners of Prussia east of the Elbe were great growers of rye, and they were being hit because the cheapness of wheat was causing a decline in the consumption of rye. So there was a move over to protection for foodstuffs after 1879. A fair statement, however, showed that increase of costs had as much as low prices to do with the complaints of German agriculturists. It is curious that the trend towards protection should have followed the adoption of gold, if the gold standard was to facilitate international trade. And as international trade on the whole was growing in spite of protection, it is perhaps not in the region of internal prices, but in that of 'world prices', that we should look for the influence of the gold standard. And in so far as a certain amount of gold would have to pass in settling international accounts we should expect the monetary authorities to be preoccupied with the problem of holding their stocks of gold, and their actions might be quoted as showing that there was not enough gold for the purpose of international trade, when it was really some of the other factors that were at fault. We should also have to watch the effects of exports of capital on gold movements. Obviously the best remedy for undue transfers of gold was to use as much as possible such devices as bills of exchange for facilitating international trade. How far that device was developed may be inferred from the well-known illustration of the 'triangular trade' which was carried on before the war. Thus we paid for our imports of grain, cotton, etc. from the United States by exporting cotton goods and other manufactured articles to India and the Far East, from which in turn the United States imported a good deal. This complicated trade was carried on by means of bills of exchange. It could hardly have been done smoothly if there had been violent changes in the rate of discounting bills in the chief centres on which bills were drawn. London was of course the most important of these centres, and perhaps it is a testimonial to the way in which the gold standard was worked in the city of London that the apprehension with which Bagehot just before his death saw the prospect of the United States following France and Germany in the adoption of gold as the basis of currency, when the United Kingdom had already been taking a fourth or fifth of the new supplies of gold, was not more fully justified. There were at times, of course, violent changes in the rate of discount, as when the Bank of England raised its rate to 10 per cent at the time of the Baring crash, and at certain stages in the familiar trade cycle changes are usually made.

Perhaps from our point of view the most disturbing influences which affected the working of the gold standard in the latter part of this period are connected with capital movements. The British investor made some strange pilgrimages in these years – possibly haunted by the spectre of a 2 per cent rate of interest. (Mulhall actually did show a drop from 4·17 per cent in 1850–60 to 3·3 per cent in 1880–5.) He had made some bad bargains in American railways in the seventies, so in the eighties he turned his attention to Argentina, Australia and New Zealand. The Argentine investments ended in the Baring crash in 1890; those in the latter Dominions were not too successful, much of the money being ill applied. Hence the stagnation of the nineties, with a bank rate of 2 per cent as at present. In this time the transactions between creditor and debtor were being liquidated. Either the debtors had let too much gold go, which upset the basis of their currencies, or they had to pay with increased amounts of exports. The parallel with the position in recent years is striking, except that besides the countries of primary production Germany was also a leading debtor in the post-war situation. Hence the prolonged fall of the prices of primary produce in the late eighties and nineties is, like that of recent years, largely due to the efforts of debtor countries to pay their debts. We may say then that the earlier fall of prices was due to the increased areas of production and the new railways; the later fall to the enforced liquidation. The adequacy of the gold standard in itself is not necessarily called in question if international trade and finance had been more wisely handled. It is often said that the increased gold supplies from the Rand put things right. Perhaps from more than one point of view they did—for after the stagnation of the early nineties the new mines were the first big thing which excited the interest of the British investor.

3 The Great Depression of English Agriculture, 1873–1896

T. W. FLETCHER

This article was first published in *The Economic History Review*, XIII(2) (1960–1).

I

The nature and extent of the Great Depression of trade and industry during the last quarter of the nineteenth century have been argued for many years. In contrast, the existence of a great depression in agriculture was, and is, universally accepted, and farmers' sufferings have been wept over by generations of mourners. 'Since 1862 the tide of agricultural prosperity had ceased to flow; after 1874 it turned and rapidly ebbed' – Ernle's splendid narrative leaves us in no doubt as to the severity of depression.[1] Venn, discussing the supply of gold and the price level, believed agriculture to have suffered more than most industries, 'being plunged indeed into the abyss'.[2] The general opinion is perhaps best summarized by Halévy; 'if the position of industry was doubtful, about agriculture there could be no doubt. It was in an advanced state of decay'.[3]

The evidence for this sort of textbook generalization is of two kinds, the statistical, with the Gazette price of wheat and Sauerbeck's food index illustrating the fall in farm prices and the Agricultural Returns mirroring output, and the descriptive, which leans heavily on Ernle and the proceedings of the two Royal Commissions of 1879–82 and 1894–7. Additional evidence, but playing little or no part in the genesis of this

[1] R. E. Prothero (later Lord Ernle), *English Farming Past and Present* 4th ed. (1927), p. 374.

[2] J. A. Venn, *The Foundations of Agricultural Economics* 2nd ed. (1923), p. 474.

[3] E. Halévy, *A History of the English People in the Nineteenth Century* – V, 2nd ed. (1951), pp. 293–4.

orthodox view, is the Schedule A assessments of the Inland
Revenue Board and the recent work on rent by Mr Rhee and
on output by Dr Ojala.[1] It is the view of the present writer
that much of this evidence is biased in that most commentators have adopted, albeit unconsciously, an attitude towards
agriculture and consequently towards the Great Depression
that is inappropriate and misleading in the economic climate
of Victorian, and later, England.

The depression is usually dated 1873–96, which fairly
coincides with the turning points of both the wheat price and
Sauerbeck's index. This seems satisfactory until the question
is asked, how important was wheat to the English farmer and
what does Sauerbeck's index measure? According to Dr
Ojala, who does not underestimate its importance, the wheat
crop contributed 13 per cent of the gross output at current
prices of the agriculture of the U.K. in the period 1867–76
and this fell to 4 per cent by 1894–1903.[2] An estimate for
England alone shows percentages of 22 and 7.[3] Sauerbeck's
index, from the point of view of the commodities and prices
selected, is probably a better measure of price changes of
foods entering international trade than it is of the products of
English farms; for example, the whole of English dairying is
represented by one price series, that of Friesland butter, out
of nineteen, all equally weighted, and fourteen of these series
relate to import not home product prices.[4] A further drawback
is that the weighting remains unaltered throughout the period
and by the 1890s is ludicrously unrepresentative of the output
from English farms.

Neither the coincidence of Sauerbeck's vegetable food
index with the curve of the wheat price nor the relatively small
part played by wheat in farm output would matter so much if
changes in the price of wheat accurately reflected changes in

---

[1] H. A. Rhee, *The Rent of Agricultural Land in England and Wales* (Central
Landowners Association, 1946); E. M. Ojala, *Agriculture and Economic Progress*
(1952).
[2] Computed from Ojala, op. cit., Table XVI, p. 208.
[3] See Appendix.
[4] Sauerbeck's food index, base 1867–77, is an unweighted average of 19 price
indices, 8 of them forming his vegetable food index, 7 his animal food index
and 4 covering sugar, tea and coffee; details can be found in the *Journal of the
Statistical Society*, XLIX (1886), pp. 592–648.

agricultural prices generally or if Sauerbeck's import prices were representative of prices received by English livestock producers. But neither of these suppositions is tenable: the price of wheat notoriously fell by more than other cereal prices and very much more than livestock prices (except wool), and although home livestock prices are neither abundant nor easily found, such price series as can be constructed exhibit a smaller fall during the Great Depression than the respective import series.[1] On the output side, to judge by the *Agricultural Returns*, there is little evidence of any contraction of production, except in the case of wheat and, to a much smaller extent, of barley; on the contrary the acreage of oats, fruit and vegetables, and the numbers of most categories of livestock increased significantly.[2]

Thus the most widely used statistical evidence of agricultural depression appears, on examination, to relate mainly to the price and acreage changes of wheat. A closer look at the Great Depression seems called for; it is proposed to begin with the general demand and supply situation and pass on to a consideration of the nature of English agriculture and of the contemporary scene.

II

The demand situation facing English farmers was encouraging. Between 1851 and 1871 the population of England increased at the rate of 1·3 per cent per annum; between 1871 and 1901 the annual rate of growth was 1·5 per cent, or, in absolute terms, whereas in the twenty years of the 'Golden Age' less than 5 millions were added to the population, in the thirty years covering the Great Depression an additional 10 million mouths appeared. Again, between 1851 and 1871 real wages rose by less than 1 per cent per annum; between 1871 and 1901 the rate was approximately 2 per cent.[3] The contrast is the more marked in that there was little change for a decade and a

---

[1] See p. 34, note 2.

[2] The numbers of cattle, pigs and farm horses in England increased by 22, 18 and 19 per cent respectively; the number of sheep fell by 18 per cent, between 1868–71 and 1894–8.

[3] W. T. Layton, *An Introduction to the Study of Prices* (1912), p. 150.

half after 1851 and the 'take-off' into significant growth of real wages occurred as late as the half dozen years after 1868. Thus with population increasing faster than during the Golden Age and accompanied for the first time by a marked upward surge in real wages the aggregate demand situation for food was exceedingly favourable for the producer.

It is a commonplace that with rising income civilized man prefers to purchase the more expensive and appetizing proteins rather than the cheaper starches. And when, as during the Great Depression, the price of bread and cereals falls by more than the price of animal products, a growing fraction of income becomes available for expenditure on protein. Contemporary references to the changing pattern of food consumption abound and were neatly paraphrased by Graham in 1899 in his well-known phrase, 'the sort of man who had bread and cheese for his dinner forty years ago now demands a chop'.[1]

The effect on English farmers of this changing pattern of demand was naturally to stimulate the production of meat, milk and dairy products at the expense of wheat and potatoes. Not that this shift began in the seventies. Since 1846 the price of meat and dairy products rose slowly relative to the price of wheat, but the prophesied flood of cereal imports was unexpectedly restricted until the seventies; it was in this decade that a revolutionary change in relative livestock and cereal prices began to be observed.[2]

Demand forms only one blade of the economist's 'abhorred shears': on the supply side a prominent feature of the period was the growth in food imports. The quantity of wheat and flour imported into the U.K. increased by 90 per cent, that of meat by 300 per cent, and that of butter and cheese by 110 per cent between 1871–5 and 1896–1900; the repercussions on home output were not, however, identical.

To judge from estimates of total supply available for con-

---

[1] P. A. Graham, *The Revival of English Agriculture* (1899), p. 9.
[2] Early advocates of a change from corn to meat, dairy and green crop production include J. Caird, *English Agriculture in 1850–51* (1852), pp. 483–7 *passim* and G. Beasley, *A Report on the State of Agriculture in Lancashire* (Preston, 1849), who argued 'upon the presumption that permanently low prices of grain will in future be established' (p. 67).

sumption in the U.K., demand for wheat increased more slowly than population. Foreign supplies were plentiful following the opening up of virgin territory abroad and the fall in rail and shipping rates, and the price at English ports fell drastically. Wheat was to all intents a homogeneous product, it sold on the classic international wheat market, and the price received by the English farmer was a direct function of the world price; it fell from 56s. 0d. a quarter in 1867–71 to 27s. 3d. in 1894–8[1] and was accompanied by a decline in the English acreage from over 3 to 1¾ million acres.

The situation was different in the case of meat. Demand grew faster than population, and home output rose by some 10 per cent in spite of a severe thinning of the country's sheep flocks by the outbreak of disease in the years 1879–81. Imports were generally inferior in quality to the home product and priced accordingly, and price differentials widened over the period of the Great Depression.[2] Imports of butter and cheese, already considerable, increased further to satisfy the growth in consumer demand which, in face of the attractions of the lucrative liquid milk trade, could not be supplied by English farmers. Most foreign supplies on the English market fetched lower prices than the home product and, as with meat, the price difference widened.[3] The responsible factor, apart from quality, was undoubtedly the price of liquid milk which, immune from foreign competition, showed little or no overall fall. To generalize in terms of grave import competition reducing agricultural prices is inadmissible against a back-

---

[1] *Gazette* prices. The period 1867–71 is chosen, whenever possible, as more representative of pre-depression prices than say 1870–6 which covers the marked cyclical peak of the early seventies; 1894–8 is taken as the end of the depression in the trough of the nineties.

[2] For example, the price of best English beef at Smithfield between 1867–71 and 1894–8 fell by 11 per cent compared with imported fresh beef which fell by 23 per cent. Imported mutton was even less competitive; first quality lightweight mutton and lamb rose by eight per cent as against a fall in average import prices of some 30 per cent (*Agricultural Returns*).

[3] Sauerbeck's best imported Friesland butter fell in price by 22 per cent between 1867–71 and 1894–8; Lancashire farm butter by about 13 per cent. Cheese imports declined in price by over 20 per cent; best Lancashire and Cheshire by some 10 per cent. (For Lancashire prices see my forthcoming article 'Lancashire livestock farming during the Great Depression' in *British Agricultural History Review* (reprinted in this volume).)

ground of generally falling prices. Some farm prices fell, others did not; some fell in the seventies, others in the eighties and nineties.

A fourth group of imports was that comprising maize, coarse grains and oilcakes. In that the quantity imported doubled between 1867–71 and 1894–8, during which time the average price fell by about 40 per cent, while livestock numbers increased by only about 10 per cent,[1] a significant increase in productivity is suggested, in the form, for example, of higher yields per cow. The question is prompted, what changes occurred in the output of English agriculture during this period?

III

The one published estimate that provides sufficient data to check the various series contributing to the final sum is Dr Ojala's, and it is unfortunate that it is computed for the U.K. as a whole, so divergent were the interests and experiences of farmers in the four countries concerned, but the difficulty of allocating imports within the U.K. and the paucity of figures relating to Anglo-Irish trade may well justify Dr Ojala's decision in this respect. It is otherwise with some of his price series which rely overmuch on Sauerbeck's import prices, in particular for meat and dairy output. Using Dr Ojala's basic data but substituting home for import prices, a revised index of the U.K.'s gross farm output at current prices moves from 100 in 1867–9 to 108 in 1870–6 to 90 in 1894–1903.[2] An estimate for England falls from 100 in 1867–71 to 87 in 1894–8.[3]

A net output calculation to determine the margin of farmers' profits is hazardous, in that small opposed movements of gross output and total costs squeeze or magnify the margin severely; nevertheless the subtraction may be attempted for the U.K. Deducting from the revised gross output figures for

[1] In terms of Livestock Units, which provide a method of adding different categories of livestock standardized in terms of feed requirements; see *Rations for Livestock*, Ministry of Agriculture, Bulletin No. 48.

[2] Dr Ojala's estimates are for the groups of years 1867–9, 1870–6, 1877–85, 1886–93, 1894–1903.

[3] For details see Appendix.

1867–76 and 1894–1903 Dr Ojala's costs – to which must be added 'rent' and 'wages etc.' derived from Mr Bellerby's estimates – the total net income at current prices of U.K. farmers declined from £85·4 million to £79 million, a fall of some 7·5 per cent.[1] In view of the predominance of imports in farm costs it is impossible to assign a figure to English farmers alone, but their fall in income was perhaps greater than in the U.K. as a whole, because of the greater importance of wheat. Wales, Ireland and Scotland were predominantly livestock farming areas. It would seem, however, that although English farmers as a group did not, as did farm labourers,[2] manage to augment their money incomes during the Great Depression, although their real incomes appreciated, they did not suffer to the same extent as landowners, to judge by the fall in gross rents.[3] But in all these cases crude average figures mask crucial differences. The contrast between the movement of wages, rents and profits in arable and livestock counties is noticeable. In the northern counties wages rose by some 17 per cent between 1867–71 and 1894–8; in the eastern counties the gain of the seventies was lost by the mid-nineties.[4] The experiences of land-owners were more extreme; for example, the Earl of Derby's Fylde rents, which rose by 18 per cent between 1870–1 and 1896, may be compared with those of the Cambridgeshire estates cited by Mr Rhee which declined by 35 per cent between the same dates.[5]

Profits are not directly measurable but output changes are. At constant 1894–8 prices, arable output declined from 1867–71 by about 5 per cent, livestock output increased by some 20 per cent; using 1867–71 prices the changes shew as —9 and

[1] See J. R. Bellerby, *Agriculture and Industry Relative Income* (1956), Table 1, p. 56. These farmers' net income figures are of the same order of magnitude as those shown by Dr Ojala (less Mr Bellerby's rent and wages), but are significantly larger than those computed by Mr Bellerby.

[2] Whose wages on average rose by 11 per cent; see A. Wilson Fox, 'Agricultural wages in England and Wales during the last fifty years', *Journal of the Royal Statistical Society*, LXIV (1903).

[3] See Rhee, op. cit., Table II, pp. 44–6. Mr Rhee's rent series are heavily weighted by rents from the corn-growing counties and thus probably overestimate the national average fall in rents.

[4] Wilson Fox, op. cit.

[5] Lancs. Record Office, DDK (Fylde Rents); Rhee, op. cit.

+18 per cent, respectively. The fall in gross output, at current prices, is entirely accounted for by the decline of wheat, and if the gross output sum be divided into its two components, crops and livestock, the distinction is clear; while arable output declined from £65 million to £41 million, livestock output increased from £64 million to £71 million. On the eve of depression arable output equalled that of livestock; by the mid-nineties it was only three-fifths its value. Wheat is preeminent in 1870; it accounts for nearly half of total arable output and over a fifth of gross output, and equals in value beef and mutton together. By the mid-nineties wheat accounts for little over a sixth of the diminished arable output and has been surpassed not only by dairy produce, beef, mutton and pig meat severally but is rapidly being overhauled by poultry.[1] Thus, while livestock farmers increased their quantum of output appreciably and even significantly raised its value, wheat growers suffered the brunt of the price fall and cut back their acreage severely.

There are a number of considerations relevant to such a gross and net output computation. Firstly, helped by the greater freedom of cropping achieved by the tenant farmer during the period, an increasing proportion of cereal growers sold oats, hay and straw off the farm as feed for non-farm horses the numbers of which in England may well have increased by as much as 50 per cent, although no census returns were collected after 1872.[2] Fertility was raised and yields increased on the shrinking arable acreage by the greater supplies of town manure available, the growing numbers of farm livestock, the larger manurial residues from the growing import of feeding stuffs and the increasing import of fertilizer.

Secondly, there were changes in the quality of products and

---

[1] See Appendix.

[2] Dr Ojala's estimate shows an insignificant increase in non-farm horses in Great Britain during the Great Depression. The only available census figures are for Ireland, where the non-farm horses almost doubled in number. In that the population of England increased by roughly 50 per cent, as did both the volume of trade and of railway frieght, an equivalent increase in the number of non-farm horses seems not improbable. For the numbers of non-farm horses 1831–72 inclusive, see *Report from the Select Committee of the House of Lords on Horses*, H.C. 325 of 1873; it was called to investigate the 'alleged scarcity of horses in this country'.

in the relative quantities sold by farmers of the several qualities of a single product, themselves changing in relative price, as exemplified in the shift from wether mutton to lamb that is apparent from an analysis of sheep numbers given in the *Agricultural Returns*. And when this shift from a lower to a higher quality output is reinforced by a widening of the price differential in favour of the better qualities, an upward bias in farmers' returns results which is not reflected in a simple quantity times average price computation.

Thirdly, although the emphasis in this brief appraisal of the Great Depression is on the overall change between 1867–71 and 1894–8, a further contrast between livestock and crops emerges when the timing of price changes is considered. Corn prices plunged after 1874 from their Golden Age plateau and never recovered, declining further in the mid-eighties and again in the mid-nineties. Livestock prices on the other hand rose rapidly in the sixties and early seventies and, apart from the one year 1879, hardly fell significantly from these new heights until the mid-eighties. Even then they did not fall below their 1867–71 level and the further fall in the mid-nineties was slight compared with that of cereal prices. In 1896 a corn grower could look back on over twenty years of almost continually falling prices; a livestock farmer would be gradually re-acclimatizing to a price level regrettably somewhat lower than in the prosperous seventies and early eighties but not very different from that of twenty-five or thirty years earlier, and in compensation he could always point to his lower feed costs.

Finally, there is the nature of the information provided by aggregate models of the gross output kind. An abstraction like the 'national farm' can neither suffer depression nor enjoy prosperity: suffering and joy are attributes of human beings, in this context of the thousands of farmers who form part of the agricultural community. What is ideally needed are the numbers of English farmers to whom wheat was the lynchpin of their systems and the numbers who were in livestock, in sheep, milk or beef. At the one extreme were those livestock farmers who had abandoned the plough before or during the Great Depression, together with many others whose arable acreage was negligible. At the other extreme there were no farmers specializing solely in wheat, although a significant number, concentrated in certain localities such as the Fens, south-west Lancashire and the neighbourhood of large towns, kept few if any livestock and were wholly dependent on the sale of arable crops such as corn, hay, straw and potatoes. Between these extremes was to be found every conceivable type of farming, classifiable into two main groups, those farmers who relied primarily on the sale of corn and to whom livestock were principally a source of fertility,[1] and those mainly dependent on livestock and whose ploughing was ancillary to their needs. During the Great Depression the numbers in this second group increased as mixed farmers abandoned the plough or fed their corn to stock rather than sell it on the market.

IV

Accurately to divide the total number of farmers in the country into these categories is impossible, but, as a first approximation, use can be made of the division of England into agricultural regions introduced into the *Agricultural Returns* in 1868. Basically this is a single division into the 'grazing' counties of the north and west and the 'corn' counties of the south and east, following a line not unlike that drawn by Caird[2] and an argument used by Cobbett[3] even earlier. There were of course arable farms in the grazing counties, but they were undoubtedly out-numbered by livestock farmers in the south and east, from the Lincolnshire and Leicestershire graziers, the dairymen of the midland vales and the environs of towns, to the sheep masters of Romney Marsh, with the result that a simple comparison of 'grazing' with 'corn' counties exaggerates the relative number of arable farmers. Nevertheless the

---

[1] As late as 1867, J. J. Mechi, the well-known Essex farmer, was 'of the opinion that, although livestock do not pay directly, they are essential to the well-being of the farm as providers of the best and cheapest manure'; more categorically, 'will any livestock (pigs, sheep or cattle) pay market price for their food? – No'. *Chester Courant* (16 October 1867).

[2] J. Caird, op. cit., map, p. 1.

[3] W. Cobbett, *Rural Rides* (1930), ed. G. D. H. and Margaret Cole, III, pp. 696–9.

comparison is worth making. The greater area, 18 million acres as against 14·5,[1] lay to the north and west and contained many more agricultural holdings over 5 acres in size, 172,000 compared with 118,000 in the south and east. The average size of these holdings was smaller in the 'grazing' counties, 70 acres as against 100 in the 'corn' counties,[2] as was the ratio of farm workers to farmers at approximately 220:100 compared with 600:100 in the south and east.[3] Justification for the descriptions 'grazing' and 'corn' applied to these two areas is provided by the statistics of crops and livestock. For example, the ten leading wheat-growing counties were all situated in the east of the country and, although covering less than a quarter of the area of crops and grass in England, provided almost a half of the wheat acreage: at the other extreme, the ten counties with the highest numbers of milk cows contained between them practically a half of the country's total population of milk cows; these counties all lay in the north and west. The 'grazing' counties between them supported 68 per cent of England's milk cows,[4] that branch of farming which, together with hill sheep and their crosses, another activity predominant in the north and west, proved most continuously profitable during the Great Depression.

Without wishing to press the geographical division too closely, it is this distinction between the livestock farmer and the arable farmer that is crucial to an understanding of the Great Depression. It was not simply that arable farmers, mainly in the south and east, suffered a steep fall in the prices of their principal output products while livestock farmers, predominant in the north and west, enjoyed more favourable prices, but that every fall in the price of cereals, so damaging to corn growers, was to them, the livestock producers, clear

[1] These figures represent total acreage; the acreage of crops and grass (excluding rough grazing) was 12·0 million in the north and west, 11·8 million in the south and east.

[2] *Agricultural Returns*, 1885; all these figures are insignificantly different from those of the next size of holding investigation in 1895.

[3] Census of 1891.

[4] These comparisons refer to the year 1896; there is little difference between the nineties and the seventies, e.g. the figure quoted was 69 in 1872. For a geographer's views on this divison see W. Smith, *An Economic Geography of Great Britain* (1949), p. 53 et seq.

gain, because it meant a reduction in the price of their most important input – feed. Further, every fall in the price of bread to the consumer, other things equal, stimulated the demand for livestock products. Livestock farmers gained on either hand and their economic interests were aligned with those of the manufacturing population to the extent that cheap bread meant cheap livestock feed and an expanding industry meant full employment, high wages, and a stronger demand for meat, milk, eggs and dairy products.[1] Attempts to assess the impact of the great, or any other, depression upon agriculture considered as a single form of economic activity are not very meaningful. Agriculture in these islands is not one industry but several; in particular it consists in the two sectors, arable and livestock, whose aims are basically incompatible. Arable farmers want a high price for their output of cereals, hay and straw: livestock producers want low cereal and fodder prices because corn is to them an input not an output.

This division was not of course a phenomenon suddenly emerging in the 1870s; throughout our history, for geographical reasons, the east and south have yielded most of our corn, whereas the north and west have been in the main producers of livestock.[2] But in the second half of the nineteenth century two developments, on the one hand improvements in transport, the opening up of foreign supplies, and the extension of international trade, and on the other, rising living standards and changing patterns of food consumption among the working classes, helped to produce a situation in England in which livestock products were in rapidly growing demand, especially so relative to the arable bread and potatoes, and cheap cereals were in abundant supply.

This was the hard truth that faced English corn growers as

---

[1] This was explicitly recognized by some livestock farmers; for examples of anti-corn law Free Trade farmers see W. Cooke Taylor, *Tour of the Manufacturing Districts* (1842), p. 87 and *Preston Guardian*, 27 September 1884, 10 December 1892, 13 April 1895.

[2] The implications of this division in the field of agrarian history are far reaching and little explored. Cf. the highland and lowland zones in R. G. Collingwood and J. N. L. Myers. *Roman Britain and the English Settlements* (2nd ed. 1937), pp. 1–15.

the prophecies of thirty years earlier were demonstrably ful-
filled in the seventies and eighties. There was no lack of warn-
ing in the agricultural press; contributors to the *Journal of the
Royal Agricultural Society* in the sixties pointed to the growing
importance of livestock farming[1] and in 1872 a leader writer
in the *Agricultural Economist* went so far as to ask why grow
corn at all? Why not pursue a rotation of two year's pasture,
one year's meadow, and one year's green crop in order to
keep more stock? But such a radical suggestion was premature
and received the traditional reply, 'wheat and barley are the
breakfast and dinner and something more to the farmer'.[2]
The same belief was expressed, and with more justice, in the
1830s;[3] it continued to be voiced by such as 'Squire' Chaplin,
owner of some 23,000 Lincolnshire acres and for fifty years
agriculture's spokesman in the House of Commons.[4]

The persistence among influential agriculturalists of this
belief in the crucial importance of corn growing and the
desirability, if inexpediency, of protection was paralleled by
the persistence in the public mind of that tripartite image of
an immutable English agriculture based on 'Squire', 'Giles'
and 'Hodge' so beloved of successive generations of cartoonists.
But was this general 'official' picture adequately representative
of the views and practices of the scores of thousands of farmers
throughout the country, few of whom subscribed to the
agricultural journals,[5] and even fewer read *The Times*, *Punch*,
or *The Economist*, and whose farming, to judge by the *Agricultural Returns* and the *Journal of the Royal Agricultural Society*,[6]
was not in fact so indissolubly attached to wheat-growing as

[1] For example, *Journal of the Royal Agricultural Society*, 2nd series, II (1866), p.
45.

[2] *Agricultural Economist*, 1 August 1872 and 1 September 1872.

[3] See *Report from the Select Committee of the House of Lords on the State of Agriculture* (H.C. 464 of 1837), QQ. 528–9, 3267–3271.

[4] See, for example, *The Economist*'s report (5 December 1879) of 'Mr. Chaplin
on Protection', and *Royal Commission 1879–82, Final Report*, C. 3309 of 1882,
supplementary memorandum by H. Chaplin, pp. 37–8.

[5] The *Agricultural Economist* (1 February 1882) was of the opinion that 'farmers
do not read'; it declared itself the only paying agricultural journal on the occasion
of Morton's appeal, as editor, for more readers, in the *Agricultural Gazette* (26
December 1881).

[6] The Farm Prize Reports in the *Journal of the Royal Agricultural Society* between
1870 and 1891 illustrate the diversity of English farming.

one is led to believe? Whom in reality did 'Squire' Chaplin represent?

V

The weather of 1879 was so bad that in July Chaplin moved for a Royal Commission.[1] He was opposed by S. C. Read, member for South Norfolk and the only 'legitimate tenant farmer'[2] in the House. Read expressed the opinion that less corn and more grass should be grown, and cited Suffolk, which he said was all dairies before the Napoleonic War and should now be sown down again. It may be noted that Read lost his seat in the election of the following year. Chaplin's view prevailed and a commission was appointed. Its title was the Royal Commission on the Depressed State of the Agricultural Interest. Who or what was the 'Agricultural Interest'?

The members of the Commission were classified by the *Agricultural Economist* as four 'aristocrats',[3] including the chairman the Duke of Richmond, and two 'landed gentry',[4] all of whom were extensive landowners south of the Trent, six 'others'[5] who 'may be considered farmers' representatives', together with two future Chancellors, G. J. Goschen and C. T. Ritchie, Bonamy Price and Sir William Stephenson, 'both great in political economy',[6] Joseph Cowen, M.P. for New-

---

[1] This was not universal; for instance, a Cornish farmer later asserted that 1879 was his best year (*Royal Commission 1894–7*, Q. 37432).

[2] *Agricultural Economist*, 1 August 1879.

[3] The Duke of Richmond (1818–1903), the 'farmers' friend', Lord President of the Council and first chairman of its agricultural committee, 1884; the Duke of Buccleuch; Earl Spencer and Lord Vernon, the former also a member of the Privy Council's agricultural committee. For this classification see *Agricultural Economist*, 1 September 1879.

[4] Chaplin and Col. R. N. F. Kingscote, chairman of the finance committee of the Royal Agricultural Society and governor of the Royal Agricultural College, for whose family background see *Gloucestershire Studies*, ed. H. P. R. Finberg (Leicester, 1957), pp. 159–73.

[5] C. Howard, Wm. Stratten, J. Wilson (later Agricultural Adviser to the Board of Agriculture and Director of the Land Division), H. Rodwell, J. Clay, R. Patterson.

[6] Price was Drummond Professor at Oxford; Stephenson began his career with a clerkship in the Treasury in 1827 and was for fifteen years chairman of the Inland Revenue Board.

castle,[1] and three spokesmen for Ireland.[2] Excluding the Irishmen, twelve of the seventeen members were directly concerned in or considered to be sympathetic to the fortunes of agriculture.

Assistant Commissioners went out to their selected districts. Druce, Assistant Commissioner for the Home Counties, was also secretary to the Farmer's Club, and, in December, attended an important meeting of the Central Chamber of Agriculture in London where it was decided that local associated chambers should be circularized and local committees formed to furnish Assistant Commissioners with the 'facts' and to 'select men who could supply the information required, viz., evidence of fall in profit or fall in output or rise in cost of production'.[3] Besides Druce, two other Assistant Commissioners were present at this London meeting and, after some debate, the Chamber's business committee was instructed to 'observe' all this activity because some members of the committee served on the Commission and were thus unable to 'act'.

Among the witnesses called before the Richmond Commission, together with landowners, land-agents for both individuals and corporate bodies, civil servants and others, were 35 farmers, almost all tenants. Of these 35 only one farmed less than 100 acres, 31 farmed more than 300 acres, 25 of them farming more than 500 and 10 more than 1,000, at a time when the average size of farm in England was perhaps less than 100 acres.[4] It is also illuminating to notice where these witnesses farmed. 26 came from the 'corn' counties of the east and south and 9 from the 'grazing' counties of the north and west; only 4 of the 35 hailed from north of the Trent, and of these 4, 2 farmed in the arable East Riding. The ten leading

[1] Described in *Who Was Who* (1897-1916) as an 'old radical, imperialist, and anti-socialist', and assumed by the *Agricultural Economist* to be the 'representative of the working man' on the Commission.

[2] M. Henry, J. L. Naper, J. Rice.

[3] *Agricultural Economist*, 1 December 1879. In its *Final Report* the Commission put on record its view that the 'evidence [was] collected, we believe, with the greatest care and impartiality'. (*Royal Commission 1879-82*, C. 3309 of 1882, p. 33.)

[4] No precise figure is available, but the average size of 'holding over five acres' in England according to the *Agricultural Returns* was 84 acres in both 1885 and 1895.

wheat growing counties produced between them 14 witnesses; the ten leading dairy counties contributed only 5.

Decided views and attitudes regarding, for instance, size of farm – 270 acres was described as 'small' – and the nature of agriculture – almost synonymous with corn-growing – were unconsciously revealed.[1] Moreover, as appears in their questioning of witnesses, members of the Commission assumed *a priori* that depression was general, and much of their interrogation consisted in the kind of amicable discussion, with hearsay evidence prominent, of the weather, markets, taxes, yields, diseases and so on that is indulged in at all times among farmers, agents, merchants and others of the agricultural community when all participants share a common interest and expertise.[2]

Thus with the Commission itself firmly led by the landowning aristocracy and gentry, all with large properties in the south and Midlands, with farmers' views screened and organized by the Central and Associated Chambers of Agriculture whose headquarters, like those of the Farmers' Club and the Royal Agricultural Society, were in London, with farmer witnesses overwhelmingly reflecting the interests of corn growers, and with almost all concerned sharing a similar set of assumptions as to the nature of English agriculture, a fairly clear idea emerges of what was meant by the 'agricultural interest' and of where its centre of gravity lay.

The evidence before the Commission showed that the immediate cause of depression was the weather, and that the only price fall, other than the short-lived general fall of 1879, was that of wheat which no longer rose in price as compensation for a diminished output. Nevertheless the view prevailed that depression was universal, 'no description of estate or tenure has been exempted',[3] and critics of this view received short shrift.[4]

In its *Final Report* the Commission listed an impressive

---

[1] *Royal Commission 1879–82*, QQ. 49768–9, 33138–9.

[2] Ibid., QQ. 33109–10, 138.

[3] *Royal Commission 1879–82, Preliminary Report*, C. 2778 of 1881, p. 24.

[4] As, for example, did Giffen on calculating that agriculture's gross output had fallen by no more than 6 per cent between 1870 and 1880 (ibid., Q. 64733 ff.; *The Times*, 7 January 1882).

number of burdens on the farmer, including tithe and local rates, farm labour which was increasingly costly and, as always, less efficient – the 'very widespread complaint among farmers that the present system of education operates prejudicially to the interests of agriculture', meaning simply that children were kept at school when they might be 'usefully employed upon the farm',[1] rents that had been unduly raised, railway rates that discriminated in favour of imports and so on. The numerous recommendations ranged from a 'shift in the incidence of Local Taxation from real property to the Consolidated Fund'[2] to the desirability of one public department for agriculture. The government in its turn did little beyond introduce a second Agricultural Holdings Act in 1883, approve Lord Cairn's Settled Land Bill in the following year, and in 1889 create a Board of Agriculture.[3] By how much all this raised farmers' incomes is a nice question.

However the weather improved, prices held, the threat of imports seemed to slacken, and grumbling among themselves, the agricultural interest carried on, some in new ways, others in the old. Prices, and this time including livestock prices, fell in the mid-eighties but subsequently recovered somewhat and the later eighties witnessed some mild rejoicing.[4] The next outcry had to await another bout of deplorable weather initiated by the drought of 1893. But the weather experienced in different parts of the country varied even more markedly than in the seventies; in 1893 London experienced 114 days without rain, Manchester and Stoneyhurst only 30,[5] while in north Derbyshire the 'oldest inhabitant could scarcely remember a more productive year'.[6] Nevertheless the cry of distress was formidable and a second Royal Commission was granted; against the advice of *The Economist* which maintained that, in respect of what might be *done*, the Richmond Commission had

[1] *Royal Commission 1879–82, Final Report*, p. 27.

[2] Ibid., p. 25.

[3] Of which Chaplin was first president with a seat in the Cabinet.

[4] See the annual reviews of the preceding year in the *Agricultural Economist* of 1 January for 1889; 1890 and 1891.

[5] Weather statistics from *Journal of the Royal Agricultural Society* LXIV (1893), pp. 849–56.

[6] *Royal Commission 1894–7*, Q. 5133.

already elicited all the facts, that no new developments had occurred, and that another Commission would merely waste time and money:[1] but time on occasion can be a valuable commodity to government.

VI

The members of the new Commission appointed by Gladstone's government were a mixed body compared with their predecessors. The 'aristocracy' had shrunk to Lords Cobham and Rendel, the one a liberal Lyttleton, the other an ex-engineer, although the 'landed gentry' were still powerfully represented in the persons of Chaplin, Kingscote and W. H. Long.[2] The Commons also provided the chairman, Shaw-Lefevre,[3] first commissioner of works with a seat in the Cabinet, R. L. Everett, an East Anglian farmer, and F. A. Channing,[4] ex-chairman of the Central and Associated Chambers of Agriculture, also, and untypically, Liberals. The Civil Service contributed R. Giffen, late of *The Economist* and now at the Board of Trade, C. N. Dalton, an expert on local government taxation and C. Whitehead, technical adviser to the Board of Agriculture. The Committee was completed by W. C. Little, another East Anglian farmer and late Assistant Commissioner to the Richmond Commission, G. Lambert, C. I. Elton, a lawyer, O. Thomas from Wales and J. Gilmour and J. Clay from Scotland.

As compared with the Richmond Commission, agriculture's representatives had both declined in number and changed in character. Whereas in the seventies leadership of the agricultural interest was firmly in the hands of the landed aristocracy, prominent in the House of Lords and the Privy Council,

---

[1] *The Economist*, 15 July 1893.

[2] The Long estate of some 14,000 acres in Wiltshire was of ancient descent; for the family see *V. C. H. Wiltshire*, VII (1953), index, pp. 233–4.

[3] G. J. Shaw-Lefevre (1831–1928); Lord Eversley, 1906; ex-member of the Privy Council's agricultural committee, and a member of every Liberal government, except Gladstone's of 1885, since 1866. In Lord Rosebery's administration of 1894–5 Shaw-Lefevre remained in the Cabinet as president of the Local Government Board.

[4] Author of *The Truth About Agricultural Depression* (1897).

in the nineties the farming interest was struggling to wean itself from the now politically embarrassing aristocracy and to make its voice heard in the more hostile Commons. The establishment of a Board of Agriculture in 1889 opened a new avenue of advance for the agricultural interest via White-hall and 'delegated legislation'.

Change is also noticeable among the farmer witnesses; not perhaps in terms of size of farm, as only 5 of the 39 whose acreage is known farmed less than 300 acres and 27 farmed more than 500 acres, but certainly in their regional dispersion. The majority, 22, still came from the east and south, but the north and west were now represented by no fewer than 18, and although the corn counties provided 13 witnesses, the dairy counties followed them close with 12.

Happily for the agricultural interest the Conservatives were returned in June 1895 and the balance of power within the Commission shifted decisively. Chaplin and Long joined the government as presidents of the Local Government Board and the Board of Agriculture respectively, Everett and Chan-ning moved into opposition, and the chairman, Shaw-Lefevre, lost both office and seat.

Conflict of interest among the members of the Commission was apparent on the publication, after nearly two years work, of the second report in February 1896. Although the chief cause of depression was 'unanimously attributed' to the fall in prices,[1] the majority Report, with Cobham,[2] Chaplin, Long and Kingscote as leading signatories, was expressly confined to a discussion of rates and land tax and the question of state loans to agriculture. It concluded with a nasty rider to the effect that 'it would be inexpedient for any member of the commission to submit for presentation to the Secretary of State a counter report or memorandum in connection with the ad interim report agreed to by the members of the commission

---

[1] *Royal Commission 1894–7, Second Report*, C. 7981 of 1896, p. 7. The first report of one page appeared in May 1894 as C. 7400 of 1894; cf. *The Economist*, 7 March 1896, pp. 290–2 – 'Divided counsels on agricultural relief'.

[2] It would seem that Cobham's support was less than wholehearted in view of what Sir H. Fowler in the Commons described as his 'singular reservation' disagreeing with any reduction in the rate of assessment of land (*Parliamentary Debates*, 4th series XXXIX, 20 April 1896).

dealing with questions which have not been considered by the commission'.[1] A minority of three, led by the chairman, now clearly powerless to curb Chaplin and Long, and backed by Rendel and Giffen, expressed their disgust at this majority resolution and ignored it. Their own position was clear. 'The depression has been and still is far more serious in the eastern and southern counties of England, over an area of rather more than one third of England and Wales, than in the other parts of Great Britain.'[2] The causes of this were (1) the east and south suffered unfavourable seasons beginning in 1892 and including two years, 1893 and 1895, of exceptional drought, the former being 'quite unprecedented', while the north and west had 'enjoyed far more favourable conditions'; (2) the east and south suffered greater in proportion because they were the chief wheat-growing districts; (3) there was a comparative absence of small farms in the south and east and small farmers had done better owing to a preponderance of family labour, more attention to smaller products, and more dairying than corn-growing; (4) 'burdens on land' in the south and east in the shape of tithe, land tax, and local rates were as a rule much heavier.[3]

The minority then proceeded to discuss prices, wages and remedial measures, which latter, as might be expected, were limited to landlord-tenant agreements, rent levels, railway rates, 'co-operation with a view to getting rid of middlemen' and the mitigation of some of the grosser inequalities of the so-called 'burdens on land'. This was as much as could be done 'short of tampering with the currency, debasing the gold standard or adopting protective duties'.[4] The intrepid trio then demolished the 'burdens on land' case by showing that in fact the 'burdens' had diminished, and the chairman, in a supplementary solo, stated, 'there appears to be a general impression among farmers and others connected with the agricultural interest that the actual average payments in respect of local rates on land have considerably increased during the last twenty-five years. This however is not in accord with the facts supplied from official sources, or with the

---

[1] *Royal Commission 1894–7, Second Report*, p. 21.
[2] Ibid., p. 22.   [3] Ibid.   [4] Ibid., p. 23.

experience of the great majority of individual cases so far as they have been laid before the Commission.'[1] Two months later, in April 1896, Shaw-Lefevre resigned.

The gravamen of Shaw-Lefevre's charge against the majority of the Commission was that Chaplin and Long privately prepared an Agricultural Rating Bill at the Local Government Board and then bulldozed the Royal Commission into endorsing its recommendations in the fortnight between 26 January, when they first acquainted the Commission with their plan, and 11 February when Chaplin, ignoring Shaw-Lefevre's plea for longer consideration, gave notice in the Commons of his intention to introduce the Bill. In Shaw-Lefevre's words, bearing in mind the 'constitution of the Royal Commission, how could they refuse a scheme for relieving land of three-quarters of its rates put before it by the government?'[2]

The *Final* (majority) *Report* in 1897[3] under the signature of Cobham as chairman, and which was almost rivalled in bulk by memoranda, reservations and two impressive minority reports, took the form of a tour of the country and vindicated Shaw-Lefevre's views. Beginning with Essex, the worst-hit county, eight pages described the 'corn' counties; two sufficed for the 'grazing' counties. Recommendations were insubstantial and the only concrete financial measure was the Agricultural Rates Act of 1896,[4] the result of the Commission's two-year deliberation on the 'burdens on land'.

The *Final Report* is a discordant compendium of many voices. Pertinent questioning by Liberals and free traders, who were not prepared to accept uncritically the agricultural interest's cry of a ruined agriculture, disclosed new problems and discredited some of the evidence. For example, Giffen's survey of world agricultural output unexpectedly revealed that the supply of wheat was not running ahead of population and

[1] *Royal Commission 1894–7, Second Report*, p. 32.

[2] *The Times*, 27 April 1896; for the controversy between Shaw-Lefevre and Chaplin see *The Times*, 29 and 30 April and 1 May, and *Parliamentary Debates*, 4th series XXXIX, 27 April, when Chaplin referred to Shaw-Lefevre's letter in *The Times* and was strongly attacked by the opposition.

[3] *Royal Commission 1894–7, Final Report*, C. 8540 of 1897.

[4] 59 & 60 Vict. Cap. 16; by which the Exchequer was to contribute annually a sum equal to half the amount raised from agricultural land in 1895.

therefore the fall in price must have been due to restricted demand.[1] Farm accounts submitted to the Commission as evidence of depression were criticized as unrepresentative, '50 of the 69 [which 'gave sufficient detail to enable them to be checked'] relate to the eight chief corn-growing, and therefore most depressed, counties, and the whole 69 are collected from only 16 of the 52 counties of England and Wales'. In the same context, the sceptical view is expressed that 'opinions of tenant farmers . . . cannot, any more than those of landlords and agents, be accepted as the views of disinterested witnesses'.[2]

For all the gathering and sifting of evidence no common understanding of the decisive changes that were occurring in the agriculture of the western world is to be observed among the members of the Commission. In particular, although the *Final Report* was cast in the form of a comparison of the north and west with the east and south, the Commission seemed curiously blind to the full implications of this contrast. The differential fall in farm prices, the growth of dairying and so on were pointed to and no more; out of nearly 200 pages exactly two were devoted to production costs and these included three paragraphs only on feeding-stuffs and manures.[3] That the fall in price of feed relative to changes in the price of livestock products during the Great Depression was of more importance to livestock farmers than this space apportionment would indicate is suggested by what may be termed the livestock: feed price ratio, which expresses the relationship between the average of dairy and livestock prices and the cost of feed in the two periods 1867–71 and 1894–8. It moved in the producers' favour from 100 to about 150.[4]

---

[1] *Final Report*, App. V. p. 73; 'people consume less cereals per head because with increase of resources, they consume more meat, which *pro tanto* displaces the cereals'.

[2] Ibid., pp. 118–19. The Commission was also interested to know why 'in sixteen instances (seven of which refer to Essex), profits were earned between 1889 and 1894 from 5 to 24 per cent on the capital employed, the rents ranging from 9s. 7d. to 34s. 5d. per acre'.

[3] *Royal Commission 1894–7, Final Report*, pp. 87–9, paras. 313–15.

[4] Average livestock and dairy prices are assumed to have fallen by 10 per cent; the cost of imported maize and oilcakes fell by 40 per cent.

VII

Very clearly the basic conflict of interest, felt rather than formulated, between the two main groups of English farmers, and masked by the ambivalent rural-urban, protection-free trade division, prevented the formulation of any coordinated view, any single, forceful, agricultural policy, any effective cooperation.[1] And in the absence of unanimity, with on the one hand a declining corn-growing interest nostalgically looking to the past and on the other hand thousands of live-stock farmers – with the small hard-working family farmer in the majority, motivated by profit and with a keen eye to the main chance – quietly increasing their output with the aid of cheap, imported cereals, the vacuum left by these divergent interests was easily filled by the confused idealism of Free Land Leaguers, Georgists and anti-landlord radicals, bi-metallists and all the advocates of peasant ownership, small-holdings and the return to the land.

Finally, it may be asked why, if arable farming did not pay and livestock farming did, East Anglian corn growers per-sisted in unprofitable practices? The short answer is that time was needed to distinguish an apparent cycle from an un-mistakably secular trend, and it may be argued that a certain rigidity, not merely of system but of mind, was the penalty paid by the third generation for the undoubted success of their forebears' 'Norfolk system'. The Earl of Leicester, son of the great Coke, grassed down his home farm and ran sheep at a profit, but, as he explained in a letter to Shaw-Lefevre, he almost despaired of his tenants having the sense to follow his example.[2] As a Lancashire farmer observed after touring Essex in 1896, 'new-comers are going in for milk, cheese, butter, fruit, and sheep but with the average Essex farmer it is

---

[1] The great London agricultural conference of December 1892, convened by the Central Chamber of Agriculture and addressed by Chaplin and Lowther, split on the question of protection which Professor J. P. Sheldon described as the '*ignis fatuus* leading our southern and eastern farmers away from their true interests' (*The Future of British Agriculture* (1893), p. 142). A similar conflict obtained among the members of the Royal Commission on Agriculture of 1919–20 over the problem of whether to continue government support of corn prices (see *Interim Report*, Cmd. 473 of 1919).

[2] *Royal Commission 1894–7*, C. 7400 of 1896 IV, 596–7.

corn, corn, corn.'[1] The difference in attitude is apparent in the evidence of farmers and landowners before the two Royal Commissions. Some, and not only in the north, farmed for the market and produced only that which paid them to do so; others continued in the ways of their fathers.[2]

The outcry died down as the century drew to its close and the agricultural interest learned to accept, if not embrace, the new England. Apart from the social problems associated with the spread of urban values and the political decline of the landed interest, what, in the narrower economic field, did the Great Depression achieve? It dethroned 'orient and immortal wheat' and turned English farmers in a new direction, that is to the production of quality livestock products. It inflicted suffering on a particular section of farmers, the large corn-growers. Output figures show that agriculture was not ruined; on the contrary an important internal revolution was effected during a period of falling prices. Seemingly unheedful of the cries of distress that sounded for over twenty years, the majority of farmers pursued the path of self-interest as they saw it; others, protesting loudly or lamenting quietly, were impelled by the logic of their bank balances to change their systems; some few, to whom cow-keeping, the laying down to grass or the selling of hay and straw were distasteful violations of the canon, went to the wall.[3] It needed war or the threat of war to revive their kind.[4]

[1] *Preston Guardian*, 24 October 1896.
[2] See also the examples of successful farming during the depression described in the minority reports of Lambert and Channing (*Royal Commission 1894–7, Final Report*, pp. 204–379), and by Shaw-Lefevre (ibid. C. 7400 of 1896, IV, 611–14); for instances of change in Essex, see R. Hunter Pringle's series of articles in the *Agricultural Gazette* of 1887, July onwards, especially 10 October 1887.
[3] This latter frame of mind is well treated in the earlier novels of A. G. Street as, for example, in *The Gentleman of the Party* (1936).
[4] The traditional view of farmers as men who grow corn persisted into the twentieth century. For example, the first effective post-1921 legislation gave help to sugar beet (1925) and wheat (1932), such was the persuasive, political power of the 'voice of Norfolk' against which Viscount Astor and Dr K. A. H. Murray pleaded vigorously in the 1930s (see *Land and Life* (1932) and *The Planning of Agriculture* (1933)).

D

APPENDIX

Two gross output estimates, one for the agriculture of the U.K. and one for that of England, have been computed. They are based on Dr Ojala's work, the main change being the substitution of more appropriate home prices for the Sauerbeck series of import prices used by Dr Ojala, in the case of Hay and Straw, Fruit, Vegetables, Beef, Mutton, Pig meat, Milk, Poultry and Eggs. Beef and Mutton prices are based on the Smithfield series of home-produced beef and mutton given in *Agricultural Statistics*. Milk and Poultry and Egg prices are derived from material in *Report on Wholesale and Retail Prices in the U.K.* (1903), the two Royal Commissions of 1879–82 and 1894–7, and Lancashire sources (see *supra*, p. 34, note 3). The Hay and Straw, Fruit, Vegetables and Pig meat prices are estimated from data in *Agricultural Statistics*, Lancashire

The Gross Output of the Agriculture of the U.K. and England (£ million)

	U.K.			England	
	1867–9	*1870–6*	*1894–1903*	*1867–71*	*1894–8*
Wheat	35·38	27·56	7·72	28·44	7·64
Barley	16·78	17·56	9·43	12·62	7·54
Oats	10·54	9·07	8·07	4·28	4·23
Potatoes	14·02	13·82	11·34	3·00	3·00
Hay and Straw, Fruit, Vegetables	20·11	19·40	21·75	14·00	17·00
Other crops	7·34	7·58	3·64	3·09	2·06
ARABLE	104·17	94·99	61·95	65·43	41·47
Beef	34·90	45·67	42·05	14·59	16·02
Mutton	25·92	30·51	25·20	14·60	12·59
Pig meat	18·60	22·95	19·13	9·59	10·52
Horses	1·50	2·00	3·00	1·00	2·00
Milk	33·78	38·51	43·56	15·40	20·29
Wool	7·49	8·27	3·24	5·62	2·36
Poultry and Eggs	4·57	6·96	10·00	3·50	7·00
LIVESTOCK	126·76	154·87	146·18	64·30	70·78
TOTAL	230·93	249·86	208·13	129·73	112·25
Index	100	108	90	100	87

newspapers and *Agricultural Statistics of Ireland* 1910 (Cd. 5882). Revised quantities for the output of Oats and Hay and Straw follow from the re-estimate of the numbers of non-farm horses (*supra*. p. 36, note 2) and of Potatoes from a reconsideration of the Irish potato crop.

The final series are not claimed to be definitive; in particular the dairy, the poultry and the fruit and vegetable outputs could be improved by the discovery of further prices and by the estimation of more accurate quantities. It is considered, however, that these crude alterations to Dr Ojala's estimates contribute to a more realistic measure of the Great Depression. Details of individual series and of methods of estimation may be obtained from the author.

4 Agricultural Changes in the Chilterns, 1875–1900[1]

J. T. COPPOCK

This article was first published in the *Agricultural History Review*, IX(1) (1961).

While the broad outlines of the agricultural depression which affected British agriculture from the late 1870s until the end of the century are well known, few local studies have been made. The Chilterns and the adjoining clay lowlands (Fig. I) provide a suitable area for investigating the changes which occurred, for they contain a wide variety of country within a small compass. The Chilterns themselves, rising to over 800 feet, have stony soils of low fertility, the clay lowlands to north and south are poorly drained and difficult to cultivate, while the gravel terraces of the Thames and the Icknield belt below the escarpment have free-working loams which make good arable soils.

In the 1870s the Chilterns were primarily rural. It is true that many of the towns were growing rapidly, but they were still small, and most of the land, though much interrupted by blocks of woodland, was used for agriculture. In those parts nearest London there were also numerous parks and mansions. The clay vales to the north, where there were few parks and little wood, were almost entirely farmed, but south of the Chilterns parks were again numerous. There were marked regional differences in the kind of farming practised, differences of fairly long standing, determined mainly by soil and by near-

[1] The cost of extracting the statistical data on which this paper is based was met by a grant from the Central Research Fund, University of London. The author is grateful to Mr J. Bryant who drew the maps. Statements which are not supported by references are either derived from the parish summaries of the agricultural returns (which have been extensively used in the preparation of this paper) or generalizations made from sources too numerous to list.

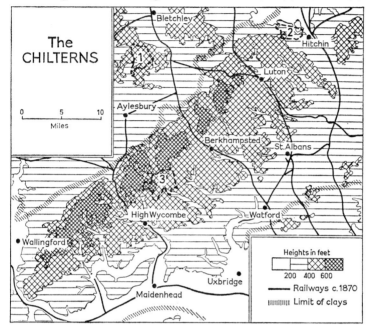

Figure I

ness to London markets. The easily worked loams of the
Icknield belt and the Thames terraces were almost entirely
arable, as were the Chilterns, where the only extensive stretches
of grass lay in the landscaped parks or along the few streams.
The amount of grass decreased with elevation; a typical farm
at Swyncombe, for example, had only 7 out of 372 acres under
grass. On the clays to the north, more land was under permanent grass, though the proportion varied from all-grass
farms in the low-lying Vale of Aylesbury to mixed farms with
a preponderance of arable around Bletchley. Generally between
one and two-fifths of the land was under the plough, and a
farm at Waterstock, with 208 acres of grass and 118 of arable,
was fairly representative.[1] The clays of south Hertfordshire and
Middlesex were nearly all under permanent grass, but the reason

[1] *Second Report, Commissioners on the Employment of Children, Young Persons, and
Women in Agriculture*, Appendix, Part II, Parliamentary Papers, XIII (1868–9),
p. 326.

for this was only partly the heavy soil. London, with its large population of horses and dairy cattle, made heavy demands on the adjacent counties for hay, straw and other fodder crops, and four-fifths of the grass was cut for hay each year (Figure IIa).

The stock kept and the crops grown also varied considerably. On the Chilterns and in all the main arable areas, the Norfolk four-course rotation, or some variant of it, prevailed (Figure IIb). Cereals, turnips and clover accounted for four-fifths of the arable, the remainder being occupied by other fodder crops such as peas and vetches. On Hoo Farm, Kimpton, for example, there were in 1870 113 acres of wheat, 88½ of barley, 73 of clover, 20 of beans and 99½ of turnips.[1] The better land supported an additional corn crop and usually carried more wheat and barley than oats. Thus, in the Hertfordshire Chilterns, where soils were generally better than further west, a five-course rotation was common and wheat and barley were the leading cereals;[2] in the poorer Oxfordshire Chilterns, a four-course rotation, with oats the second cereal, was general. On the clays, cropping was more varied, and rotations often longer.[3] Wheat was everywhere the chief crop, occupying a third or more of the arable. Beans were also a characteristic crop, and a larger proportion of land was bare-fallowed; but some oats, barley, clover and turnips were also grown. On Manor Farm, Upper Stondon, wheat, occupying 99 acres, and beans, 52 acres, were the leading crops in 1868, the remainder of the arable being occupied chiefly by 50 acres of clover, 37 of turnips, 24 of barley, 22 of oats and 18 acres of fallow.[4] On the little arable on the clays to the south of the Chilterns, wheat was again the leading crop.

Specialized cropping was rare. Market-gardening was important only on the Middlesex gravel terraces and potatoes were grown only in small quantities, except in the market-gardening areas and on the sandy soils around Leighton

[1] Accounts, Hoo Farm, Kimpton, Hertfordshire Record Office.

[2] H. Evershed, 'Agriculture of Hertfordshire', *Journal of the Royal Agricultural Society*, XXV (1864), p. 272.

[3] *Second Report on the Employment of Children*, etc., loc. cit., p. 75; ibid., *First Report*, Appendix, Part I, Parliamentary Papers, XVII (1867–8), p. 124.

[4] Bedfordshire County Record Office, DDX 159/3.

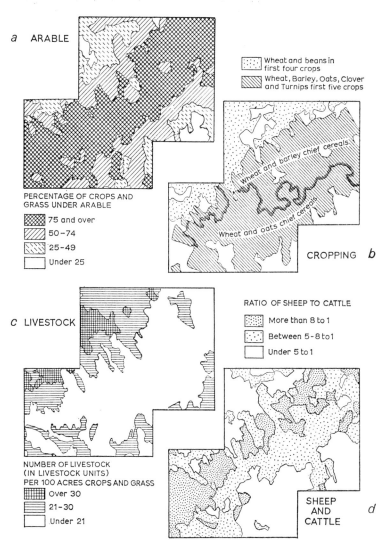

a ARABLE

Wheat and beans in
first four crops

Wheat, Barley, Oats, Clover
and Turnips first five crops

Wheat and barley chief cereals

Wheat and oats chief cereals

CROPPING *b*

PERCENTAGE OF CROPS AND
GRASS UNDER ARABLE

75 and over

50 – 74

25 – 49

Under 25

c LIVESTOCK

RATIO OF SHEEP TO CATTLE

More than 8 to 1

Between 5-8 to 1

Under 5 to 1

NUMBER OF LIVESTOCK
(IN LIVESTOCK UNITS)
PER 100 ACRES CROPS AND GRASS

Over 30

21 – 30

Under 21

SHEEP
AND
CATTLE

d

Figure II

Buzzard. Wheat and barley were the principal cash crops; on one Hertfordshire farm they accounted for 84 per cent of crop sales.[1] Within easy reach of London, however, oats, hay, roots, and straw were sold; the importance of oats in south Hertfordshire was probably due to the demand for oats and oat straw rather than to the quality of the soil.

Most observers noted the considerable uniformity of cropping on farms, particularly in the Chilterns, and their impressions are supported by the agricultural returns. To what extent this uniformity was due to lease restrictions it is impossible to say; clauses in leases ranged from general injunctions to cultivate the land in a husband-like manner to specific instructions to follow a particular rotation, as on a farm at Mapledurham, where the farmer was enjoined to cultivate the land on a four-course system and was forbidden to take two crops of the same kind of grain in succession or to crop more than half the land with grain.[2] There were limitations on growing other crops; a tenant of a 640-acre farm on the Ashridge estate was prohibited from growing more than 2 acres of potatoes.[3] There were also restrictions on the disposal of hay, straw and roots grown on the farm. It is true that such restrictive covenants were not necessarily enforced and practice seems to have varied from estate to estate; only one specific example of the enforcement has been noted, where a tenant on a farm at Chenies was ordered to plough up and fallow a field sown to oats because of 'too great a liberty in the extent of his White-Strawed Cropping'.[4] The object of the covenants was, of course, to protect the land, and farmers were usually allowed to sell crops, hay and straw when sufficient dung could be brought back to replace their manurial value.[5]

The importance of livestock varied inversely with the proportion of arable,[6] except on the clays to the south of the

---

[1] 'Remarks concerning a Herts farm', *Herts Illustrated Review*, I (1893), pp. 647–8.

[2] Agreement, April 1883, Blount MSS., Bodleian.

[3] Hertfordshire County Record Office, Leases, Ashridge Estate.

[4] Bedford Office, Bedford Estate Reports, 1887.

[5] Evershed, op. cit., p. 284.

[6] No winter returns of livestock were made, but there is evidence of fattening of cattle in winter in the arable areas.

Chilterns where the hay crop severely limited grazing (Figure
IIc). On the Icknield belt and on the Chilterns sheep were the
principal livestock, especially on the higher parts where water
was scarce. They were arable sheep, folded on roots, and were
kept primarily to manure the soil. Horses accounted for one-
third of the total livestock, and a few dairy cattle, beef cattle
and stores were also kept. Stocking on these farms is exemplified by Hoo Farm, Kimpton, which carried 702 sheep, of
which 408 were breeding ewes, 32 cattle, 23 horses and 75
pigs. Lower down the Chilterns, where water was more
abundant, fewer sheep and more cattle were kept (Figure
IId). South of the Chilterns farms kept mainly cattle, and
nearer London some dairying was practised. The chief areas
of livestock farming were, however, the clay lowlands to the
north, especially the area around Aylesbury, which Read had
called 'the pastoral garden of the county'.[1] Cattle were the
chief livestock, but both arable and grass sheep were kept.
The mainly grass farms near Aylesbury fattened beef cattle,
particularly Herefords, but the mixed farms, which covered
most of the clays, practised dairying and rearing as well as
fattening. Dairying was typical of the poorer grassland and
was still largely concerned with butter production; only in
well-placed areas was much milk sold.[2]

Stocking, too, was affected by lease restrictions, though less
frequently than the use of the arable land. Some leases merely
enjoined the farmer to stock the farm adequately; but occasionally restrictions were more specific, as on Park and Rose
Farms, Mapledurham, where the tenant was required to keep a
sufficient flock of sheep and to pen and fold them on the farm.[3]

This brief statistical account inevitably minimizes the rich
variety of farming; nevertheless, the prevailing impression is
one of considerable uniformity within regions which differed
markedly from each other.

In the late 1870s a series of bad harvests coincided with a

[1] C. S. Read, 'Report on the farming of Buckinghamshire', *Journal of the Royal Agricultural Society*, XVI (1855), p. 281.
[2] J. C. Morton, 'Dairy farming,' *Journal of the Royal Agricultural Society*, 2nd Series, XIV (1878), p. 689, and report of Daily News Special Commissioner, reproduced in *Bedford Times*, 13 September 1879.
[3] Agreement, April 1883, Blount MSS.

period of falling prices. Although the weather improved, grain prices, particularly of wheat and barley, continued to fall; they were joined in the 1880s by a similar, though smaller, fall in the prices of livestock and livestock products. These falling prices were met in two main ways; part of the burden was shouldered by landlords, who remitted and later reduced rents, and part by farmers, who attempted to reduce their losses by farming less intensively, by avoiding expensive cultivations, and by concentrating on those products which were least affected by the fall in prices. But none of these remedies was adopted uniformly over the whole area.

The reductions in rents are the best documented of the changes and were almost universal. At first landowners granted temporary remissions; in 1880 for example, the Duke of Bedford allowed 25 per cent off the year's rent to all tenants on the estate.[1] But gradually, as it became clear that this was not a temporary recession, there were permanent reductions. These were made necessary both to retain existing tenants and to attract new, and it was said that in parts of Hertfordshire no rent at all was paid, the landowners being glad merely to keep a tenant on the farm.[2] There was often a succession of reductions; the rent of Flint Hall Farm on the West Wycombe estate, for example, was reduced by £30 in 1882 and by a further £40 in 1886. Revenues from rents fell steadily; on the West Wycombe estate the rental fell by 19 per cent between 1876 and 1888,[3] and on the Bedford estates in Bedfordshire and Buckinghamshire average farm rent fell by 48 per cent between 1876 and 1895.[4] Reductions were most marked on heavy arable clays, which were expensive and difficult to work, and on poor soils which gave a low return; on the thin soils of the Oxfordshire Chilterns, for example, rents fell by 50 per cent between 1880 and 1893.[5] On good grassland, or

[1] Bedford Estate Reports, 1880.

[2] *Royal Commission on Agriculture, Reports of Assistant Commissioners*, Parliamentary Papers, XVI (1881), p. 368.

[3] Rentals, West Wycombe Estate papers.

[4] Duke of Bedford, *The Story of a Great Agricultural Estate* (London, 1897), p. 224.

[5] *Royal Commission on Agriculture, Minutes of Evidence*, Parliamentary Papers, XVI, Part I (1894), p. 57.

where there was easy access to a market, reductions were much less; in the Vale of Aylesbury reductions were generally 20–25 per cent, and near the railways south of the Chilterns from 10–25 per cent.[1]

The most general of the agricultural adjustments was an extension of the grass acreage (Figures IIIa and b). Since wages changed little, labour costs, the largest single item in the outgoings of the arable farmer, could be reduced only by curtailing expensive cultivations. It is difficult to be sure how much land was laid to grass. The agricultural returns show a progressive increase in the amount of permanent pasture; and while this may be due in part to a more complete enumeration of the smaller holdings, which would tend to be largely grass, there is no reason to suppose that it does not reflect an actual trend. Naturally the permanence of price reductions was not appreciated at first and many farmers simply left leys down for more than one year; these would be returned as temporary grass, and only later would they be regarded as permanent. It is true that the assistant commissioner who reported on Bedfordshire in 1895 thought that the amount of permanent grass was being overestimated and that of temporary grass underestimated;[2] but the returns themselves suggest that an expanded temporary grass acreage often concealed the extent of the conversion of arable to permanent pasture. His observation that fields were allowed to lie in grass for a number of years with the intention of ploughing them when prices improved is probably correct; but prices did not improve, and the fields remained in grass. The point at which such leys should be regarded as permanent is in any case debatable; cropping records on a number of farms on the Panshanger estate show fields which, having been under a ley for two or three years, are recorded in the succeeding year as pasture.[3]

Farmers increased their acreage under grass in a number of ways; by sowing more temporary grass and allowing it to stay

[1] *Royal Commission on Agriculture, Report of A. Spencer on the Vale of Aylesbury and the County of Hertford*, Parliamentary Papers, XVI (1895), p. 17.

[2] *Report of H. Pringle on the Counties of Bedford, Huntingdon, and Northampton* Parliamentary Papers, XVII (1895), p. 41.

[3] Panshanger Estate Papers, Hertfordshire County Record Office.

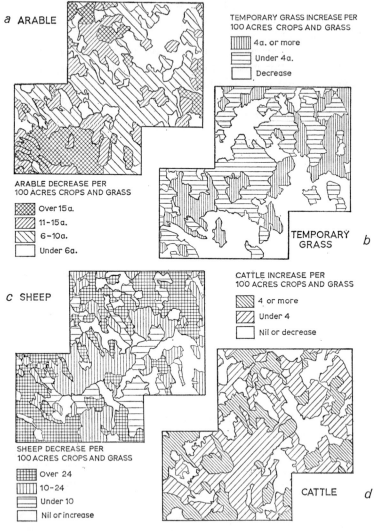

a ARABLE

TEMPORARY GRASS INCREASE PER
100 ACRES CROPS AND GRASS

- 4a. or more
- Under 4a.
- Decrease

ARABLE DECREASE PER
100 ACRES CROPS AND GRASS

- Over 15a.
- 11–15a.
- 6–10a.
- Under 6a.

TEMPORARY
GRASS *b*

c SHEEP

CATTLE INCREASE PER
100 ACRES CROPS AND GRASS

- 4 or more
- Under 4
- Nil or decrease

SHEEP DECREASE PER
100 ACRES CROPS AND GRASS

- Over 24
- 10–24
- Under 10
- Nil or increase

CATTLE *d*

Figure III

down longer, by laying down arable to permanent pasture, and by abandoning arable to colonization by self-sown grasses and weeds. The contribution made by each varied in importance in different parts of the area. The proportion of the arable occupied by leys increased nearly everywhere, and in the Chilterns the increases were on such a scale that, despite the diminishing arable, the acreage of temporary grass expanded (Figure IIIb). The Chilterns were said to be unsuited to permanent grass, though they could support leys of up to three years.[1] But these leys were left down and subsequently recognized as permanent pasture; in 1901 Rider Haggard noted that most of the grass in the Oxfordshire Chilterns was originally seeded as two- or three-year leys.[2] On the clays the increase in temporary grass was often ephemeral, and after bad seasons had passed the acreage was reduced (Figure V, Stewkley).

On better land, particularly the claylands where mixed farming was practised and the establishment of good grass was known to be possible, land was intentionally laid down as permanent grass, either directly or under a nurse crop. But 'it is a very expensive luxury'; the seeds alone cost 30s. an acre, and the Duke of Bedford estimated the total cost at £15 an acre.[3] It is likely to have been widespread, therefore, only on the estates of wealthy landowners. The duke himself laid down 1,308 acres on the 28,274 acres of his Bedfordshire and Buckinghamshire estates between 1880 and 1897. The landowner usually provided the seeds and the tenant the labour; in 1880, for example, two arable fields on stiff clay at Hill Farm, Potsgrove, were laid down to permanent pasture, the Duke of Bedford providing the seeds on condition that the fields were not again ploughed up.[4] The farmer himself sometimes provided both seeds and labour, though he had frequently to obtain the landowner's consent first. In general, once the fields were laid down to permanent grass they were subject to the same prohibitions on ploughing up as the

[1] *Royal Commission on Agriculture, Minutes of Evidence* (1894), p. 57.
[2] Rider Haggard, *Rural England* (London, 1902) II, p. 118.
[3] *Royal Commission on Agriculture, Minutes of Evidence*, Parliamentary Papers, XVII (1881), 618, and Duke of Bedford, op. cit., p. 197.
[4] Bedford Estate Report, 1880.

existing grass; a lease on a Datchworth farm stated that the tenant was not to break up fields which at the determination of the tenancy should have been under seeds for six years.[1] Increases in permanent grass were widespread, particularly on the clays, and in the Oxfordshire Chilterns and in north-east Berkshire (though here accessibility to markets rather than the nature of the soil was the important consideration).

Much was made by contemporaries of the abandonment of cultivated land and of fields that 'tumbled down to grass'. Agricultural historians have perhaps been too influenced by the 'terrible map, dotted thick with black patches' (Clapham's phrase) which accompanied Pringle's report on Essex in 1893. But there is no evidence that abandonment was widespread here; a return in 1881 of abandoned farms and fields in Buckinghamshire, for example, gave a total of 1,102 acres, out of 403,673 acres of agricultural land.[2] It is possible that abandoned land might escape enumeration (though there was no fall in the total acreage returned); but Pringle himself could find none in Bedfordshire. Some of the farms on owners' hands through lack of tenants may well have been neglected; land on such farms at Wallington and Bygrave was said to be almost out of cultivation.[3] But even the extent of land on landowners' hands seems to have been exaggerated. Although one witness reported, at second hand, that on Lord Camoys's estate in the Oxfordshire Chilterns only two out of thirty tenants remained in 1882, this area seems to have been exceptional.[4] Spencer suggested in 1895 that rather more than 20 per cent of the cultivated area was in hand in Hertfordshire, and agricultural returns for 1887 of the acreage of land farmed by owners suggest that over most of the area the proportion was even smaller.[5] Moreover, farms were sometimes taken in hand to prevent the land being neglected by tenants who had lost heart or resources. This seems to have been the practice on the Bedford estate. What is clear is that standards of farming fell. Lord Macclesfield's agent said in 1892 that he did not

---

[1] Hertfordshire County Record Office, Abel Smith Papers.
[2] Manuscript figures, parish summaries 1881, Ministry of Agriculture.
[3] Spencer, loc. cit., p. 22.
[4] *Royal Commission on Agriculture, Minutes of Evidence* (1881), p. 847.
[5] Spencer, loc. cit., p. 22.

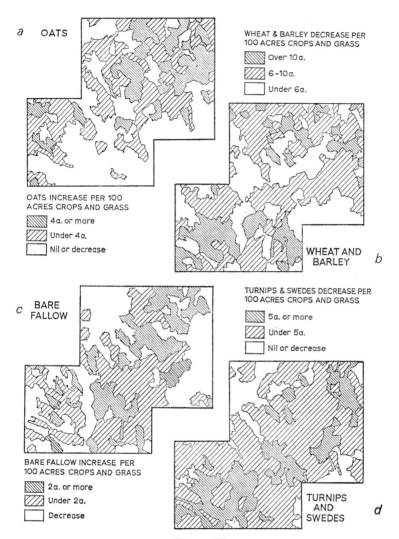

_a_ OATS

WHEAT & BARLEY DECREASE PER
100 ACRES CROPS AND GRASS

Over 10 a.

6-10 a.

Under 6 a.

OATS INCREASE PER 100
ACRES CROPS AND GRASS

4 a. or more

Under 4 a.

Nil or decrease

WHEAT AND
BARLEY _b_

_c_ BARE
FALLOW

TURNIPS & SWEDES DECREASE PER
100 ACRES CROPS AND GRASS

5 a. or more

Under 5 a.

Nil or decrease

BARE FALLOW INCREASE PER
100 ACRES CROPS AND GRASS

2 a. or more

Under 2 a.

Decrease

TURNIPS
AND
SWEDES _d_

Figure IV

know a parish where the land was being well farmed, and that he had just taken over one farm without a clean acre.[1] A bad season might lead to temporary abandonment; this is suggested by the laconic entry 'thistles' in the cropping record of one farm in 1880.[2] The increase in the acreage of bare fallow, particularly in the Chilterns (Figure IVc), may also conceal such temporary neglect. Fields did tumble down to grass; one such field is recorded on Great Green Street Farm at Chenies in 1887, where the land became covered with couch and weeds which provided only poor herbage. Self-sown grass was auctioned annually in Bedfordshire and was let at very low rents;[3] but even here the extent was exaggerated and an observer who had been told that a good deal of land around Toddington was 'laying itself down with twitch' found the fields fairly clean.[4] It seems likely that in so far as self-sown grass was widespread, it was to be found chiefly on poor arable clays and on very light land.

In whatever way land was converted to grass there was everywhere a reduction in the tillage acreage. The fall was least on the free-working loams at the foot of the escarpment, and on the predominantly pastoral clays around Aylesbury and in south Hertfordshire, where the need and scope for additional grass were limited. It was greatest on mixed farms on the clays and on the steep slopes and stony soils of the western Chilterns, especially in Oxfordshire. Three sample parishes show the range of variation, Stewkley (Bucks.) representing the heavy clays, Pirton (Herts.) the Icknield belt, and Great Missenden (Bucks.) the Chilterns (Figure V). That they are fairly typical of the areas in which they lie is confirmed by the maps in Figures III and IV.

Of course, these averages conceal considerable variation between different farms. It is possible to find farms which delayed conversion of arable until the 1900s. Furthermore, the process on any one farm was not as continuous as the graphs

---

[1] *Royal Commission on Labour, Report upon the Poor Law Union of Thame*, Parliamentary Papers, XXXV (1893–4), p. 52.

[2] Panshanger Papers, Digswell Lodge Farm.

[3] Pringle, loc. cit., p. 22.

[4] *Royal Commission on Labour, Report upon the Poor Law Union of Woburn*, Parliamentary Papers, XXXV, I (1893–4), p. 18.

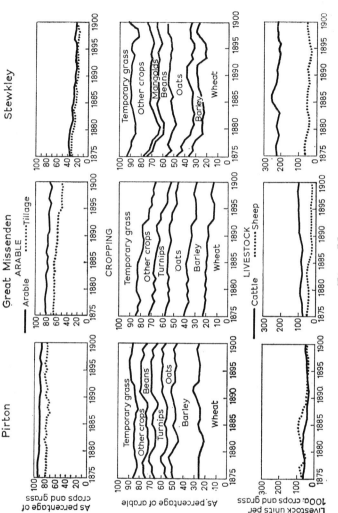

Figure V

suggest; fields would be laid down at intervals between which the arable acreage was constant. A change in tenancy was frequently the occasion for an increase in the grass acreage since it was hard to find good tenants for arable farms on indifferent or heavy soils. Thus, on the 260 acres of Lodge Farm, Chenies, 81 acres were laid down to grass for a new tenant in 1884. The change in emphasis is well seen in a sale catalogue for the Wargrave Manor Estate, which, though largely arable in 1876, was advertised in 1896 as being mainly grass and having only 100 acres of arable, and that of high quality.[1] The great majority of farms increased their grass acreage between 1878 and 1900, and although the sequence of events and the proportion of arable converted to grass varied from farm to farm, there seems to be no doubt that the picture of steady conversion was true of the farms of any area as a whole.

In so far as it was deliberate, this increase in the grass acreage was effected primarily to reduce labour costs; but it was generally accompanied by changes in the stocking of farms. With less arable fewer sheep were needed to fertilize the land, and numbers fell, particularly where sheep had been most numerous, on the High Chilterns, below the escarpment, and in the clay vales (Figure IIIc). There was a corresponding increase in the number of both store and dairy cattle, save in the areas which remained largely arable (Figure IIId). In favoured parts, such as south Oxfordshire, the numbers of cattle increased at a faster rate than the grass acreage, suggesting that here the increase in stock was the cause and not the consequence of more abundant grass; but more commonly the increase in numbers of cattle seems to have been a by-product of the expanding grass acreage.

The extension of dairy farming was the most significant of the livestock changes; progressive farmers like Lawes established dairies because, as he put it, 'foreign nations cannot so easily sell us milk'.[2] Dairying had tended to increase in the traditional livestock areas on the clays north of the Chilterns ever since 1865, when the cattle plague decimated the

[1] British Museum, Wargrave Manor Estate, Maps 137 c. 13.
[2] *Royal Commission on Agriculture, Minutes of Evidence* (1881), p. 949.

population of the London cowhouses. Transport was the chief limitation on the production of milk for sale, and within two or three miles of a railway station farmers began to substitute milk production for butter-making. With the decline in arable farming, other favourably placed farms along the railway lines adopted dairying as their grass acreage expanded, though they had frequently to await the construction of suitable buildings; a prospective tenant at Digswell in-

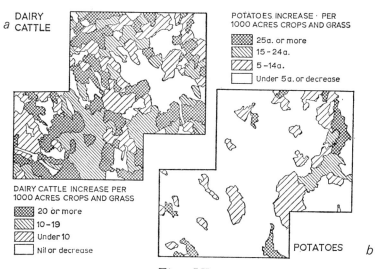

DAIRY
a CATTLE

POTATOES INCREASE · PER
1000 ACRES CROPS AND GRASS

25a. or more
15 - 24a.
5 -14a.
Under 5a. or decrease

DAIRY CATTLE INCREASE PER
1000 ACRES CROPS AND GRASS

20 or more
10 -19
Under 10
Nil or decrease

POTATOES   *b*

Figure VI

sisted on a cowhouse for forty cows as a condition for taking over the farm. In addition to the London market, local markets for milk were provided by the condensed milk factory at Aylesbury and by the biscuit factory at Reading; the considerable increase in dairying in the Oxfordshire Chilterns is undoubtedly due in part to this local demand. The growing towns in the area, such as Watford, also provided local markets. The absence of water precluded dairying in the higher parts of the Chilterns, and the chief areas in which dairying increased lay in the lower south and in the major valleys. Figure VIa shows the general correspondence between areas of greatest increase and the major valleys, most of which carried railway lines from London. In the clay vales to the north there were both an increase in the number of dairy cattle and a further switch from butter-making to milk selling, especially for the London market.[1] Unfortunately there are no records by which this change in the use of milk can be measured; but one contemporary writer reported that in 1888 some 60,000 gallons of milk were sold each week out of the Vale of Aylesbury, more than half of it to London, and that 'Aylesbury butter has lost its prestige'.[2]

The increased interest in cattle-keeping was partly due to the immigration of livestock farmers from the West Country and from Scotland, who were attracted by the low rents and the ease with which farms could be got. On the Knebworth estate, for example, in 1895 Scottish farmers outnumbered English by nine to six,[3] and so numerous were the newcomers when Rider Haggard made his survey of Hertfordshire in 1901 that he was led to ask 'But where are the home people?'[4] The Scots were particularly associated with dairying while the Devon and Cornish farmers were said to be more concerned with stock-rearing.

On the reduced acreage of arable there were also adjustments in cropping (Figure IV). Restrictive covenants could no longer be enforced, both because of the difficulty of finding tenants and because farmers' working capital had been reduced; on the Bedford estate, where the strict enforcement of cropping restrictions has previously been noted, there was relaxation,[5] and on the claylands convenience had become 'the controller of rotations'.[6] Apart from the increase in temporary grass, the most general changes were the greater emphasis on oats at the expense of wheat and barley, and the marked reduction in the acreage of other fodder crops, especially turnips on light land and beans on heavy land. Oats replaced

---

[1] Evidence of Mr Perkins, *Journal of the British Dairy Farmers Association*, VI (1890), p. 126.

[2] R. Gibbs, *A History of Aylesbury* (Aylesbury, 1888), pp. 666–7.

[3] Spencer, loc. cit., p. 14.

[4] R. Haggard, op. cit., I, p. 510.

[5] Royal Commission on Labour, p. 17, and J. Caird, *English Agriculture in 1850–1* (London, 1852), p. 436.

[6] Pringle, loc. cit., p. 40.

wheat as the leading cereal over most of the western Chilterns, and replaced barley as the second cereal in the Hertfordshire Chilterns, where the oat acreage increased despite the falling arable. Fewer sheep were one cause of the reduced turnip acreage, but high labour requirements were also a factor, and the place of turnips in the root break was partly filled by an increase in the acreage of bare fallow. On the clays beans occupied a smaller proportion of the diminished arable and the acreage under mangolds rose; but while there was a marked increase in bare fallow in the early years of the depression, this expansion was not maintained (Figure V, Stewkley, other crops). The least change in cropping occurred on the loams of the Icknield belt.

As with the laying down of land to grass, these generalizations conceal differences between farms. These can be illustrated by the Panshanger estate, where cropping records for a number of farms in close proximity permit comparison of the average acreage under different crops for the periods 1874–6 and 1889–91. On Lower Handside Farm, for example, the acreage under wheat fell 8 per cent, while the acreages under barley and oats rose 5 per cent and 8 per cent respectively. On Digswell Lodge Farm the wheat acreage declined less than 1 per cent, the barley acreage 11 per cent, while the oat acreage increased 10 per cent. At Attimore Hall the oat acreage rose 2 per cent, and acres under wheat and barley declined slightly, while on Birchall Farm the wheat acreage rose 5 per cent, the barley 1 per cent and the oat acreage fell 4 per cent. Nevertheless, although there was much variation from farm to farm, the trend on most farms was similar.

While in many parts of the country farmers met falling cereal prices by growing potatoes and vegetables, few farmers in the Chilterns adopted these crops. Market-gardening spread westward along the Thames terraces in south Buckinghamshire, and southward from the mid-Bedfordshire market-gardening area towards the foot of the Chilterns. But on the Chilterns and in the clay vales soils were either too poor or too heavy to encourage vegetable growing, while much of the area was too inaccessible; even Barton-in-the-Clay, little more than three miles from the nearest station, was held to be too far away for it to be suitable for market-gardening.[1] The stony soils of the Chilterns were also unsuited to potato-growing, which increased mainly in the Vale of St Albans and the Hitchin Gap (Figure VIb). Three causes promoted this expansion: the lighter soils, the immigration of Scottish farmers, who brought not only dairying but potato-growing and ley farming, and the abundant supplies of manure which London provided. It was this last consideration which restricted potato growing to a narrow belt near the railway lines; manure cost only 4s. 6d. a ton at the station, but its price was more than doubled five miles away by transport charges.[2] Figure VIb shows how highly localized this expansion was, though the parish returns, which include more distant farms which did not grow potatoes, minimize the size of the increase. On the 340 acres of Digswell Lodge Farm an average of 43 acres of potatoes was grown in 1882–9 by a new Scottish tenant, whereas none had been grown in 1873–9 by the former tenant, a local farmer whose family had occupied the farm for six generations.[3]

There were other minor changes. Although fruit-growing never became a major activity in the Chilterns, additional orchards were planted, often by smallholders, along the foot of the escarpment, particularly between Totternhoe and Ivinghoe, and in places such as Holmer Green on the plateau. Poorer soils were sometimes taken out of cultivation altogether and planted with trees, usually conifers; many small parcels of arable were planted in the western Chilterns and are usually distinguished from the surrounding beechwoods by their conifers, their straight boundaries and their names, e.g. Jubilee Plantation (Hambleden).

It is clear that the regional pattern of agricultural change was determined mainly by the nature of the soil and by accessibility. Where land was easy to cultivate and moderately fertile it remained in arable, often with little modification in its cropping; where soils were heavy arable fields were laid down

[1] Bedfordshire County Council, Smallholdings File, Bedfordshire County Record Office.

[2] Minutes of Evidence, Select Committee of the House of Commons on Railway Bills, Q. 9223 (1881), BTC 899, in British Transport Commission Archives.

[3] Panshanger Papers.

to grass and pastoral farming was widely adopted; and where soils provided poor arable but were also unsuited to grass, pastoral farming was adopted almost involuntarily by leaving temporary grass unploughed. On the flatter terrain and somewhat better soils of the Hertfordshire Chilterns changes were less marked than further west, and the differences were accentuated by the relative ease with which manure could be got. While the importance of the supply of manure is probably exaggerated by the farmer who said that without the abundant supplies of dung he would not have the land as a gift,[1] Spencer in his report on Hertfordshire did not see how the poorer land could have remained in cultivation without the advantages conferred by the railways.[2] The closer network of lines in Hertfordshire (Figure I) reinforced the advantages of greater nearness to London and better soils which the county enjoyed over Buckinghamshire and Oxfordshire. Railways facilitated the adoption of dairying and potato-growing, and their importance was generally recognized in higher rents near railway lines, away from which, said one farmer, was 'agricultural death'.[3]

The effects of other factors are more difficult to estimate and their incidence was probably more localized. Wages fell little, but there was continued emigration to the towns and many complaints of the quality of the remaining labour. How far the adjustments in farming were caused by labour shortage or by high labour bills is uncertain; but it seems probable that the need for economy was more important than the shortage of labour.[4] The presence of immigrant farmers, introducing new ideas, also affected the local pattern of change; they were among those most successful in riding the depression, partly because their farming suited the new conditions, partly because they were less conservative than the local farmers and partly because they worked hard and lived hard. Adjustments also depended on landlords; wealthy landowners might retain tenants by temporary remissions of rent and facilitate

[1] Rider Haggard, op. cit., I, p. 542.
[2] Spencer, loc. cit., p. 22.
[3] Rider Haggard, op. cit., I, p. 511.
[4] H. Rew, *Report on the Decline of the Agricultural Population of Great Britain*, Parliamentary Papers, XCVI (1906), p. 37.

change by providing necessary buildings, while tenants of poorer landowners would have been left to fend for themselves. But this consideration, while it undoubtedly modified local details, can hardly have determined the broad regional pattern of change.

The main effect of the events of this twenty-five year period was to emphasize differences which had only been latent before, and to diversify further the pattern of farming. The agriculture of 1875 could still be recognized in the haymaking on the London Clay, the corn and sheep farming on the Chilterns, and the pastoral farming in the clay vales; but these differences were becoming muted, and other differences were arising in their place. The contrast between the arable Chilterns and the grasslands to the north and south became less marked, but that between the eastern and western Chilterns and between valley and hilltop farm increased. A further thirty years were required to complete the process; but the foundations of change were clearly laid in this period.

5 Lancashire Livestock Farming during the Great Depression

T. W. FLETCHER

This article was first published in the *Agricultural History Review*, IX(1) (1961).

The phrase 'Great Depression' fairly describes the usual view taken of the condition of agriculture during the last quarter of the nineteenth century. The ruin of her farmers was the price paid by Britain for the benefits she obtained, and conferred, as the great free trading nation of the world. Such is the usual verdict.[1] Of course depression did not press equally heavily on all farmers. According to Clapham, 'north of the Humber . . . there was not so much wreckage as further south'; Lancashire was in the 'half-light' and Cheshire, long famous for its dairies, 'suffered less than any county'.[2] But this was somehow marginal; depression was universal; it was merely that some luckier areas suffered less than the majority.

This paper explores the impact of the Great Depression upon the livestock farmers of Lancashire, the home of the cotton industry, of Cobden, Bright and Free Trade, and, perhaps less widely appreciated, one of England's leading agricultural counties. It ranked sixth among English counties in area of agricultural land (*c.* 1890), and at least as high in terms of gross output per 100 acres. Like its neighbours, Cheshire, Derbyshire, the West Riding, Westmorland and Cumberland, Lancashire was predominantly a livestock district, but unlike

---

[1] The standard work is R. E. Prothero (Lord Ernle), *English Farming Past and Present*, 4th ed. (1927), chapter 18, 'Adversity'; typical of the general historian is R. C. K. Ensor, *England 1870–1914* (1936), p. 115; 'British agriculture . . . was thrown overboard in the storm like an unwanted cargo' (1870s); and p. 284: 'Agriculture was ruined a second time over' (1890s).

[2] J. H. Clapham, *An Economic History of Modern Britain*, 1951 ed., III, pp. 80, 81.

them, it contained within its borders an area of extremely intensive arable farming concentrated on the sands and mosses of the south-west. So different was, and is, this arable culture from the livestock farming of the north-west that it has been excluded from this study. As an example of pure arable farming that weathered the depression unchanged it merits separate treatment.[1]

LANCASHIRE FARMING

South of the Ribble and east of the arable plain, Triassic sandstones give way to the coal measures and gritstones of the east Lancashire Pennines where the towns and villages of the cotton trade are strung along the valley bottoms, and in their interstices and on the hillsides are squeezed the small grass farms of the east Lancashire cow-keepers, men specializing in the retail sale of milk to the customers at their farm gates.

Agricultural writers of the nineteenth century say little of east Lancashire.[2] The best brief description is Rothwell's of 1850. 'The district . . . is principally occupied as small dairy farms, there being a great demand for milk and butter; and not much adapted, from the nature of its soil and climate, for arable cultivation.'[3] The system had not changed at the end of the century; the agent of an estate in the Blackburn–Oswaldtwistle area described his tenancies in 1895 as 'all milk and butter farms'. 'They [the farmers] barter the products themselves in the large, adjoining towns; they retail it as you will understand.'[4]

Although arable farming was only to be found in the south-

---

[1] Contemporary descriptions may be found in *Journal of the Royal Agricultural Society*, XXXVIII (1877), pp. 462–526; XLVI (1885), pp. 547–90; XLVII (1886), pp. 120–71.

[2] For example, J. Holt, *General View of the Agriculture of the County of Lancashire* (1795), p. 210: 'Capital, labour, ingenuity and attention are in this county diverted from agriculture'; G. Beesley, *A Report on the State of Agriculture in Lancashire* . . . (Preston, 1849), p. 7: 'Occupiers of land in this district can scarcely be considered farmers'; W. J. Garnett, *Prize Report of the Farming of Lancashire* (Preston, 1849), p. 8: 'Altogether a coal district' with 'not much to interest a farmer'.

[3] W. Rothwell, *Report of the Agriculture of the County of Lancaster* (1850), p. 20.

[4] *Royal Commission on Agricultural Distress 1894–7*, Q. 40,649–50 (J. Howson); the Alphabetical Digest (C. 8146 of 1896) enables individual witnesses to be traced to their appropriate volume.

west, milk production south of the Ribble was not confined to east Lancashire. Every town was supplied by producer-retailers on its outskirts whose methods were similar to but less intensive and more flexible than those of the east Lancashire men in that some crops were grown, to be sold when relative prices were favourable but otherwise fed to their cows. Such mixed farming was common in the Leigh–Wigan–Bolton–Chorley belt of country between the hills and the arable plain proper.

Lancashire, north of the Ribble, was a 'purely agricultural district'.[1] The Fylde plain between the gritstone hills of Bowland on the Yorkshire border to the east and the coast to the west had been the county's granary in the eighteenth century but by 1870 was an important dairying district and, like Cheshire, specialized in cheese production.[2] Milking stock were reared and dry cows fattened for the butcher. It was also famous as a horse-breeding centre, well situated for supplying the industrial towns to the south.[3]

North of Lancaster stretches a narrow coastal strip, partly of limestone, where oats, roots and seeds were grown for consumption on the farm by sheep and cattle on a system similar to the Scottish. Cattle were mainly of the dairy type, though at Holker, north of the sands, the Duke of Devonshire maintained a celebrated herd of beef shorthorns. But, as Beesley had noted long before, 'pedigree, shorthorned stock . . . are confined to gentlemen, or amateur farmers';[4] Booth's shorthorns were too beefy; in Lancashire milk was demanded. The extraordinary growth of Barrow-in-Furness during the last third of the nineteenth century would yet further concentrate interest on the dairy rather than the beef animal. In the hills of Bowland and Furness, sheep and cattle rearing was universal. Butter was made on most farms, and with the increasing de-

[1] Garnett, op. cit., p. 16.
[2] W. Smith, 'Agrarian evolution since the eighteenth century', *British Association Report* (Blackpool, 1936), Appendix, p. 44; *Royal Commission on the Depressed Condition of the Agricultural Interest 1880–2*, C. 3375–IV (Coleman's Report), p. 40; J. P. Sheldon, *The Future of British Agriculture* (1893), p. 114.
[3] *Preston Guardian*, 1 April 1885; article on the development of shire breeding in Lancashire; *Royal Commission 1880–2*, Q. 67,733–4 (J. Clay).
[4] Beesley, op. cit., p. 47.

mand for milk cows, the by-products were used to rear dairy stock rather than children. Lamb, mutton, butter and dairy heifers constituted the main output of these farms.[1]

Farms generally were small in Lancashire. The average size of 'holding' over 5 acres of crops and grass in 1875 was 40 acres compared with an average for England of 80 acres. In east Lancashire the comparable figure was 30. Only 8 per cent of all holdings over 5 acres were larger than 100 acres although accounting for more than 30 per cent of the total agricultural acreage of the county. Associated with the small size of farm was the importance of family labour. According to the 1871 Census the proportion of farmers and farmers' relatives to farm workers was 43:57, which was not very different from that of twenty years earlier (41:59) when Danson and Welton discovered to their surprise that south Lancashire was more densely populated with agriculturalists than any of the 'agricultural' counties.[2] Because of the relatively large contribution to the total labour force made by farmers themselves, the money cost of labour was a less important farm expense in Lancashire than on the larger farms of the arable east, even though pastoral settlement and industrial development had brought high farm wages. Wilson Fox's wage indices show that in 1867–71 average wages in the northern counties were 14s. 9d. a week compared with 11s. $11\frac{1}{4}$d. in England and Wales and 11s. $4\frac{3}{4}$d. in the eastern counties.[3] Lancashire wages, particularly south of the Ribble, were frequently higher than Wilson Fox's average for the northern counties.[4]

[1] Information from the Kelsall family's diaries and notebooks relating to the hills of the Lancaster area which have been kindly lent to the writer by Mr W. Kelsall of Quernmore.

[2] T. A. Danson and J. T. Welton, 'On the population of Lancashire and Cheshire, 1801–1851', *Historic Society of Lancashire and Cheshire*, XII (1859), p. 63: 'No facts are here before us which would justify an attempt to indicate the circumstances under which this ratio of agricultural population has been obtained, in the very heart of our district, usually regarded as pre-eminently, if not exclusively, favourable to manufacture and commerce. But the fact must be noticed as one of the most remarkable of those yet divulged by this enquiry.'

[3] 'Agricultural wages in England and Wales during the last 50 years', *Journal of the Royal Statistical Society*, LXIV (1903).

[4] Wages of labourers on the Park farm of the Hesketh estate ranged up to 16s. (County Record Office, DD He/62/31, 32, 33, 1867–71); cowmen near Manchester were paid 18s. (*Manchester Guardian*, 9 February 1872).

The pattern of Lancashire's farm output is shown by the Agricultural Returns first collected in 1866.

TABLE I *Crops and Stock per 100 acres of Crops and Grass*

Average of 1870, 1874, 1875[1]	*Crop acreages*				*Livestock numbers*			
	Arable	*Corn*	*Oats*	*Pota-toes*	*Cattle*	*Milk Cows*	*Sheep*	*Pigs*
England	57	32	6	1	17	7	81	8
Lancashire East	31	14	7	4	30	16	43	5
Lancashire North	5	2	1	—	37	22	46	4
Lancashire	27	13	7	2	32	15	61	5

Compared with England on the eve of the depression, Lancashire possessed more permanent grass, and a greater proportion of its corn acreage was devoted to oats for feed. The county was relatively densely stocked with cattle and particularly so with milking stock, but there were relatively fewer sheep and pigs. County totals, like England's, conceal fundamental regional differences. Lancashire's 31 per cent of arable was an average of extremes, of 5 per cent in east Lancashire and of 60 per cent in the arable south-west; north of the Ribble about a quarter of the agricultural acreage was under the plough.

The leading products of Lancashire's livestock farms were milk, sold retail and wholesale, butter, cheese and mutton and lamb. Poultry were kept in increasing numbers, but information is scanty for the nineteenth century. Most of the beef production in the county was cow beef, a by-product of dairying; more important was the rearing of milking stock, mainly by hill farmers north of the Ribble whose fortunes during the Great Depression were thus linked with those of the milk sellers of the Fylde and south Lancashire.

Among farmers' expenses other than labour, feed and rent

[1] The years 1870, 1874 and 1875 (the intervening years are unavailable) were chosen to avoid using the earlier, more unreliable, years; data were abstracted from the original parish and 'collection' summaries in the possession of the Ministry of Agriculture.

predominated. Milk producers in the county had long been familiar with purchased feeding-stuffs, and the plentiful supply of brewers' wastes and the accessibility of imports at Liverpool encouraged a growing dependence on purchased feed by grassland farmers wishing to produce winter milk. The price movements of this crucial purchase during the Great Depression are of primary concern. Rent, as befits its many-sided character, is treated separately.

DEMAND

The population of Lancashire increased by some 50 per cent between 1867–71 and 1894–8; other things equal, demand for food would increase *pro rata*. But other things were not equal. Whatever form the Great Depression took, it was not a period of depression for the working classes, by comparison with whom the inhabitants of Lombard Street were insignificant as consumers of food. Earnings in the Lancashire cotton trade rose by some 25 per cent between 1867–71 and 1894–8[1] at a time when retail prices fell by about 26 per cent.[2] *Per capita* real income thus increased by some two-thirds, an annual rate of growth appreciably greater than during the 'good years' of 1850–70. Associated with rising income was the growing preference for protein rather than starch, for livestock products rather than cereals and potatoes. The oatmeal, coarse bread, cheese and fat bacon of the farm labourer no longer sufficed for the more delicate appetites of the less robust cotton workers. Tea with milk, white bread and butter, meat and eggs were their favourite dishes.[3]

---

[1] G. H. Wood, *The History of Wages in the Cotton Trade during the Past Hundred Years* (1910), p. 128.

[2] W. T. Layton, *An Introduction to the Study of Prices* (1912), p. 150.

[3] See *Preston Guardian*, 28 April 1894: of the 'operative classes in our large towns' – 'their fondness for eggs, tea and other "luxuries" having taken the place of their liking for the plain and wholesome tuber'. Lancashire budgets collected by G. von Schulz-Gaevernitz in 1891 illustrate the prominent place of dairy products and meat in the diet of cotton operatives. The average of five detailed family weekly budgets shows 6s. 4d. spent on bread, flour, cereals and potatoes, 9s. 5d. on milk, butter, eggs and cheese, and 6s. 8d. on beef, mutton, pork, bacon and ham. – *The Cotton Trade in England and on the Continent* (1895), trans. O. S. Hall, pp. 178 ff.; see also W. E. Bear, 'The food supply of Manchester', *Journal of the Royal Agricultural Society*, LVIII (1897), p. 511.

Most vital to the Lancashire farmer because of its immunity from competition was the demand for milk. On the conservative assumption that *per capita* intake of liquid milk in the county increased by a quarter between 1867–71 and 1894–8 (see Appendix A), total demand would rise by 88 per cent. Depending on quality and price relative to the imported product, the demand for lamb, eggs and butter may well have risen to a similar, if not greater, extent. Lancashire farmers were keenly aware, as they had been for generations, that their prosperity was linked with that of trade and industry as reflected in consumer demand rather than with the protectionist policies of the 'agricultural interest' who seemed mainly concerned with the effects of weather and imports on the home wheat crop.[1]

SUPPLIES AND PRICES

By contrast with demand, more specific information about farm supply is available as a result of the decision to collect agricultural statistics in 1866. In view of acreage uncertainties due to the declining use of local measures such as the Lancashire and Cheshire customary acres during the Great Depression, Graph A shows simply the numbers of the various classes of livestock in Lancashire between 1867 and 1900. Table II gives figures for the nineties comparable to those shown in Table I for the 1870s. Assuming that the increase in area of agricultural land from 748,000 to 823,000 acres resulted from the displacement of customary measure by the statute acre,[2] it is clear that little change occurred in Lancashire farming

---

[1] For example, a Brindle producer-retailer complained that 'since business became bad at Gregson Lane Mill things have not been half so good for the farmers in the district' (*Preston Guardian*, 20 April 1895); cf. the Burnley milk-producer of fifty years earlier who was converted to a 'corn-law repealer' by the discovery that the 'closing of a mill in his neighbourhood suddenly deprived him of all his best customers'. – W. Cooke Taylor, *Tour of the Manufacturing Districts* (1842), p. 87.

[2] The most common customary measures used in Lancashire were of 2·1 and 1·6 statute acres; see E. H. Smith, 'Lancashire long measure', *Historic Society of Lancashire and Cheshire*, CX (1958), pp. 1–14.

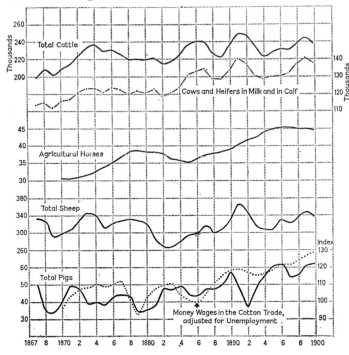

A. LIVESTOCK 1867–1900

during the last thirty years of the nineteenth century other than an intensifying of existing systems.

(i) *Dairy Produce.* The total number of cattle rose from 226,000 in 1870, 1874 and 1875, to 230,000 in 1894–8, an in-

TABLE II   *Crops and Stock per* 100 *acres of Crops and Grass*

Average of 1894–8 inc.	Crop acreages				Livestock numbers			
	Arable	*Corn*	*Oats*	*Pota-toes*	*Cattle*	*Milk Cows*	*Sheep*	*Pigs*
England	47	23	8	1	18	8	64	9
Lancashire East	31	13	10	5	31	18	44	8
Lancashire North	2	1	1	—	39	27	38	8
Lancashire	23	10	7	3	37	19	70	8

crease of some 2 per cent; the number of cows and heifers in milk and in calf increased by 10 per cent.[1] This concentration on the productive milk cow was most noticeable in east Lancashire, where, with total cattle numbers rising no faster than in the county as a whole, cows and heifers increased by some 20 per cent. Nevertheless, the number of milk cows per 1,000 of the population of Lancashire, which in 1871–5 was 42, fell to 32 in 1894–8. Lancashire's milk supply could thus only be maintained by increasing yield per cow, by increasing the output of liquid milk at the expense of butter- and cheese-making or by importing milk into the county.

If the yield per cow in Lancashire is assumed to have been 350 gallons per annum in 1870 and to have increased by 20 per cent to 420 in 1894–8, if *per capita* consumption is taken as a quarter of a pint a day rising by 25 per cent, and if 30 per cent of total milk production was sold in the form of butter and cheese in 1870 with absolute output remaining constant thereafter, an overall picture emerges which is shown in Table III.[2] Considerable latitude may be allowed in the assumptions without affecting the general position.

TABLE III

Lancashire — *million gallons*	(i) *Milk* *production*	(ii) *Butter and* *cheese*	(iii) *Milk* *sales* *(i–ii)*	(iv) *Liquid* *consumption*	(v) *Import* *(iv–iii)*
Average of 1870–1	32·7	9·7	23·0	32·8	9·8
Average of 1894–8 inc.	47·1	9·7	37·4	61·2	23·8

The import of milk into Lancashire was not easy: little was produced in the hills to the north and north-east, while over the Pennines to the east the industrial West Riding was barely self-sufficient. To the south the famous dairying county of Cheshire supplied the bulk of Lancashire's needs. The demands of other concentrations of consumers, however, notably

[1] The growth of cattle numbers in north and east Lancashire was partly offset by a decline in the arable south-west of the county.
[2] For a discussion of these estimates see Appendix A.

E

the Great Wen itself, facilitated by the railway companies'
use of differential rates to encourage the long haul, were, by
the 1870s, stretching into Staffordshire, Derbyshire and many
parts of Cheshire.[1]

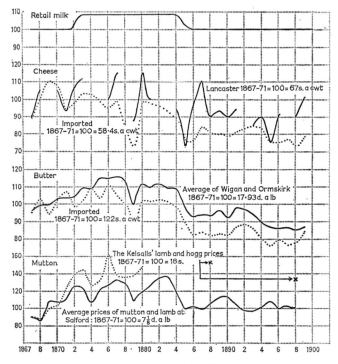

B. PRICE INDICES

Local producers had thus every incentive to increase their
output of liquid milk, and most butter- and cheese-makers in
Lancashire, like those of Cheshire, were within competitive
range of the large liquid markets of Manchester and Liverpool
at a time when their dairy produce was subjected to growing
import competition. But, as may be seen from Graph B,

[1] See E. A. Pratt, *The Transition in Agriculture* (1906), pp. 18–23; *Royal Commission 1880–2*, Q. 5,777–800, Q. 30,491; *Royal Commission 1894–7*, Q. 35,345–6;
Report from the Select Committee on Railways, H.C. 374 of 1881, Q. 8,029; *Agricultural Gazette*, 11 October 1880.

Lancashire farm cheese and butter did not fall in price to the same extent as imports; the inflexibility of supply, given the attraction of the liquid market, and the growing consumer preference for better quality, account for the relative rise in price of the superior Lancashire grades. Evidence of change in the quantity of butter and cheese made on Lancashire farms is contradictory. Farmers are reported to have abandoned cheese-making for the more lucrative sale of liquid milk; they are also said to have improved and increased their output of Lancashire cheese, which did not reach Manchester market until the early 1890s. It was then mostly supplied from Preston, where in response to demand from urban south Lancashire the cheese market was at this time growing rapidly and supplanting that of Lancaster.[1] Local farm butter was unknown in the Manchester market; it was mainly sold retail in the producing areas, either by producer-retailers to their milk customers – the usual method of disposing of surplus milk – in the local market, or by private contract to customers who preferred fresh farm produce and were prepared to pay a higher price for it.[2] Those hill farmers of north Lancashire who were unable or unwilling to sell liquid milk continued to produce butter for local sale.[3]

Price movements in Lancashire seem to have been as follows. The price of butter rose, as did liquid milk, during the 1860s and 1870s and did not significantly break until 1878. The fall of 1879 was acute but of short duration: by 1880 butter and cheese prices seemed normal enough. But with the trade depression of 1883–6 prices fell, touching bottom in 1886 and bringing down both wholesale and retail milk prices. Recovery

[1] *Royal Commission 1894–7*, Q. 11,320 (A. Wilson Fox); cf. *Manchester Guardian*, 29 March 1883: 'It is a notorious fact that the demand for milk in our largest cities is increasing at a rapid rate, so much so that many who have made cheese and more who have been making butter have given up both for milk selling.' *Preston Guardian*, 12 October 1895; Bear, *Journal of the Royal Agricultural Society*, LVIII (1897), *Preston Guardian*, 1 December 1894: cheese fairs were instituted at Preston in 1879; in 1881 the total pitch was 769 cheeses, in 1893 17,618, and in 1894 18,622 cheeses.

[2] *Royal Commission 1894–7*, Q. 40,650 (J. Howson), Q. 12,593 (T. Worthington); *Preston Guardian*, 18 April 1891, 24 January 1891; Graham, op. cit., p. 144.

[3] Kelsall Diaries; but even in Furness whole milk selling was common, with that surplus to market requirements being made into butter, the skim milk 'finding a ready sale' (*Preston Guardian*, 22 September 1881).

was hesitant and partial, and the break of 1890–3 in the upward surge of real wages checked demand and some prices gave way again after 1892.[1] Demand picked up in 1894, and the Lancashire milk cow population, which had fallen steeply from a suspiciously prominent peak in 1891, resumed its increase.[2] The price of imported butter and cheese, like that of meat and eggs, fell sharply after 1893 to a minimum in 1897–8 and impressively larger quantities were imported. While milk prices held, local butter and all but top-quality cheese prices continued to sag until import prices recovered in 1898.

The most significant feature was the stability of the retail milk price and the limited movement of the wholesale price. As milk production was the most important single activity of Lancashire farmers, and as approximately three-quarters of the total dairy output took the form of liquid milk, the maintenance of the milk price during a period of generally falling prices was clearly a powerful factor in supporting farmers' incomes and encouraging expansion of output.

It seems that a fair degree of equilibrium existed between farmers' net returns from the sale of milk and the making of cheese or butter, except for poor quality cheese and, after 1885 possibly and after 1893 almost certainly, for butter sold in the local market.[3] In these circumstances the less efficient producers would be persuaded to improve the quality of their product, particularly in the case of cheese where relatively high returns might be achieved,[4] improve its marketing, more feasible in the case of butter,[5] or enter the liquid market. A

[1] This is true of market butter but not of better quality cheese which held its price until 1895, when it suffered from a 'record' supply due to the hot summer (*Manchester Guardian*, 3 October 1895, *Preston Guardian*, 18 April 1896), a diminishing demand as a result of the cold spring (*Royal Commission 1894–7*, Q. 62,411), and the cheapness of frozen mutton (ibid.).

[2] 'Suspicious' because there is nothing in the state of trade or the movement of prices in 1888–91 to account for the steep fall in cow numbers after 1891. A possible explanation put forward at the time is that high meat prices led to abnormal slaughterings: certainly dairy stock were highly priced and in short supply in 1893–4 (*Preston Guardian*, 7 October 1893, 10 November 1894).

[3] Cf. Ruth Cohen, *A History of Milk Prices*, pp. 21 et seq.

[4] For example, even in the 1890s 70s. a cwt was obtained at Preston in the spring (*Manchester Guardian*, 29 March 1893, 29 March 1894, 27 March 1895).

[5] For the advantages of marketing butter privately, see *Preston Guardian*, 24 January 1891, 18 April 1891 and *Royal Commission 1894–7*, Q. 21,761, 35,331–48.

shift to liquid sales was also encouraged by a fall in rail transport costs which, between the 1870s and 1890s, approximately halved within the area supplying Manchester.[1]

Normally butter was made on the farm all the year round, frequently from milk surplus to retail liquid requirements, whereas cheese-making was usually a seasonal occupation when the cows were out at grass. Thus price relationships varied seasonally, as they did in different parts of the country, and local opportunities offered scope to the enterprising to market their milk in its most profitable form. Peter Blundell, the well-known Fylde farmer and horsebreeder, made cheese all the year round, whereas some of his neighbours confined their cheese-making to spring and autumn; in the height of the summer they sold liquid milk into the spreading seaside resorts.[2] Others combined cheese with winter butter or winter milk; all depended upon circumstance. Intermittent developments of this nature during the Great Depression, the fruit of innumerable decisions by thousands of small farmers, produced a remarkable increase in the supplies of liquid milk and improved the quality of farm butter and cheese.[3] The existence of local preferences for farm produce should warn the unwary against the use of import prices to measure farmers' receipts.

(ii) *Sheep.* The remaining livestock product of importance in Lancashire was mutton. The total sheep population of the county was 319,000 in 1870, 1874–5; it fell steeply to a trough in 1882–3 from natural causes of weather or disease common throughout the country, and recovered by 1894–8 to some 4 per cent above its original level. Sheep numbers declined in east Lancashire owing to the growing industrial exploitation of these hills as quarries, reservoirs and gathering-grounds, and to the competition of retail milk selling. Most of Lan-

[1] *Manchester Courier*, 28 March 1872; *Report from the Select Committee on Railways* (1881), Q. 8021, 8029; *Report on Railway Rates and Charges Provisional Order Bills* (1891), Q. 8499 and p. 946; Bear, *Journal of the Royal Agricultural Society*, LVIII (1897), p. 508.

[2] *Preston Guardian*, 20 April 1895, 13 October 1894.

[3] Some help was given by both County Council and private landowners in the form of attempts to improve the quality of farm butter and cheese, mainly in the direction of standardization by the encouragement of scientific methods; see, e.g., *Preston Guardian*, 18 April 1891, 30 April 1892.

cashire's sheep were to be found north of the Ribble in the hills of Bowland and Furness, and here total numbers increased by over 20 per cent.

There was a fundamental difference in the type of sheep kept on arable and hill farms in the nineteenth century. The former were heavy, often long-woolled breeds, and their owners suffered from the extreme fall in wool prices and the import competition, particularly of frozen mutton after 1883, which lowered the price of their fat mutton. In contrast, wool was less important to the hill farmer; it was only of carpet quality, and even when it fetched 1s. a lb in the early seventies brought in but 3s. a ewe as against 25s. for her lamb. The lean horned hill ewe and her crosses bred the small lambs and lightweight mutton that were in growing demand and with which, during this period, the foreign supply was not directly competitive. It is significant that the ratio of lambs to total sheep in Lancashire increased by almost 10 per cent during the Great Depression, and the explanation of this shift from wether mutton to lamb production is to be found in the relative movement of their prices which reflected the impact of changes in consumer demand upon the supply situation. As with cheese, the better quality home produce was considered superior to the imported and priced accordingly. Newspaper reports of Salford market, the largest livestock market in the county, stress throughout the period the high demand for lamb and lightweight mutton.[1] Fat wether mutton, like the live and frozen imported, sold at well below the price of English and Scotch lamb.[2] The difference was particularly wide in 1895 when frozen imported mutton could be bought in London for 2d. a lb at a time when first quality English lamb was fetching up to 11d. at Salford. The general position was that particularized by the market reporter in 1895: 'Choice small sheep were scarce and in good demand at late full rates, but heavy and

---

[1] For example, *Manchester Guardian*, August 1871: 'Choice lambs ... were very scarce and much sought after'; ibid., 3 October 1894: 'Good demand for choice lightweight sheep.'

[2] For example, *Manchester Guardian*, August 1871: 'Foreign sheep were of such indifferent quality that they were almost unsaleable'; ibid., 4 October 1871: foreign sheep were a 'drug on the market'; ibid., 3 June 1885: 'inferior qualities sold slowly at a reduction'; ibid., 3 June 1896: 'heavy and fat sheep not quotable'.

inferior sold slowly at lower [compared with the previous week] prices'.[1] Mutton (including ewe) prices at Salford fell slightly from 7·2d. to 7·1d. a lb between 1867–71 and 1894–8; lamb prices rose from 7·5d. to 8·1d.

Lancashire sheep farmers would undoubtedly agree with the Yorkshireman who, quoting the price of 'small mutton' as 'well worth 8d. a lb' to the Royal Commission in November 1895, admitted 'we have not been doing badly at all. Taking the depression during the last twenty years the sheep have held up wonderfully'.[2] Following consumers' preference and increasing their rate of turnover in the process, sheep farmers abandoned the rearing of heavyweight, low-priced wethers in favour of an annual crop of lightweight, high-priced lambs.

(iii) *Poultry and Pigs.* The number of pigs in Lancashire increased by about a third during the Great Depression; the number of poultry also increased but no figures are available. Total imports of pig meat into the U.K. more than doubled between 1871–5 and 1894–8, and prices of imported fresh pork and bacon fell by 8 per cent and 13 per cent respectively; no local quotations have been found. From 1867–71 import prices of eggs rose in the early seventies but gradually declined to about the original level by 1894–8; unlike import prices local prices at Stockport did not fall after 1886. The profit to be derived from poultry and their growing importance in Lancashire were frequently discussed.[3] In that feed accounts for some 80 per cent of production costs, as with pigs, the steep fall in purchased feed prices during the Great Depression constituted a clear profit incentive for the farmer to increase his output, particularly of eggs, which, as the price indicates, were in high demand and, as today, were preferred fresh from the farm.[4]

The Yorkshireman's verdict was applicable to all the main output products of the Lancashire farmer during the Great Depression when considered in relation to the general course of prices. Even the price of his poorest cheese did not sink to the depths reached by the wheat price. The decline in world

[1] *Manchester Guardian*, 2 October 1895; cf. *Preston Guardian*, 2 January 1892.

[2] *Royal Commission 1894–7*, Q. 61,014 (P. Norfolk).

[3] For example, *Journal of the Royal Agricultural Society*, 1877, p. 492; *Preston Guardian*, 11 April 1885, 2 April 1892, 15 September 1892, 20 April 1895.

[4] See *Royal Commission 1894–7*, Q. 62, 166–230, and *Final Report*, p. 254.

cereal prices certainly affected Lancashire livestock farmers, but most agreeably, as the note on feed prices indicates.

(iv) *Labour*. Lancashire Census data provide only a crude picture of variations within the agricultural population which in total fell from 51,000 to 40,000 between 1871 and 1901. The changes recorded in the numbers of both farmers and their relatives are suspect, but whereas the decline in the number of farmers is exaggerated a spurious increase is shown in the number of relatives.[1] The total of farmers and relatives is perhaps not too inaccurate and its proportion to that of male farm workers rose slightly from 43:57 in 1871 to 47:53 in 1901. The number of farm workers in the county fell by 28 per cent during these years, from 29,400 to 21,100. Alternative employment was close at hand south of the Ribble, if less so to the north, and the exodus of labour from farms was facilitated by the gradual introduction of mowing machines, 'hay collectors', and other machinery to cope with the haytime peak of the grassland farmer's year. As always, farmers' sons and daughters were 'flocking to the towns', bringing home in 1894 'from £2 to £3. 10s. a week'.[2]

Farm wages in the northern counties, already higher than elsewhere in 1867–71, were raised yet further during the Great Depression. In 1894-8 they stood at 17s. 4½d. a week, an increase of 18 per cent compared with average wages in England and Wales which had risen by 12 per cent to 13s. 4½d.[3] Wages throughout the country rose in the seventies but whereas in the north gains were consolidated, in some areas a slipping back was evident. Almost all Wilson Fox's Lancashire evidence was collected from the Fylde where the weekly wages of a stockman were 17s.–18s. in both 1891 and 1901. South of the Ribble £1 a week was commonly quoted in the nineties.[4] To

[1] Exaggerated by the exclusion of retired farmers after 1871; decennial numbers of farmers from 1861–1901 were, in thousands, 16·8, 16·0, 14·8, 13·5, 12·2; female relatives were included in 1901 in contrast to the preceding three Censuses; for a critical analysis of these figures see Lord Eversley, 'The decline in number of agricultural labourers in Great Britain', *Journal of the Royal Statistical Society*, LXX (1907), pp. 267–319.

[2] *Royal Commission 1894–7*, Q. 14,274 (J. Barlow).

[3] Wilson Fox, op. cit., p. 332.

[4] *Royal Commission 1894–7*, Q. 12,580 (T. Worthington): '19s. to £1'; Q. 27,290 (T. Mercer): '£1'; *Preston Guardian*, 20 April 1895: '20s.'

the farm worker the period was one of slowly growing comfort. Like the cotton operative he benefited from the fall in retail prices, but increases in his cash income of 18 per cent compared unfavourably with the 25 per cent increase of an initially higher income enjoyed by his fellows in the factory: here was the continuing incentive to leave the farm.

With a decline of 28 per cent in the number of paid workers and an increase of some 18 per cent in average wages, the total wage bill paid by Lancashire farmers declined by 15 per cent during the Great Depression. Many Lancashire farmers employed no regular labour other than their families, and of those who did, almost all worked alongside their men. Their whole way of life contrasted vividly with that of the large tenant farmers of the corn-growing areas.

(v) *Feed*. On dairy farms feed was much the most important cash outlay. A Fylde farmer in 1885 spent £651. 10s. 1d., or approximately £13 a cow, on feed for his cows, which numbered between 48 and 52; his rent and rates for 98 acres were £338. 8s. 6½d.[1] On more intensive dairy farms expenditure on feed was relatively greater. Thomas Barlow of Rossendale in east Lancashire spent £400 a year on provender in the nineties for 31 milking cows, which again averaged some £13 a cow but at prices lower than those of the preceding decade. His farm was 44 acres and probably rented at about £90.[2] Such intensive stocking was not uncommon among the producer-retailers of east Lancashire:[3] the hill farmers of the north were more self-sufficient.

The Royal Agricultural Society's judges remarked in 1877 on the 'abundant supply of feeding stuffs in the great port of Liverpool',[4] where imports of maize increased from an average of 4·3 million cwt for the years 1867–71 to 13·1 million in 1894–8, and of oilcakes from 18,200 to 97,500 tons. The fall in price was the fact mainly responsible for this increase in the quantity of feed purchased by farmers, which was in turn, apart from slow advances in breeding and management, the

[1] *Journal of the Royal Agricultural Society*, XVLII, 1886, p. 146.
[2] *Royal Commission 1894–7*, Q. 14,280 (T. Barlow); the rent is estimated.
[3] Stocking on the Thwaites's estate was equivalent to 'one head for every 1 ac. 1 r. 35 p. of land'. – *Royal Commission 1894–7*, Q. 40,661 (J. Howson).
[4] *Journal of the Royal Agricultural Society*, XXXVIII, 1877, p. 504.

means whereby milk and livestock output was so signally and, it would seem, profitably expanded. In the case of the two important items maize and oilcakes, overseas trade figures for the U.K. show a fall in price of 45 per cent and 37 per cent respectively between 1867–71 and 1894–8, and it seems reasonable to suppose that the cost of feed to the Lancashire farmer fell by at least a third during this period.

With labour an overhead on the ubiquitous family farm, many dairy farmers on the plain both north and south of the Ribble continued to grow oats and other crops for livestock feed. In such circumstances the market price of his oats was not the farmer's chief concern; more apposite was the relationship between the oat price and the cost of a comparable feed. As the Wiltshire man explained to the Royal Commission in 1895, he had grown and sold oats at 24s. 6d. a quarter and purchased Russian barley for '13s. 9d. delivered'.[1] It is unlikely that such opportunities escaped the Lancashire man. Twenty years earlier south-west Lancashire arable farmers were purchasing maize at 6s. 6d. a cwt to feed their farm horses, their oats they sold for 8s. 9d.[2] If the Lancashire farmer in search of profit dared deprive his horses of their oats, he would certainly experiment with the diet of the more accommodating cow as opportunity prompted. These considerations partly explain the maintenance of the county's oat acreage during a period of falling oat prices, although more to the point in arable south-west Lancashire, where the bulk of the country's oats were grown, was the relationship between the prices of wheat and oats.

RENT

Rent is of peculiar interest. Net rent represents the income of the landowner; it may be thought of as the return on his investment. Gross rent is both a cost to the farmer and a measure of the demand for land and thus indirectly of the changing prospects in agriculture. Rent is somewhat insensitive in this last respect as landlords and their agents do not necessarily accept the highest bidder and the rent of a farm

[1] *Royal Commission 1894–7*, Q. 15,821 (Sir G. Goldney).
[2] *Journal of the Royal Agricultural Society*, XXXVIII, 1877, p. 486.

tenanted by the same family for decades is slow to change. Landlord-tenant relationships were important in Lancashire where the owner-occupier was a negligible figure. Owners farmed less than 10 per cent of Lancashire's agricultural land; the comparable figure for England was 20.[1] In east Lancashire, the most industrialized part of the country, the percentage was as low as 7.[2] The land-owning families of Lancashire, with the Stanleys and the Molyneuxs at their head, were of ancient descent and clung tenaciously to their estates.[3] Manufacturers who invested in land either purchased small properties within the county or, like Sir Robert Peel the elder, looked elsewhere.[4]

The lease and the covenant were rare, particularly south of the Ribble. The country-wide survey conducted by the *Mark Lane Express* in 1876 into the effects of the Agricultural Holdings Act of the previous year summarized the position in Lancashire;[5] few leases were to be found other than on Crown property north of Lancaster; nor were they desired by the tenantry who, perhaps like Peter Blundell, had 'no desire for either a lease or tenant right, regarding Lord Derby as the best landlord in England'.[6] If this sentiment be thought to represent a survival of 'feudal' instinct in rural north Lancashire, at the other extreme was Thomas Worthington of Wigan who declared before a Royal Commission, 'I have taken my farm like taking a house. When I have paid the rent I am master of the show'.[7]

[1] Estimates from *Agricultural Returns* 1890–8 inclusive.

[2] 'Collection' figures; complicated by the existence of Honour of Clitheroe copyholders whose unique tenure was, in practice, almost indistinguishable from freehold.

[3] Of 24 estates in south Lancashire of over 3,000 acres in the 1870s 19 were in the hands of families who could trace their occupation back at least as far as the reign of Henry VIII; the remaining five were also ancient estates of inheritance. – J. Bateman, *The Great Landowners of Great Britain and Ireland* (1879 ed.).

[4] For example, Mr Earnshaw, a cotton manufacturer of Bury, bought a small estate in the Fylde of 'one farm or more' (*Preston Guardian*, 20 October 1894); another Bury manufacturer, 'Squire' Mucklow, purchased 7,000 acres in Cornwall in the mid-nineteenth century (*Preston Guardian*, 29 September 1894).

[5] W. E. Bear, *The Relations of Landlord and Tenant in England and Scotland* (1876), Appendix, pp. 104–31, where the findings of the survey are usefully summarized.

[6] *Royal Commission 1880–2*, Coleman's Report, p. 38.

[7] *Royal Commission 1894–7*, Q. 12,774 (T. Worthington).

In spite of what might appear to be a lamentable absence of security, Lancashire farmers were prepared to sink large amounts of tenant's capital into their farms.[1] They found that it paid to farm intensively even though under six months' notice to quit should the land be required for building.[2] The tenant's security was rooted in 'confidence in his landlord'.[3]

The concomitant of the annual tenancy in Lancashire was the freedom from restriction. As early as 1876 every Lancashire farm mentioned in the report of the Prize Farm Competition was noted as being an 'annual tenancy' with 'no restrictions'.[4] This informality between landlord and tenant was partly due to the presence of manufacturers. The main economic incentive of many ancient families in retaining their south Lancashire estates in the nineteenth century was the prospect of mineral rights, coal royalties, ground rents and other 'casual profits' that industrial development and the growth of population brought to the landowner.

Dr H. A. Rhee's index of national farm rents rises from 100 in 1870–1 to a peak of 113 in 1877 and then slowly declines to 75 in 1899.[5] Lancashire rents were higher throughout than Dr Rhee's average for the country and ranged between 30s. and 68s. per acre.[6] Moreover no fall is apparent when 1870 is

---

[1] *Royal Commission 1880–2*, Q. 67,501 (J. Coleman): 'Tenant's capital of £15–20 an acre . . . very much larger than ordinary capital'; *Journal of the Royal Agricultural Society*, XXXIX (1886), p. 109: 'the extraordinary development of land values at their own risk by yearly tenants.'

[2] Ibid., Coleman's Report, p. 32; cf. ibid., pp. 33–4; a Stretford tenant of Sir Humphrey de Trafford had 'no special agreement as to tenant right and does not appear to want it. He said that if he knew that he was going to leave next year he could not afford to alter his management'.

[3] *Royal Commission 1880–2*, Q. 67,505–7 (J. Coleman); cf. *Royal Commission 1894–7*, Q. 27,283 (T. Mercer): 'Lord Sefton and Lord Derby own all for miles around, so we have confidence, I believe every tenant has, that they will not disturb a tenant.'

[4] *Journal of the Royal Agricultural Society*, XXXIX, 1877, p. 467.

[5] *The Rent of Agricultural Land in England & Wales, 1870–1943* (Central Landowners' Association, 1949), Table II, pp. 44–6.

[6] See, for example, *Royal Commission 1880–2*, Coleman's Report, pp. 31–41; *Journal of the Royal Agricultural Society*, XLVIII, 1886, pp. 146, 165; *Preston Guardian*, 29 October 1892; Schulze-Gaevernitz, p. 174; *Agricultural Gazette*, 17 October 1892; *Royal Commission 1894–7*, Q. 9,991 (W. Smith), Q. 12,526 (T. Worthington); ibid., C. 7400 of 1894, Appendix A IV, 413, Appendix A XIII, 429.

compared with the end of the century. Total 'agreed' rents on
the Derby estates in Fylde and Bowland rose from £16,346
in 1884 to £20,212 in 1904 with arrears running at the rate of
14 and 15 per cent respectively. In view of the possibility of
addition by piecemeal purchase, a contingency not without
significance in itself, the rents of the large manor of Trayles
were scrutinized. The gross rent increased from £4,452 in
1867 to £5,478 in 1884, from which figure there was little

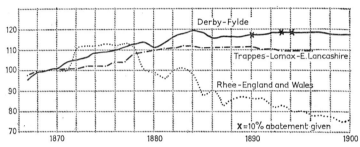

Derby, 1867–71 = 100 = £4,634 = index of agreed rents
from the manor of
Trayles, Roseacre and
Quarles.

Trappes-Lomax, 1867–71 = 100 = £3,009 = index of agreed and
paid rents from 40
identical farms.

Rhee, 1870–1 = 100 = 26s. 7d. = index of average agricultural rent per acre in
England and Wales.

C. RENT

significant change up to 1904. Arrears stood at the formidable figure of £4,996 in 1867, fluctuated downward to £2,870
in 1882, dropped sharply to £745 in 1883, and did not reach
four figures again until 1900; in 1904 arrears were £862. Only
a small fraction of these arrears were 'carried out', viz., written
off as bad; the bulk were eventually paid. 10 per cent abatements were given in 1890, 1893 and 1894.[1]

On the Trappes-Lomax estates of Clayton and Allsprings
in east Lancashire gross rents from 40 farms rose from £2,942

[1] C.R.O., DDK (Fylde Rents).

in 1867 to a maximum of £3,368 in 1883, declined slightly to £3,270 in 1893, and remained at this figure until the end of the rental in 1896. No abatements are mentioned and arrears were negligible throughout, perhaps because almost all these rents were paid in cash, as might be expected in an area of producer-retailers.[1] On the nearby Thwaites estate, agreed rents remained at an average of £2. 5s. 3d. an acre from 1875 to 1895, remissions of perhaps 15 per cent being granted in 1892 and 1893.[2] Immediately over the county boundary on the Lister estate near Halifax rents remained unchanged, after allowing for industrial loss of acreage, between 1870 and 1900.[3]

Evidence of this nature, corroborated by contemporary opinion such as Smith's to the effect that 'permanent reductions are very few, they were the exception',[4] and by comment in the *Preston Guardian* suggesting that a 10 per cent abatement in an occasional year after 1890 was as much as the Lancashire tenant could expect,[5] is indicative of the firmness of farm rents in Lancashire during the Great Depression. It is extremely doubtful, after all allowance has been made for reduction and remission in the nineties, whether by the end of the century rents actually paid had fallen to the level of 1867–71. The Tithe Act of 1891, which enforced the payment of tithe by the landowner by transferring to him the legal responsibility for its payment, appeared to make no change in the tenants' position in Lancashire. Evidence from the Derby and Hesketh (south-west Lancashire) rentals corroborates Thomas Worthington's statement in 1894 that the invariable practice after 1891 was to add the Tithe or Tithe Rent Charge to the rent;[6] this has been discounted in the Derby rent series which is net of tithe throughout.

The net income position of the landowner is obscure. Little

[1] C.R.O., Trappes-Lomax Rentals.

[2] *Royal Commission 1894–7*, Q. 40,841 (J. Howson); the percentage remitted is not given as such.

[3] Shibden Hall, Halifax, Lister MSS.

[4] *Royal Commission 1894–7*, Q. 9,979 (W. Smith); cf. President Rimmer's complaint at the Lancashire Tenant Farmers' meeting that there 'had been few reductions in Lancashire rents'. – *Preston Guardian*, 10 December 1892.

[5] See, e.g., *Preston Guardian*, 4 February 1893, 7 October 1893, 13 January 1894, 28 April 1894.

[6] *Royal Commission 1894–7*, Q. 12,527–9 (T. Worthington).

is known about estate maintenance costs and investment, but such evidence as has been found indicates that at least on some estates the level of investment was maintained,[1] even though, as was claimed, interest-free improvements were effected by the landlord in lieu of rent reductions.[2] Any appreciable fall in net income was improbable and an impoverished landowner was unlikely to be found in Lancashire, albeit his property were confined to agricultural land, which was rarely the case.[3]

As evidence of depression within the county rent reductions and abatements in the 1890s should be treated with caution. The activities of the newly formed Lancashire farmers' associations during a period when agricultural depression was widely assumed to be endemic were inevitably affected by national and political considerations.[4] Lancashire farmers were not protectionists[5] and local price changes offered only a small target; there remained the landowner, for long the recipient of criticism from urban radicals.

A continuous campaign was mounted by this vociferous

[1] See, for the Thwaites's estate, *Royal Commission 1894–7*, Q. 40,856 (J. Howson); Sir Charles Tempest, *Preston Guardian*, 7 October 1893; Trappes-Lomax, C.R.O.; Derby, *Preston Guardian*, 25 September 1886, 14 October 1893; Sefton, *Preston Guardian*, 14 October 1893; Duchy of Lancaster, *Preston Guardian*, 14 October 1893, *Royal Commission 1894–7*, C. 7400 of 1894, Appendix A XIII, p. 429; Crown, ibid., Appendix A IV, p. 413. Land reclamation continued; 500 acres of the Rawstorne property at Hutton and Howick were reclaimed from the marsh in 1887 when the rent was £1 an acre; in 1894 it was £3 10s. and 'cheap at the price' (*Preston Guardian*, 19 May 1894).

[2] This was alleged by J. Kay, an official of the Lancashire Federation and an ex-tenant of the Thwaites's estate, before the Royal Commission in March 1894 (Q. 14,009) and vehemently denied by the agent Howson in the following February (Q. 40,661).

[3] *Preston Guardian*, 7 February 1891: tenants were 'forthcoming' and 'nothing is heard of landlords being obliged to farm their estates themselves'; *Royal Commission 1894–7*, Q. 11,313 (A. Wilson Fox): 'Land-agents say the land has not gone back . . . and that farms will let easily.'

[4] The main body was the Lancashire Tenant Farmers' Association founded in January 1892; a short account of the origins and development of the various local associations since their effective beginning in 1890 is given in *Preston Guardian*, 10 December 1892.

[5] The agricultural correspondent of the *Preston Guardian*, after a tour of the Fylde, 'was surprised to find that most of the gentlemen I called upon were staunch Free Traders' (*Preston Guardian*, 13 April 1895). Lancashire farmers considered that the Great London Agricultural Conference addressed by Chaplin in 1892 was a 'profound disappointment in that it was throughout PROTECTIONIST'. – *Preston Guardian*, 10 December 1892.

minority of organized farmers against the level of rents. It was well publicized by local newspapers whose editors tended to look at agriculture through eyes conditioned by the national press, which in turn reflected the view of the corn-growing interest. Vivid contrasts and 'lessons for Lancashire landlords' were drawn between the fall in rents in the eastern counties and their immobility in Lancashire. The challenge was re-iterated that 'if the price of land did not come down in Lancashire and Cheshire, it would have to do'.[1] Such a campaign, though conducted by a minority, could not but have some effect on tenants and landlords and their agents as they engaged in their biannual commiseration over the dearth of coin in the pockets of each. The relative stability of Lancashire rents under such pressure suggests not only a continuing demand for agricultural land, which may conceivably have been misguided, but the absence of any fundamental depression.[2]

CONCLUSION

The experiences of Lancashire livestock farmers during the Great Depression are graphically illustrated by the movement of their product prices which, unlike Sauerbeck's curve of general prices in terms of which the Great Depression is seen as a period of continuously falling prices from the plateau edge of a Golden Age in 1873–4 to the trough of the mid-nineties, climbed steadily upwards into the early eighties to fall back to approximately the 1867–71 level by the nineties. With the price of feed roughly following the price of wheat and falling throughout, livestock farmers enjoyed a double incentive to expand

[1] *Preston Guardian*, 5 October 1895; repeated 3 October 1896; attributed to Chaplin, December 1892.
[2] See the exchange between Giffen and Wilson Fox (*Royal Commission 1894–7*, Q. 11,313–22), particularly Q. 11,322: 'Why should they compete for farms . . . unless it is the case that it pays them to do it in Lancashire? – One would think that would be the case. One is loth to believe them unbusinesslike, and to bid higher than they can pay.' Cf. *Preston Guardian*, 16 October 1897: 'So far the number of farms to be let in north Lancashire may be counted on the fingers of one hand, and yet have some to spare, and the small acreage of land that has this year been sold in public sales has made very good prices.'

output, namely, a fall in production costs and a continually rising demand for their products, most of which enjoyed a degree of protection, derived from transport difficulties and quality differences, against the competition of imports.

At a crude estimate the value of gross output from Lancashire livestock farms increased by a third during the Great Depression. On the other side total labour costs fell by some 15 per cent and rent may be taken as unchanged. If it be assumed that in 1867–71 expenditure on feed equalled the combined cost of labour and rent, then with a fall of a third in the price of feed, the maintenance of total costs in 1894–8 at their earlier level would permit an increase of 60 per cent in the quantity of feed purchased. As total milk output, in all forms, increased by less than 50 per cent, it would seem that such an increase of expenditure on feed was ample for the expansion envisaged. A rise in the value of output with no increase in total costs indicates a larger gross profit margin, to be divided moreover between a smaller number of farmers if Census data are even approximately correct.

Thus considering the evidence of output, prices, the movement of rent and the lack of concrete evidence of distress during a period when such evidence was specifically requested by successive Royal Commissions, it must be concluded that no great depression of agriculture existed in Lancashire during the last quarter of the nineteenth century. On the contrary, the evidence indicates substantial prosperity until 1884 and the mitigation of any subsequent adverse impact from declining output prices by a relatively steeper fall in feed costs and by an expansion of output.

In explanation of this immunity from distress a number of factors may be cited, all to some extent recognized both by contemporary and post-mortem investigators. They include the keeping of livestock, particularly milk cows, sheep, pigs and poultry; a reliance on grassland and purchased feed rather than the plough; the existence of small farms largely independent of hired labour; the presence of adjacent urban markets; the practice of direct sale to the consumer; and freedom of the tenant from restrictive covenants.

But these factors were not peculiar to Lancashire. They were to be found in various combinations throughout the country, even in the arable areas. 'Looking forward to what was coming', Sir John Lawes reluctantly installed a dairy herd and gave up a 'great deal of corn growing' at the beginning of the seventies.[1] The Earl of Leicester, son of the great Coke, abandoned the four-course, laid down his corn land to grass, and fattened sheep at a profit.[2] Even in East Anglia small farms predominated; in Norfolk, Suffolk and Essex taken together, almost a half of the total number of agricultural holdings over 5 acres were under 50 acres in size and less than 10 per cent were over 300 acres. By the 1890s few parts of the country were beyond the reach of either a local market or the ever-spreading demand of the conurbations, in particular that of London. Lord Vernon in the Midlands, like Mr Miller of Singleton Park in the Fylde, supplied regular customers with fresh butter at a price higher than that in the retail markets.[3] Lastly, long leases and restrictive covenants were disappearing as opinion turned against them and legislation endeavoured to give formal protection to the annual tenant.

It may be argued that such alternatives were perhaps feasible on the light lands of Hertfordshire and Norfolk but impracticable for heavy land farmers like those on the clays of Essex, acknowledged as the worst hit county. But even in Essex there was scope for initiative.[4] The Scottish dairying on the run-down Essex clay may be paralleled by the less publicized experiences of Lancashire men who took with them, besides milking cows, a tradition of freedom, both from technical dogma and restrictive landlords, a keen eye for opportunities and a willingness to farm according to the dictates of the market. As a Fylde farmer observed after touring Essex, 'newcomers are going in for milk, cheese, butter, fruit and sheep, but with the average Essex farmer it is corn, corn, corn'. The prices of milk, butter and cheese were as good as if not better than in Lancashire, thanks to the proximity of London which

[1] *Royal Commission 1880–2*, Q. 57,619 (Sir John Lawes).
[2] *Royal Commission 1894–7*, C. 7400–IV, Appendix E, pp. 597–8.
[3] *Royal Commission 1894–7*, Q. 21,761, 35,332; *Preston Guardian*, 18 April 1891.
[4] See R. Hunter Pringle's series of articles on the change from corn to meat and grass in Essex during the 1880s in the *Agricultural Gazette* of 1887, July onwards, especially 10 October 1887.

constituted a 'ready and paying market which they cannot flood'. 'Look at the hay they want in London,' the Fylde man expostulated, 'the butter, the beef, the milk, to say nothing of the cheese and eggs. But when we were down in Chelmsford we learnt that the town was often short of milk and didn't hear of any farmer who made cheese.'[1]

Perhaps the fundamental explanation of Lancashire farmers' prosperity during the depression is not the presence of favourable circumstances—after all these did not appear fortuitously —but the character of the farmers themselves. In the eyes of Essex men, Lancashire farmers were 'more boisterous, more energetic in temperament than our people. The same enters into your work, I have noticed. Our folk want to work genteelly; they don't put that energy, that enterprise, that wholehearted zeal into it that you do.'[2] Undoubtedly the 'mercantile enterprise of Liverpool and Manchester merchants . . . imbued the agriculturalists of the district with the same impetus,'[3] but the 'pregnant wit'[4] of the Lancastrian long antedated the Industrial Revolution, however subsequently it may have been sharpened by the economic fluctuations of the nineteenth century which not only closed cotton mills but thereby deprived the milk-selling farmer of all his best customers. But granted these virtues in the Lancashire farmer, it can scarcely be maintained that with the exception of a scattered handful beyond the Lyme he enjoyed a monopoly of vision and enterprise. The question thus arises: to what extent was the period really as tragic as the orthodox picture claims? Have the agonized cries of corn-growers and the simple symbolism of the wheat price continued to hypnotize twentieth-century observers as they did nineteenth-century participants? A study of more relevant evidence than that considered by the Royal Commissions of 1880–2 and 1894–7 and viewed with rather more

[1] *Preston Guardian*, 24 October 1896: Report of the tour of Essex organized by the *Preston Guardian* for Lancashire farmers; see also September to December inclusive in the same year for accounts of Lancashire emigration to Essex.
[2] Ibid.
[3] *Journal of the Royal Agricultural Society*, XXXVIII, 1877, p. 464.
[4] A. A. Mumford, *The Manchester Grammar School, 1515–1915* (1919), p. 11: in the School Statutes of 1525. Professor Redford kindly drew my attention to this point and provided the reference.

impartial eyes might suggest a radical reappraisal of the
accepted view.[1]

APPENDIX

A. Milk Output and Consumption

Yields per cow in Lancashire are taken to be greater than those
assumed by Dr E. M. Ojala for the U.K. (*Agriculture and
Economic Progress*, 1952, pp. 204–5) in view of the greater proportion of specialist milk producers in the country. The
general pattern of milk consumption estimates between those
of J. C. Morton (*Journal of the Royal Agricultural Society*, 1865,
1878) and those of A. R. Prest (*Consumers' Expenditure in the
U.K. 1900–1919*, 1954) suggests a rise from about a quarter of
a pint to a third of a pint a head each day. Assuming the more
conservative increase of 25 per cent between 1870 and 1894–8
and using *Agricultural Returns* for the number of cows, and
Dr Ojala's U.K. estimate of yields, the output of farm butter
and cheese in England and Wales appears to have constituted
about 45 per cent of total milk production in 1870, falling to
30 per cent in 1894–8 and 23 per cent in 1907 (this latter figure
is taken from the *Agricultural Output of Great Britain*, 1908,
Cd 6277 of 1912) but with absolute output changing little.
For Lancashire with its many liquid milk sellers a proportion
of 30 per cent was assumed for 1870 with absolute output unchanged thereafter.

B. Milk Prices

(i) Retail. Of 29 Lancashire retail milk quotations covering the
Great Depression, 16 give 3d., 5 less than 3d., and 8 over 3d. a
quart as the ruling price. Prices were higher in the larger towns,
reaching 4d. at Liverpool, and lower in the more rural areas,
but little significant change in the average level of prices
occurred until 1909–10 when a general rise to $3\frac{1}{2}$d. took place.

---

[1] For example, much evidence furnished to the Commission of 1894–7 received
scant attention; see the *Minority Reports* of G. Lambert and F. A. Channing, both
of whom complained that the majority ignored examples of successful farming. –
Final Report, pp. 204–376, C. 8540 of 1897.

For sources see *Manchester Guardian* and *Manchester Courier* for February and March 1872, and *Preston Guardian*, 29 September 1892.

It appears that a general rise occurred in or about 1872, a time of rising prices, and that some, if not all, of this increase was lost before 1891 when, as in 1900–1 outside the Liverpool and Manchester areas, the commonest price was 3d. a quart. As it is doubtful whether all the gain of 1872 was lost by the nineties, e.g. the Manchester price was above 3d. in 1897 and 1901 and very probably so in 1891, and as moreover it seems that outside the largest centres of population the price rose to 3d. *c.* 1872 and never thereafter fell, it follows that the retail price of milk could scarcely have fallen between 1867–71 and 1894–8.

For the purpose of Graph B a price of 3d. has been taken for 1867–71 rising to 3¼d. (in practice 3d. in summer and 3½d. in winter) in 1872 and falling again to 3d. in 1886, the trough year of the trade cycle. In corroboration of the view that the retail price was constant over a long period was the practice before 1910 in east Lancashire of using pint measures permanently marked internally into thirds: at a price of 3d. a quart, milk could thus conveniently be sold in pennyworths and half-pennyworths (information from Mr E. Fitton of Bury; cf. also *Preston Guardian*, January 1936).

(ii) Wholesale. Price quotations of wholesale milk in Lancashire are scarce.

Date	Source	Comment	Price in pence per gallon		
			Summer	Winter	Average
1871–2	*Manchester Courier*, 14 February 1872	near Manchester	6–6½	7–7½	6¾
1876	*Journal of the Royal Agricultural Society*	near Lancaster	—	—	8
1880–2	*Royal Commission*	near Stockport	8	10	9
1886	*Journal of the Royal Agricultural Society*	near Lancaster	—	9	(8)
1894	*Preston Guardian*, 13 October 1894	{Blackpool {Fylde	10 7–8	— —	— —
1897	*Journal of the Royal Agricultural Society*	a Manchester dealer (so probably refers to Cheshire supplies)	6	7½–9	78

If, as seems probable, quoted prices are those paid by buyers and nominally received by producers, then the fall in rail transport costs between the seventies and the nineties of approximately ½d. per gallon would offset by that amount any fall in price. The evidence is slender, but such as there is falls into the familiar Lancashire product curve pattern, rising in the seventies and falling back in the eighties. No Lancashire witness before the Royal Commission of 1894–7 who gave evidence in the years 1894–96 complained of a fall in the price of milk, either wholesale or retail. On the contrary, it was specifically stated by the Assistant Commissioner for the county that the 'price of milk had not fallen' (R.C. *1894–97*, Q. 11,396, A. Wilson Fox; and see *Preston Guardian*, 14 October 1893); in the context Wilson Fox was referring to the period since the mid-eighties. The milk price in Cheshire was said to have fallen by about 10 per cent from 1880 to June 1894 (R.C. 1894–97, Q. 26,014, T. Parton). Prices at the former date were significantly higher, perhaps 20 per cent, than ten years earlier, so that after allowing for cheaper carriage it is difficult to see how any overall net fall could have occurred between 1867–71 and 1894–8. It is just possible that some temporary unrecorded reduction took place in 1895 and (or) 1896 in the trough of the general price cycle.

C. Butter and Cheese Prices

(i) Butter. The original series of Lancashire butter prices was taken from the *Wigan Observer* in the absence of any continuous Preston series. It is an annual unweighted average of prices at Wigan market on the first market day of each calendar month throughout the year. The spread of prices on any one day was narrow—½d. or 1d. a lb; very frequently only one price was quoted. Comparable prices at Ormskirk market were taken from the *Ormskirk Advertiser*; here too the spread was narrow or non-existent. North Cheshire butter and egg prices were published in the *Manchester Guardian* and the *Stockport Advertiser* from 1884–5 onwards. Stockport prices moved conformably with those at Wigan and Ormskirk. Prices at Wigan declined by 15 per cent between 1867–71 and 1894–8; at Ormskirk by only 11 per cent as a result of an advantage that was gained between 1873 and 1876 and never thereafter lost. The Kelsall butter prices, which are an annual average of fifty-two weekly quotations weighted by weekly quantities sold, fit the Ormskirk–Wigan pattern. The average of 1872–77 inclusive = 110 = the average of Wigan prices in the same years; the mean of the 1896 and 1900 prices = 87. It may be tentatively concluded that farm butter prices at Lancashire markets declined by some 13 per cent between 1867–71 and 1894–8.

(ii) Cheese. No unbroken single source of Lancashire farm cheese prices has been found. Some Preston prices were occasionally published in the *Preston Guardian*. The *Manchester Guardian* quoted prices at various markets, including Lancaster, Preston, Crewe, Derby, Nottingham and Leicester, sporadically throughout the period. The *Agricultural Gazette* gives some Preston and Lancaster prices between 1888 and 1894. The *Wigan Observer* abandoned the reporting of cheese prices at Wigan after 1882. A Staffordshire cheese factory price series, from 1874 to 1893 inclusive, is the most complete annual series discovered but is of limited value in assessing changes in the price of Lancashire farm cheese.

Market prices were usually quoted for two or three grades, variously defined, but this was not universal. The spread of prices in any one year may be considerable, e.g. William Kelsall made 80s. in May 1875 but only 60s. in October, or again at Preston in 1886 April prices ranged from 50s. to 65s. while October prices were 70s. to 80s. As between adjacent districts price movements could vary widely; the *Manchester Guardian* (10 October 1892) reported of Chester October fair: 'As compared with last year there was a downward tendency of 5s. per cwt for fine and 10s. to 15s. for other qualities', whereas two days later at Lancaster the 'prices realized were from 5s. to 10s. per cwt more than at the last October fair'. A further complication is the suggestion of a shift during the Great Depression from late-maturing cheeses which were stored on the farm over winter to the quick-ripening cheese consumed in the season of its manufacture (see *Preston Guardian*, 12 October 1895).

In these circumstances the best single series, although incomplete, is that of prices each year at Lancaster autumn fair and this has been graphed. William Kelsall's prices in the 1860s and 1870s have also been shown. A price curve of inferior qualities has not been drawn but a decline of some 20 per cent is indicated.

D. *Mutton and Lamb Prices*

Mutton and lamb prices are taken from Salford Tuesday market reports published in the *Manchester Guardian* and the *Manchester Courier*. Salford was the largest market in the county and dealt mainly in native live sheep; the numbers and prices of foreign and Irish sheep were usually given separately. The aim has been to obtain a price series applicable to Lancashire sheep, almost all of which were sold off grass; the majority were hill or hill-crosses lambed during March, April and early May (see *Preston Guardian*, 31 March 1894). In some years, particularly the later, *Manchester Guardian* reports are sufficiently detailed to provide a seasonal picture of sources of supply. The best representation of Lancashire prices is obtained by averaging weekly prices during July to October inclusive. Prior to July few Lancashire lambs were marketed, and there is, moreover, the difficulty of distinguishing shorn sheep from those 'in the wool'; after October numbers at the market fall off rapidly.

Prices were quoted in pence per lb except occasionally when lambs were quoted per head. Graph B is the mean of two price series, one for lamb and the other for mutton, excluding imported sheep but including ewes. A typical October report reads (*Manchester Guardian*, 3 October 1894): 'good Cheviot wethers and well-finished North Country lambs $8\frac{1}{2}$, strong North Country sheep $7\frac{3}{4}$–8, Cheviot and Half-Bred ewes $6\frac{1}{4}$—$6\frac{1}{2}$, 1st class Irish wethers $7\frac{3}{4}$, heavy ditto $6\frac{3}{4}$–$7\frac{1}{2}$, ewes 6; (number at market 10,376)'.

6 The Landlord and Agricultural Transformation, 1870–1900[1]

RICHARD PERREN

This article was first published in the *Agricultural History Review*, XVIII (1) (1970).

I

By now the distinguishing features of the fortunes of English agriculture between 1870 and 1900 are well known.[2] The succession of wet seasons culminating in that of 1879, accompanied by the drastic fall in the prices of cereals throughout the 1880s spelt disaster for many farmers in the cereal-growing regions of the south-east of England, especially if they happened to work heavy clayland farms. For the livestock producer, though the initial situation in 1879 was still serious, in the long run it was less gloomy. With rising real wages for much of the time, and a rising population, the demand for livestock products was promising. Meat prices did not fall till after 1885, and then the decline was much smaller than for cereals. *Per capita* consumption of meat and dairy products rose continuously right up to 1914. A good deal of this rising consumption was supplied by overseas producers, but not all of it; there was still an opportunity for home producers to supply this buoyant market with those foods where their advantage as producers was greatest, such as high quality meats, dairy foods, poultry, eggs and fresh milk. But to do this successfully required from the farmer increased specialization and the

[1] I am grateful to the Archivist, Mr F. W. Stitt, and the staff of the Stafford County Record Office for making the documents I have used available to me so readily. I am also grateful to Mr E. J. T. Collins for valuable suggestions made during the preparation of this article. The responsibility for the opinions stated is my own.

[2] T. W. Fletcher, 'The Great Depression of English agriculture, 1873–96', *Economic History Review*, 2nd series, XIII (1961).

adaptation of his enterprises to the changed market conditions after 1879, if he had not taken steps to do so before that date.

Of course to some extent British agriculture had changed its emphasis in the twenty years before 1873.[1] As early as 1849 Caird had anticipated an improvement in vegetable and live-stock product prices as a result of rising population, and a relative deterioration in cereal prices as imports increased. The fall in cereal prices did not come till the 1880s, but in the meantime there is no doubt that there was a marked im-provement in animal product prices after 1850.[2] This en-couraged farmers on mixed farms to increase their produc-tion of livestock by making it more profitable for them to use the grain they produced as feed, rather than selling it for cash. A further impetus to livestock farming was given by the imports of oilcake from Europe and further afield which grew from 273,000 tons in 1856 to 740,000 tons a year by the 1880s.[3] These developments required increased capital both from the tenant farmer and from the landlord. From the tenant more capital was required to buy in more livestock and also for purchased feeding if they were used; from the landlord increased livestock usually implied heavier expendi-ture on new buildings to house them, especially if the farmer concentrated on stall- or yard-feeding.[4] In the 1850s and 1860s this type of farming spread from mixed farming regions, where it had originated, to the dairying parts of Cheshire and Gloucestershire and into parts of Cornwall and Cumberland which had previously depended on grain.[5] Developments after 1879 encouraged further reliance on livestock. Prices of cereals and oilcake fell, acting as a stimulus for farmers

[1] E. L. Jones, 'The changing basis of agricultural prosperity, 1853–73', *Agricultural History Review*, X (1962).

[2] E. L. Jones and E. J. T. Collins, 'Sectoral advance in English agriculture, 1850–80', *Agricultural History Review*, XV (1967), p. 79.

[3] F. M. L. Thompson, 'The second agricultural revolution, 1815–1880', *Economic History Review*, 2nd series, XXI (1968), pp. 67–8.

[4] W. Wilson, *British Farming* (1862), pp. 437–8; W. Wright, 'On the improve-ments in the farming of Yorkshire . . .', *Journal of the Royal Agricultural Society*, XXII (1861), p. 91; M. Evershed, 'Early fattening of cattle', *Journal of the Royal Agricultural Society*, 2nd series, XIV (1878), p. 162; J. A. Clarke, 'Practical agriculture', loc. cit., pp. 498–503.

[5] Jones, loc. cit., p. 229. footnote 4.

to use purchased cattle foods, and the greater efficiency of fattening cattle in covered fold yards, where they put on weight more rapidly with less inputs than if they had been fed in the open, was especially attractive to farmers at a time when profit margins were under severe pressure and every economy was desirable. Furthermore, the fact that the provision of new buildings was, on most estates, the landlord's responsibility relieved the tenant of the need to make outlays in this direction. But even in areas where more intensive methods of cattle feeding were not adopted there was generally still a need for landlords to undertake increased expenditure when greater reliance was placed upon livestock farming. With marginal arable land converted to pasture there would still be a need for extra buildings to carry the increased number of stock in winter, and even the 'arable dairy farming' practised in parts of Essex still required milking parlours and accommodation for the dairy herds.[1]

Thus successful adaptation, whether it was carried out before 1879, or after, required from the landowner a certain level of expenditure, both on land and on farm buildings. The purpose of this article is to examine statistics of income and expenditure on these items for eight estates in different parts of England between 1872 and 1892, and for one estate between 1870 and 1900, to find out the extent to which landlords seemed to be incurring the extra costs of transformation before 1879, and how the process proceeded after that date. Also, some attempt will be made to judge the success of this work by seeing how far large estate expenditures on buildings and land are correlated with small declines in the rents of such estates (Part II). Part III is concerned with a comparison of two sets of estates, namely, the Shropshire and Staffordshire estates of the Dukes of Sutherland and the Bedfordshire and Buckinghamshire estates of the Dukes of Bedford, to see what other factors besides mere levels of estate expenditure affected the success, or otherwise, of agricultural transformation.

[1] Sir W. Gavin, *Ninety Years of Family Farming* (1967), p. 86.

II

In February 1894 the second Royal Commission on Agriculture
sent out a letter[1] to a number of large landowners in England
and Scotland explaining that 'The Commission desire to be
informed at first hand by the experience of landowners in
different parts of the country, of the effect upon rents of the
present agricultural depression, as compared with a period of
15 or 20 years ago; and of the way in which the diminution of
gross income has been accompanied by a diminution of the
owner's outlay under different heads'. The Commissioners
asked for information between 1872 and 1892, though not all
the replies they received went back as far as 1872. Of the
thirty replies they got for England some sixteen did so,
though not all of these are suitable for purposes of comparison.[2] In all, eight were found to be suitable, four of these
were in counties which were predominantly arable areas and
four were in counties where livestock farming predominated. In
certain cases, because the landowner did not want his identity
to be disclosed, it is not possible to identify the precise location
of the estates. (See Table I.) In the arable group of estates this
problem presents the least difficulty as regards Suffolk which it
is admitted was heavily committed to cereal production at this
time. Also the Duke of Bedford's estates were described as
being largely comprised of 'some of the best wheat land in
England'[3] and the Duke of Richmond has been regarded as the
champion of the corn-growing interest;[4] nor does the inclu-
sion of the Holkham estate in this group require any justification. In the livestock counties, the estates in Cheshire and
Northumberland present no problem as these were predominantly livestock counties, and so, too, was Gloucestershire. Also, Harewood Hall was situated in the West Riding
of Yorkshire which was predominantly livestock-oriented.[5]

[1] *Royal Commission 1894–7. Particulars of Expenditure and Outgoings on Certain
Estates in Great Britain, and Farm Accounts*, p. 4.

[2] For example, one estate in Middlesex gave no figures for its acreage, and
some of the others were plainly very small outlying estates of large landowners.

[3] Duke of Bedford, *The Story of a Great Agricultural Estate* (1897), p. 55.

[4] Fletcher, op. cit., p. 425.

[5] *Royal Commission 1894–7, Final Report*, p. 7 and map facing that page, which
defines arable and livestock counties in 1895.

As we would expect, the estates in the arable counties showed a greater fall in rents and net estate income than the estates in the livestock counties between 1872–4 and 1890–2. The Cheshire estate was the best off, with a rise in net estate income, and though the major part of this comes from a falling off in expenditure in 1890–2 these years do also see a small increase in rent over the early seventies. At the other end of the

TABLE 1[1] *Eight estates: comparison of average annual acreage rent, expenditure and net income between 1872–4 and 1890–2*

([2])	Estates	Years	Acres	Rent	Expen-diture	Net income	Per cent change
				£	£	£	
	LIVESTOCK COUNTIES						
8–9	An Estate in Cheshire	1872–4	16,110	31,378	13,676	17,702	
		1890–2	16,110	31,890	9,454	22,436	26·7
22–23	An Estate in	1872–4	11,333	8,864	4,030	4,834	
	Northumberland	1890–2	11,483	8,023	3,631	4,392	9·2
6–7	An Estate in Yorkshire[3]	1872–4	28,221	37,396	12,461	24,935	
	(Earl of Harewood)	1890–2	28,193	31,735	10,375	21,360	−14·4
18–19	An Estate in	1872–4	17,379	36,773	10,087	26,686	
	Gloucestershire	1890–2	18,387	31,742	9,499	22,243	−16·6
	(Lord Fitshardinge)						
	ARABLE COUNTIES						
12–13	An Estate in Norfolk[3]	1872–4	44,037	58,833	20,243	38,590	
	(Holkham Estate)	1890–2[4]	45,177	44,492	14,275	30,217	−21·7
32–33	Goodwood Estate,	1873–5	14,247	18,550	7,752	10,797	
	Sussex	1890–2	14,247	13,794	5,637	8,157	−24·5
	(Duke of Richmond)						
16–17	Estates in Beds. and	1872–4	30,619	48,849[5]	26,067	22,782	
	Bucks.	1890–2	24,634	31,366	17,997	13,369	−41·3
	(Duke of Bedford)						
14–15	An Estate in Suffolk	1872–4	15,075	20,182	2,730	17,452	
		1890–2	15,326	11,514	5,160	6,354	−63·6

[1] *Royal Commission 1894–7. Particulars of Expenditure . . . and Farm Accounts.*
[2] These are the page numbers of the returns.
[3] These estates identified in the *Final Report, Report by Mr George Lambert*, p. 207.
[4] Return starts in 1873.
[5] These figures are an overstatement of agricultural rents as those making the return inadvertently included urban property.—Duke of Bedford, *The Story of a Great Agricultural Estate* (1897), p. 65.

scale come the Duke of Bedford's estates in Bedfordshire and Buckinghamshire and the estate in Suffolk. It might be objected that the position of the Duke of Bedford's estates is made to look worse than it really was by the fall in acreage between the two periods; but even when this is taken into account the net income per acre fell from 16s. 3d. in 1872–4 to 12s. 3d. in

1890–2 – a decline of 24·3 per cent – which makes the estates equal with the Duke of Richmond's Goodwood estate. On the Suffolk estate, expenditure does rise in the period 1890–2 but even on this estate the decline in rents between the two sets of dates accounts for the major part of the decline in net estate income, as it does on the other estates.

When the Commissioners sent out the forms of reply to the landowners they left separate columns for the ordinary expenses of running the estate such as rates, taxes, management charges and repairs to fences and buildings, and for items of extraordinary expenditure, that is, money spent on new buildings and land improvements. However, when they came to the work carried out on the estate very few owners made any distinction between these two classes of expenditure in their accounts.[1] Usually money spent on new buildings was included along with sums spent on maintenance and repairs in the estate building account. From the landlord's point of view this was logical because both classes of work were carried out by the same labour as and when the need for them arose.[2] However, the failure to make this distinction does create problems if one wants to compare the sums spent on permanent improvements with the ordinary expenditure of the estate. Some estates did make returns with the items for permanent improvements separated but for the sake of comparability all cases considered so far include expenditure on both current and capital items. But Tables II and III, which deal with expenditure on the actual estate itself, make this distinction where it is possible to do so.

On the four estates in livestock counties, expenditure on land and buildings was at quite high levels in the seventies, in no case being much below 20 per cent of the rent received. On the Cheshire estate the level of expenditure shows a tendency to

---

[1] *Select Committee (House of Lords) on the Improvement of Lands* (1873), Q. 1964, 1698–1700.

[2] R. J. Thompson, 'An enquiry into the rent of agricultural land in England and Wales in the nineteenth century', *Journal of the Royal Statistical Society*, LXX (1907) p. 602, considered the distinction between 'repairs' and 'permanent improvements' in many cases a purely artificial one. While it would not be fair to charge the cost of improvements, lasting over a number of years, against *one* year's rent they may be fairly charged against income over a *number* of years, as their effects would be reflected in the rents.

decline in the late eighties, but this seems to indicate that the transformation of the seventies was a success and allowed the landlord to reduce his infusions of capital without rents suffering to any great extent. This would be in accordance with much of what is already known about Cheshire, which probably fared best of all the English counties during the depression[1] because of its heavy concentration on livestock and dairying, especially milk production for which the Lancashire and Mersey-side cities provided a buoyant market. Also, the lower level of expenditure on these items for this estate, than for some others, would seem to indicate that relatively little was required to be spent on the process of transformation. The Northumberland estate seems to have undergone very heavy expenditure on new buildings and land improvements, especially between 1880 and 1885, and it would seem that more expenditure from the landlord was necessary to maintain rents on this estate than on the Cheshire estate. The Gloucestershire estate of Lord Fitzhardinge shows a lower level of expenditure on fresh items, but substantial sums were spent on repairs and maintenance and, overall, the level of expenditure on the fabric of the estate seems to have been very high.

One feature which all the estates have in common is the comparatively high level of expenditure on drainage and land improvements immediately after 1879. This is not surprising as no matter how much the landlord had spent on new build-ings the effects of the wet years 1879–81 on the actual land itself were quite independent and most estates could have some land which was particularly badly affected and would have needed immediate treatment to remedy the situation, either by drainage, expenditure on fertilizers, expenditure on grass seeds or some combination of the three.

As far as the estates in the arable part of the country were concerned (Table II) estate expenditure on these items was generally significantly lower than in the livestock area; so was it on buildings and repairs. The level was lowest of all on the Suffolk estate where the decline in net estate income was greatest. Here little expenditure on new buildings was under-

[1] T. W. Fletcher, 'Lancashire livestock farming in the Great Depression', *Agricultural History Review*, IX (1961), p. 17.

taken: even in the period 1886–92 work was only carried out during four of those years, and even normal repairs were at a very low level; the column for drainage and land improvements bears the remark 'available to ascertain'. The accounts of this estate point to very little being spent on transformation either

TABLE II[1]

		Expenditure as a percentage of rent received			
Years	Estate	Repairs, fences and insurance	New buildings	Drainage and land improvement	Total
1872–9		17·1		4·7	21·8
1880–5	Cheshire	12·2		5·9	18·1
1886–92		6·5		1·7	8·2
1872–9		5·0	18·3	9·1	32·4
1880–5	Northumberland	5·7	29·0	8·9	43·6
1886–92		7·1	17·3	5·8	30·2
1872–9	Yorkshire	16·8		2·6	19·4
1880–5	(Earl of Harewood)	12·8		5·0	17·8
1886–92		17·1		4·3	21·4
1872–9	Gloucestershire	23·6	4·5	2·6	30·7
1880–5	(Lord Fitzhardinge)	21·4	7·5	8·6	37·5
1886–92		17·3	8·2	2·0	27·5

[1] Same source as Table I.

before 1879 or after it. Also, both the Earl of Leicester's Norfolk estate and the Duke of Richmond's Sussex properties exhibited lower levels of expenditure on these items than did the estates in livestock areas. But the Duke of Bedford's Buckinghamshire and Bedfordshire estates do not follow this rule. Here expenditure was higher than on either the Yorkshire or Cheshire estates before 1879, yet the fall in rents and net estate income was much higher. This points to the fact that the landlord was not able to control the fall of rents simply by the size of his expenditure. There were other factors at work about which nothing has been said to far. These factors were, broadly, the frame of mind of the estate management towards meeting changed conditions, and the limitations which the nature of the estate itself imposed on the management in this direction.

TABLE III*

Years	Estate	Expenditure as a percentage of rent received			
		Repairs, fences and insurance	New buildings	Drainage and land improvement	Total
1872–9		13·9		0·8	14·7
1880–5	Norfolk – Holkham	15·4		1·5	16·9
1886–92		9·2		0·1	9·3
1873–9	Goodwood, Sussex	7·9			7·9
1880–5	(Duke of Richmond)	9·2		Nil	9·2
1886–92		7·6			7·6
1872–9	Beds. and Bucks.	18·4	10·3	3·6	32·3
1880–5	(Duke of Bedford)	14·2	7·7	7·0	28·9
1886–92		11·3	4·6	4·5	20·4
1872–9		4·3	0·7		5·0
1880–5	Suffolk	2·8	1·2	Nil	4·0
1886–92		5·8	9·0		14·8

* Same source as Table I.

Natural limitations would include climate, soil type, and soil fertility which would determine the sorts of farming it was both possible *and profitable* to carry out on the estate. However, the general rule for these eight estates was that the larger expenditures on repairs, new buildings and land improvements were associated with the smaller declines in rent and net estate income. This was tested by calculating Spearman's rank correlation coefficient between the expenditure on the permanent structure and land of the estates, expressed as a percentage of the rents received over the 21 years, 1872–92, and the decline in rent per acre between 1872–4 and 1890–2. This figure was found to have a value of −0·67.[1]

[1] For a sample of size 8 this value is significant at the 5 per cent level and implies a real inverse correlation between the two variables.

F

III

As our concern is to analyse the role of the landlord in this period of agricultural depression, something should first be said about the circumstances of the Dukes of Sutherland and Bedford before we go on to compare their estates. In the first place, both were substantial landowners, having other agricultural properties besides those which are of immediate interest here. In 1892 the properties of the Duke of Bedford comprised 22,845 acres in Lincolnshire, 24,792 acres in Devon and Dorset, and 25,401 acres of the Woburn estate in Bedfordshire and Buckinghamshire – 73,038 acres in all.[1] The Duke of Sutherland was the largest private landowner in the United Kingdom with 1,326,453 acres in the counties of Sutherland and Ross, a mere 1,853 acres in Stitterham, Yorkshire, besides his Shropshire and Staffordshire estates. In all he owned some 1,358,545 acres in 1880.[2] Neither of these landowners was wholly dependent on their agricultural properties for their incomes. The Duke of Bedford had substantial urban properties, especially in London, which yielded a steady income,[3] and the Duke of Sutherland had substantial industrial properties around North Staffordshire and in the Wolverhampton area, which were very profitable in the 1870s. So both these landowners had at least adequate external sources of income which would be used to meet the bills for repairs, new buildings and land improvements, supposing the normal incomes from the estates were not enough to meet these, and the other costs of running the properties. Also, both landowners took an interest in the welfare of their estates and the progress of agricultural development. The Dukes of Bedford had traditionally fostered experimental agriculture, and since 1876 the resources of the Woburn Abbey home farm had been at the disposal of Lawes and Gilbert for investigations into livestock feeding and the

---

[1] Duke of Bedford, op. cit., p. 68.

[2] J. Bateman, *Great Landowners of Great Britain* (1883), p. 361.

[3] F. M. L. Thompson, *English Landed Estates in the Nineteenth Century* (1963), p. 336; D. Spring, *The English Landed Estate in the Nineteenth Century: its Administration* (1962), p. 41 where he describes the London property as 'perhaps the most valuable land in the world'.

laying down of permanent pasture.[1] The Dukes of Sutherland had also shown an interest in agricultural improvements, both in the past by their drainage of a large portion of the Shropshire estate in the 1800s, and in the 1870s when the third Duke spent colossal sums in Scottish land reclamations.[2]

But despite this similarity in circumstances and attitudes between the two landlords, the financial history of the two estates is distinctly different during this period. The performance of the Duke of Sutherland's Shropshire estate[3] is summarized in Table IV. As in the case of most of the estate figures taken from the Royal Commission, no distinction was ever made between items of current and capital expenditure when it came to farm buildings and work on land improvements.

A number of points in the pattern of expenditure are important. Firstly, the large amount spent on buildings in the early seventies was caused by the fresh construction of farm buildings and cottages – mainly farm buildings. This suggests that the estate was taking considerable care over transformation, even before 1879, and will be referred to again later, though it is true that not everything was done in this direction before the eighties. A second rise in expenditure in the nineties is accounted for by further work on farm buildings. Secondly, as on so many of the estates looked at so far, particularly those in livestock areas, expenditure on drainage and land implements rises in the 1880s. On this estate it was a reaction to the need for drainage and the conversion of heavy arable land to pasture.

The overall effects of this expenditure was that net estate income was very well maintained throughout the eighties and

---

[1] Duke of Bedford, op. cit., pp. 162–4.

[2] E. S. Richards, *James Loch and the House of Sutherland 1812–1855*, Unpublished Ph.D. thesis (Nottingham University, May 1965); C. G. Roberts, 'Sutherland Reclamation', *Journal of the Royal Agricultural Society*, 2nd series, XV (1879).

[3] Information on the Duke of Sutherland's properties came from the Staffordshire County Record Office, series D593, the Sutherland collection. The Shropshire property comprised land in the east of the county in the parishes of Lilleshall, Muxton, Sheriffhales, Kinnersley and Longdon-on-Tern. The figures in Table IV refer to a constant acreage of farms paying £50 p.a. rental, or more, amounting to 13,953 acres – Staffordshire County Record Office, D593 G/1/24/2–27 & D593 11/14/3/19.

was in fact higher in the quinquennium 1888–92 than it had ever been in the seventies, despite the fall in rents. The most serious fall in rents and net estate income came between 1893 and 1897, partly as a result of the renewed fall in agricultural prices of the early nineties and the difficult seasons which were bound to have repercussions on rents, and partly as the

TABLE IV *Duke of Sutherland's Shropshire Estate:*
expenditure and income, 1871–1900
(overlapping quinquennial averages)

	Expenditure[1]				Income	
	Drainage and land improvements	Buildings and repairs	Other[2] expenses	Total expenses	Rents from[3] farms of over £50 rental	Net income from farms
	£	£	£	£	£	£
1871–5	1,240	7,947	4,790	13,977	23,423	9,446
1873–7	1,543	9,396	4,780	15,719	23,464	7,945
1876–80	2,239	7,927	4,816	14,982	22,590	7,608
1878–82	2,694	6,757	4,778	14,229	22,538	8,309
1881–5	2,985	6,526	4,531	14,042	22,562	8,520
1883–7	2,998	6,045	4,333	13,376	22,228	8,852
1886–90	2,849	5,754	4,120	12,723	22,657	9,934
1888–92	2,529	5,669	4,042	12,240	22,776	10,536
1891–5	2,352	7,056	4,210	13,618	21,675	8,057
1893–7	2,359	7,514	4,406	14,279	20,683	6,404
1896–1900	1,991	5,414	4,273	11,678	20,027	8,349

[1] Staffordshire County Record Office D593 F5/4/10–39.
[2] This includes general management, rates, taxes and tithes.
[3] Shropshire County Record Office, 673/2/76–81; Staffordshire County Record Office, D593 G/1/24/2–27.

result of renewed expenditure on buildings after 1892 which reduced net estate income further. The recovery of net estate income in 1896–1900 was due solely to the fact that the management felt it had done all it could by the provision of new buildings, and so in 1896 the decision was taken drastically to reduce the size of the estate building and other departments. The work done on land improvements was also reduced at this time.

Unfortunately it is not possible to present the same sort of breakdown of expenditure on the Duke of Sutherland's

Staffordshire properties[1] because this estate, on the edge of the Potteries, contained a fair proportion of urban property besides farms. At times large sums were spent on this town property and the estate accounts are constructed in such a way that it is impossible to separate these sums from purely farm expenditure. Nevertheless, the estate accounts and correspondence indicate a pattern of activity between 1870 and 1900 which was very similar to that carried out in Shropshire. Although it had a high percentage of pasture,[2] the Staffordshire estate was worse off than the Shropshire estate, especially just after 1879, because it had a high proportion of clayland. The effect of this can be seen in the decline of rents in the early 1880s. On the Shropshire estate the average rent per acre received between 1876–8 and 1882–4 fell by less than 1 per cent. On the Staffordshire estate there was a fall of over $4\frac{1}{2}$ per cent.[3] But even on the heavy land the fall was not so severe as on the Bedfordshire and Buckinghamshire estates where in 1879 half a year's rent was remitted to the farm tenants, with remissions of 25 per cent in 1880 and 1881 and 10 per cent in 1882. In 1883 and 1884 rents were paid in full.[4] On the Bedfordshire and Buckinghamshire estates by 1895 the position was as follows:[5]

	£
Total rental in Bedfordshire and Buckinghamshire in 1878	43,975
Total amount of rents remitted since 1879	132,222
The revaluation of rents made in 1895, and brought into force with effect from Michaelmas, 1895, was	20,063
Showing a reduction of	23,912
Being (say) 55 per cent.	

[1] The Staffordshire property comprised land in the parishes of Trentham, Barlaston, Blurton, Hanford, Normacot, Clayton and Hanchurch. The estate had an agricultural acreage of 6,505 acres being farms of £50 rental p.a., or over – Staffordshire County Record Office, D593 H/14/2/10 and D593 G/2/6/82.

[2] 75 per cent of the land on the Staffordshire estate was pasture in 1870, rising to 85 per cent in 1900 – Public Record Office, M.A.F., 68 (Parish Agricultural Returns).

[3] Staffordshire County Record Office, D593 G/1/24/2–4 & 8–10; G/1/22/22–24 & 30–33.

[4] Duke of Bedford, op. cit., pp. 122–3.

[5] Ibid., p. 126.

Only on the Shropshire estate of the Duke of Sutherland was anything ever approaching an overall revaluation ever carried out, and even this, which was undertaken in 1893, was only partial and amounted to only 6 per cent of the rent proper of the tenants affected, and even with the land tax and the fire insurance for the farm buildings which the landlord now took over at that date, it only came to 8 per cent.[1]

The management's attitude on the Duke of Sutherland's estates to tenants' demands for rent reductions was to resist any demand for a universal reduction. When the tenants on the Shropshire estate presented a petition in 1881[2] asking for a reduction on the grounds of low prices of farm produce, competition from both foreign grain and cattle, disease among their livestock and the gradual reduction of their capital, the estate was able to reply that, 'nothing like a case calling for a general and substantial reduction of rents has been made out, but on the contrary, all have been most liberally dealt with as to buildings. Most of the cases having a special claim have already been assisted and are in course of receiving assistance in a way most likely to render their farms increasingly valuable – and further that there is a majority . . . whose holdings would let at equal or increased rents.' Again in 1893 when a petition caused a reduction, the principle of treating every case on its merits was still adhered to. On the Bedfordshire and Buckinghamshire estates, however, the regular remissions were given as a means of avoiding a revaluation of the estates' rental which the management wanted to avoid at all costs, as it was hoped that circumstances might improve; and if a revaluation were adopted it could not be confined to the Bedfordshire and Buckinghamshire estates. Hence the policy of remissions along with assistance to tenants in the form of laying down land to grass, etc.[3] But the policy was only of limited success and with the revaluation of 1895 the estate finally accepted the inevitable. Thus, though the objects of both estate managements were similar – the avoidance of permanent or 'across the board'

---

[1] Staffordshire County Record Office, D593 G/4/17.

[2] Staffordshire County Record Office, D593 L/3/69; Memorial from sundry tenants asking for a reduction of rents. (This document gives the estate's reply to the petitioners.)

[3] Duke of Bedford, op. cit., pp. 182–3.

rent reductions, and the offering of improvements to tenants to help them adapt to the changed circumstances – the outcome in each case was dissimilar.

The reasons for this difference in outcome seem to lie with the attitude of the management and the sort of agriculture which was predominant on the estates. Both the Duke of Sutherland's estates were in livestock counties and were subject to a system of dairying or mixed farming with a strong emphasis on the livestock side. Thus it was possible to concentrate production on livestock as prices for this branch of production improved from the 1850s onwards. In 1858 the Shropshire estate was revalued and from that date, till 1881, something like £80,000 was spent on the farm buildings – the greater part of this being for additions to capital – and about £19,000 on drainage, over £10,000 of this being for fresh work. So something like £90,000 was spent on transformation in the twenty-four years before 1881. As a result of this the management told the Shropshire tenants in that year that the rise in beef and mutton prices had 'fairly met the fall in grain'.[1] The chief enterprise of the Shropshire estate was the fattening of cattle, on grass to some extent, though more were finished off in the winter on oilcakes under cover.[2] On the light land in the parishes of Lilleshall and Sheriffhales there was also some concentration on sheep and barley,[3] the sheep being folded on the root crops one year and on the barley enriched with their manure, the next. But on the Bedfordshire and Buckinghamshire estates the first place was given to corn-growing and the 1850s and 1860s saw increasing emphasis on this crop.[4] Against this sort of background the unpreparedness of these estates for the changes after 1879 is not surprising.

The experience of the Duke of Sutherland's properties after 1870 also points to a more or less successful process of transformation. Nationally the numbers of sheep dropped after 1879

---

[1] Staffordshire County Record Office, D593 L/3/69.
[2] Ibid.
[3] G. W. Robinson, *A Survey of the Soils and Agriculture of Shropshire* (1916), p. 29.
[4] W. Bennett, 'The farming of Bedfordshire', *Journal of the Royal Agricultural Society*, XVIII (1857), p. 17, where the author refers to the Duke allowing a tenant to break up second-rate pasture for corn-growing.

but this did not happen on the Shropshire estate. In 1870 the density of stocking was 86 per 100 acres of pasture; it was the same in 1885, but by 1900 it had risen to 95 sheep and lambs per 100 acres. Also the acreage of barley on the estate, which was 8 per cent of all arable and pasture land, was 10 per cent in 1900. The fattening of cattle continued to develop. In 1870 the ratio of calves to every 100 cows in milk and calf was 94, but by 1900 this figure had reached 194, which points to an increased tendency to fatten more calves bred on the farm instead of buying in from outside.[1] All this seemed to point to increased agricultural production on the estate by 1900 which was a sound basis for the preservation of rents. On the Staffordshire estate, dairying developed despite the decline in the farm manufacture of cheese after 1875.[2] The Potteries provided a ready market for fresh milk, and so did London for those farms which were conveniently placed for reaching stations on the London and North Western Railway line.

All this is not to deny that the years after 1879 imposed something of a strain on the management of the Duke of Sutherland's properties, but the cost was nowhere near as great as for the Duke of Bedford. For instance, if we consider the burden of farms in hand, between 1880 and 1899 these cost the Shropshire estate £4,398, or an average of £220 per annum.[3] On the Bedfordshire estate only, however, the cost of farms in hand amounted to £23,116 between 1879 and 1896, or an average of £1,284 per annum.[4]

The sort of assistance offered to tenants on the Duke of Sutherland's estates after 1879 appears to have been thoroughly in keeping with the needs of the times. On both estates farmers were provided with Dutch barns for the storage of fodder during the winter. The Dutch barns consisted of a galvanized iron roof resting on iron supports and needed far less maintenance than an ordinary barn. Also they saved the farmer the annual expense of having to pay for hay ricks to be thatched, which was important at a time when labour costs were rising;

[1] Public Record Office, M.A.F. 68.

[2] *Agricultural Gazette*, new series, VI (20 August 1877), p. 185.

[3] Staffordshire County Record Office, D593 F/5/4/20–39.

[4] Duke of Bedford, op. cit., p. 185. These sums are not included in the figures for expenditure in Tables I and IV.

straw also tended to be scarce as less corn was grown, especially on the Staffordshire estate. On the Shropshire estate, some tenants were offered covered fold yards to assist the winter fattening of cattle[1] and one was given a small railway along which fodder trucks full of feeding stuffs could be pushed, to save on labour costs in stall-feeding.[2] In addition, heavy arable was drained and converted to pasture on both estates as and when circumstances demanded.

In contrast the response to changing circumstances was never so positive on the Bedfordshire and Buckinghamshire estates, nor, when it was attempted, was it followed by such successful results. This was partly because these estates were forced to incur a large proportion of the expenses of transformation all at once, whereas they had been more evenly spread out on the Duke of Sutherland's estates. Also the job was much larger on estates which were largely geared to cereal production than on those where livestock already predominated. But it seems that the attitude of the management also contributed to the difficulties after 1879, being unaware of the reasons for change and psychologically unprepared to make these changes. Writing of the views of those responsible for the Bedfordshire and Buckinghamshire estates in 1880, the Duke of Bedford said,[3] 'Agriculturists and the nation at large were alike insensible to the real character of the depression. Nevertheless the causes at work were not obscure even in 1880. The gust of prosperity consequent on the continental wars of 1870 and 1877–8 had spent itself. Cheap marine transport had already thrown open the English market to the cereals of four continents. . . . It is easy to be wise after the event, but it is strange that a catastrophe which was no longer merely impending but had actually taken place should have been regarded by those best able to judge as a passing cloud.'

However, it must be emphasized that this was certainly not the attitude of those responsible for the management of the Duke of Sutherland's properties at that time. Both before

---

[1] These were offered to some tenants on the Shropshire estate in 1893 in lieu of rent reductions.

[2] Staffordshire County Record Office, D593 K/5/2/16 749–50.

[3] Duke of Bedford, op. cit., p. 181.

1879 and after, the situation had been correctly appraised and sufficient steps taken to deal with it. In 1879 the agent for the Shropshire and Staffordshire properties reported to his employer[1] that 'heavy land will generally not now bear the cost of cultivation with the corn prices which, so far I think, may be taken as practically permanent and therefore ... a change from arable to pasture is desirable – on the ground that so far as can be judged from experience it will yield more rent in that form than in any other possible at present. *This has been long recognized here and a good deal has been done in the direction of this change.*'

On the Bedfordshire and Buckinghamshire estates, in contrast, heavy land appears to have been infrequently, if at all, seeded down before 1879. We are told that in 1881 the ninth Duke of Bedford 'anxious to gain experience in this direction' had 64½ acres of arable, whose rental had been 27s. an acre in 1878, seeded down to grass. The operation cost £10. 0s. 6d. an acre initially and a further £5 an acre for incidental and necessary outlays: in the valuation of 1895 this land was put at 5s. an acre.[2] The problem here was that on the extremes of heavy clay and light sands, where the natural fertility of the soil was limited, it was impossible under any circumstances to make an expensive conversion to pasture pay. Between 1880 and 1895 the landlord converted 1,308 acres on these estates to pasture, but large areas were also converted by the tenants or else just allowed to 'tumble down'.[3] This last feature was entirely absent on the Duke of Sutherland's estates where all conversion to pasture was carried out properly, with manures and seeds from the landlord. This experience would seem to point to the fact that the Bedfordshire and Buckinghamshire estates contained a proportion of marginal land which it was profitable to turn to corn production when prices were high, but which was profitable for neither cereal nor intensive grass production after 1879 and 1885 when the prices of both corn and livestock had declined. Under these circumstances the

---

[1] Staffordshire County Record Office, D593 K/3/9/65 G. Menzies to the Duke of Sutherland, 6 September 1879 (Italics not in the original.)

[2] Duke of Bedford, op. cit., pp. 196–7 and p. 204 for further examples.

[3] Duke of Bedford, op. cit., p. 203.

landlord's verdict[1] was, 'It is best to accept the situation and accept that these lands must revert to the condition they were in before the then high price of corn justified their being broken up and brought into cultivation. If they only produce a rental of 5s. an acre it is more profitable for the landowners and farmers than if the latter lost £5 an acre by corn growing.'

IV

If the examples quoted from the Royal Commission are representative, it would seem that there was a broad correlation between the amount a landlord spent on the farms on his estate and the extent to which rent levels were maintained after 1879. Also, it would seem that landlords in livestock areas were generally willing to spend more money on their estates than landowners in the arable part of the country, both before and after 1879. The relative reluctance of landowners in the arable districts to spend money before 1879 may have been because they thought it unnecessary to do so while cereal prices were being maintained. Their failure to do so afterwards may have been because they found the costs of transformation, especially for heavy land, coming with the precipitate fall in rents, too much for them to meet. However, the availability of capital to the landlord is not the only variable which has to be taken into account. The comparisons made between the Duke of Bedford's arable estates and Duke of Sutherland's livestock-producing estates show that both the attitude of their managements and the limitations imposed by climate and soil types played an important part in affecting the success of any schemes adopted. The Duke of Bedford's managers who had stuck to cereal production in the 1860s showed more inertia and reluctance to accept changes in the structure of farming after 1879 than the managers of the Sutherland estates, who were prepared to do everything to encourage the extension of livestock production, even before the situation regarding cereals had reached calamitous proportions. But even as late as 1880 the appreciation of the situation by the management of the Bedfordshire and Bucking-

[1] Ibid., p. 206.

hamshire estates was still incomplete, and this incomplete appreciation led the management to apply measures which only imperfectly answered it. Perhaps a more satisfactory solution would have been achieved if the estate had accepted from the start that rents on this sort of land were bound to fall and that the answer was to encourage the tenants to try new systems of farming,[1] or else for the estate to run the farms which came in hand under a rigorous system of management,[2] paying strict attention to costs, with the object of making a profit, instead of spending money on the costly conversion to pasture of land which was really unsuitable for such treatment.

[1] *Royal Commission 1894-7, Final Report, Report by G. W. Lambert*, pp. 205-6 and *Report by F. A. Channing*, pp. 251-8 for accounts of successful farming, many in predominantly arable districts.

[2] F. M. L. Thompson, 'Agriculture since 1870', *V. C. H. Wiltshire*, IV (1959), p. 197; Gavin, op. cit., p. 86.

7 Where was the 'Great Agricultural Depression'? A Geography of Agricultural Bankruptcy in Late Victorian England and Wales

P. J. PERRY

This article was first published in the *Agricultural History Review*, XX (1972).

Most important questions in agricultural history are also questions of agricultural geography; studies of agricultural change must commonly be concerned with spatial as well as temporal changes and relationships. So much is this the case that an historical geographer working primarily in this field might go so far as to suggest that the essence of historical geography is the concurrent application of the methods of history and geography to examine topics which cannot be studied adequately by either discipline alone.

The agricultural depression of the last quarter of the nineteenth century has been a rather neglected topic in British agricultural history. Since Lord Ernle's classic history of English farming,[1] itself a child of the depression and disaster which he witnessed in the early 1880s, the only detailed treatments of the topic have been by Fletcher, Thompson and Coppock. Each has produced a regional study, on Lancashire, Wiltshire and the Chilterns respectively, and a more general but by no means comprehensive treatment.[2] Orwin and

---

[1] Lord Ernle (R. E. Prothero), *English Farming – Past and Present*, 6th ed. (Chicago, 1961) (with introduction by G. E. Fussell and O. R. McGregor).

[2] T. W. Fletcher, 'Lancashire livestock farming during the Great Depression', *Agricultural History Review*, IX (1) (1961), pp. 17–42; also 'The Great Depression of English agriculture, 1873–1896', *Economic History Review*, 2nd series, XIII (3) (1960–1), pp. 417–32; F. M. L. Thompson, 'Agriculture since 1870', *Victoria County History of Wiltshire*, IV (1959), pp. 92–114; also *English Landed Society in the Nineteenth Century* (London, 1963); J. T. Coppock, 'Agricultural changes in

Whetham provide a more general discussion of the depression in their book on British agriculture from 1846 to 1914.[1] To some extent the depression and its scholarship have become casualties of the substantially successful attempts of two generations of British historians to discredit the idea of a widespread and general depression during the last quarter of the nineteenth century.[2] The value and importance of their work is hardly to be disputed; it does not, however, destroy the validity of the view that British farming passed through a period of crisis and change in the last quarter of the nineteenth century.

The object of this paper is not, however, to look at every aspect of the depression in its geographical and historical context. Rather it is to use one comprehensive source to examine the extent of the depression in the early 1880s and early 1890s.

Under the Bankruptcy Act of 1869[3] notice of bankruptcy in the strict sense, or of the much employed alternative procedure of 'liquidation by arrangement', had to appear in the *London Gazette*.[4] The occupation of the bankrupt is always given, and his residence; it is therefore possible to map agricultural failures and the geography of depression using this source. The 1869 act allowed no one to go bankrupt on his own petition, hence the importance of the alternative pro-

the Chilterns 1875–1900', *Agricultural History Review*, IX (1) (1961), pp. 1–16; also, 'The changing arable in England and Wales, 1870–1956', *Tidschrift voor Economische en Sociale Geografie*, L (1959), pp. 121–30.

[1] C. S. Orwin and E. H. Whetham, *History of British Agriculture 1846–1914* (London, 1964). (Two chapters relate directly, two more marginally, to the depression.)

[2] *Inter alia*, see S. B. Saul, *The Myth of the Great Depression, 1873–1896* (London, 1969); H. L. Beales, 'The Great Depression in industry and trade', *Economic History Review*, 1st series, V (1) (1934), pp. 65–75; C. Wilson, 'Economy and society in late Victorian Britain', *Economic History Review*, 2nd series, XVIII (1) (1965), pp. 183–98.

[3] 32 & 33 Vict. c. 11. (The Bankruptcy Act 1869.) The law of bankruptcy in general and the failings of the 1869 legislation in particular are treated in the article on bankruptcy in *Encyclopaedia Britannica*, 11th ed. (1910–11), III, pp. 321–32.

[4] The set used was that of the General Assembly Library, Wellington, N.Z. A few copies are missing in most years. The equivalent Scottish publication, the *Edinburgh Gazette*, is not available in New Zealand; Scotland has therefore necessarily been excluded from consideration.

cedure mentioned above. Unfortunately this 'liquidation by arrangement or composition with creditors', as it was usually termed in the *Gazette*, lay largely outside the control of the courts set up by the act; it was easily entered into and there is no doubt that it was often abused as far as creditors were concerned. The Bankruptcy Act of 1883[1] remedied these defects and set up from 1885 the procedure which has, in broad outline, survived to the present day. The first stage in bankruptcy under the 1883 legislation was the 'receiving order'; moreover, bankruptcy on the bankrupt's own petition became possible and in fact common. It seems likely that this stricter legislation played a part in reducing the number of agricultural bankruptcies, but it should be noted that the mid and late 1880s also saw some easing of the depression. A third factor must also be remembered in this context; from the early 1880s people became aware that the depression was no ephemeral one, caused by a succession of bad seasons, but likely to be long-lasting. In these circumstances most, albeit not all, landlords were prepared to make considerable concessions to keep tenants on the land.[2]

The ease of liquidation or composition under the 1869 act has already been mentioned. Just over 150 farmers did so in 1871, almost 700 in 1881. This almost five-fold increase can be accounted for primarily in terms of the onset of the depression, but an awareness among farmers and solicitors that in some cases the provisions of the act could be operated to their advantage was probably an important secondary factor in this increase. By comparison most of the farmer's creditors were weakly placed; the act put the small creditor in a poor position, and most creditors were in no position to have the farmer adjudicated bankrupt (in the strict sense) because of the prior claims of the landowner under the law of distress.[3] Farms

[1] 46 & 47 Vict. c. 52. (The Bankruptcy Act 1883.)

[2] The evidence heard by the Royal Commissions of 1880–2 and 1893–5 contains an abundance of references to this phenomenon, as also the Assistant Commissioners' reports and the writings of contemporary agricultural journalists, for example, Richard Jefferies.

[3] This matter was raised and discussed not infrequently before the Royal Commissions of 1880–2 and 1893–5; some witnesses were inclined to think it favourable to the farmer, e.g. W. C. Little, a Cambridgeshire tenant farmer and assistant commissioner (Q. 46990, 27 May 1881), others the reverse, e.g.

became hard to let quite early in the depression; most land-lords were therefore unwilling to bankrupt or see bankrupted tenants whom they knew to be almost irreplaceable.

Does all this invalidate the source material in terms of the historical geography of the depression? The almost five-fold increase in gazette notices under the 1869 act between 1871 and 1881 suggests not, although in the light of the discussion above it may not be inappropriate to point out that it is possible to argue either a more than five-fold or less than five-fold intensification of real agricultural failure during this period according to which of the possible complicating factors is given most weight. The 1869 act certainly favoured the liquidating or compounding creditor; it seems doubtful whether, save in exceptional cases, it encouraged farmers to liquidate or compound unless they were in difficulties. Farming was the only skill most farmers possessed; leaving the land meant leaving house and home, and at a time of depression the chances of extracting their diminished capital by giving up farming were uncertain in both legal and market terms. In looking at the geography of this phenomenon, then, we are looking at a geography of the agricultural depression, a reliable geography in the general if not in the most detailed sense. (The 1883 legislation, it should be noted, raises no such problems of an interpretative kind.)

At a more mundane level the *London Gazette* material is tedious and bulky to use, that under the 1869 act more so than that under the 1883 legislation, which latter is printed in a convenient tabular form. Under the 1869 procedure three or four meetings of creditors might take place over several months; there is the resultant problem of ensuring that each bankruptcy is considered only once.[1] A more serious problem

---

S. Rowlandson, a Durham tenant farmer and landowner (Q. 35651, 25 March 1881). (Questions and dates, where referred to in the footnotes, refer to the minutes of evidence of the appropriate Royal Commission. These were printed as British Parliamentary Papers (Blue Books), 1881, XV; 1881, XVII; 1882, XIV; and 1894, XVI; 1896, XVII.)

[1] A related problem is the occasional instance where one failure is followed by those of several possible relatives in the locality or district. These must, of course, be regarded as *bona fide* failures but the phenomenon suggests some degree of financial interconnection, to the extent where one failure might have wide implications.

is that throughout the depression a large number of those farmers who failed also had non-agricultural occupations which might well have been the main cause of their difficulties. This group, commonly including innkeepers, butchers and carriers for example, have been excluded from consideration; but where farming was associated with another activity closely connected with agriculture, milling, corn-dealing and agricultural contracting, for example, the bankruptcy in question forms part of the materials of this study, together with the farmers, graziers and dairymen. This classification is arbitrary and subjective but necessary; when it is made there remain a large number of failures for consideration. Finally, because the source is so bulky, extraction and mapping the data so tedious, this study focuses on three periods, 1871–3 as pre-depression datum; 1881–3 the latter part of the first period of intense depression; and 1891–3 the earlier part of the second phase of intense depression.

The source material allows two maps to be constructed for each of the three-year periods; the location of individual failures can be shown and a value derived for each county relating the number of failures to the number of farmers and graziers recorded at the census, the first year in each of the three-year periods being a census year. The early 1870s were the Indian Summer of 'high farming', the last years of the nineteenth century in which such methods paid well, to the extent of lively competition for farms.[1] In the most failure-prone county in the early 1870s, Essex, only one in 500 farmers failed each year; in South Wales, Lancashire and Devon only one in 5,000 failed. The overall pattern at this period is of a higher level of failure in south-eastern England than northward and westward. The ten counties where the annual average of failures exceeded 0·16 per cent (Map I) were all in south-eastern England, Worcestershire alone excepted.

How is this regional concentration to be explained? Contemporary commentators would perhaps have criticized the easy-going outlook and modest energy of the south-eastern

---

[1] See, for example, William Sturge, president of the Institute of Surveyors, Q. 3754–55, 11 March 1880; J. Dunn, a Yorkshire tenant farmer, Q. 33897, 18 March 1881.

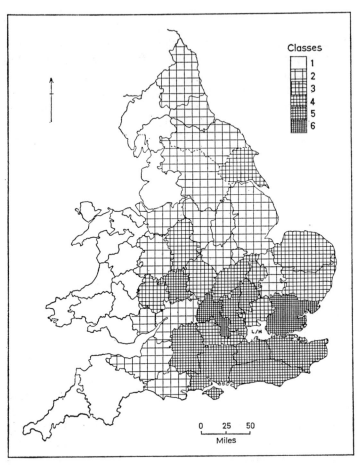

MAP I

Agricultural Failure (assignments and bankruptcies, annual average by counties), 1871–3, as a percentage of the farming population in 1871: (1) less than 0·04 per cent; (2) 0·04 per cent to less than 0·08 per cent; (3) 0·08 per cent to less than 0·12 per cent; (4) 0·12 per cent to less than 0·16 per cent; (5) 0·16 per cent to less than 0·20 per cent; (6) more than 0·20 per cent; L/M, London and Middlesex.

farmer and his poorly paid labourer in comparison with those of the north and west.[1] The economic historians of the 1950s and 1960s would probably point to the declining profitability of grain crops in comparison with livestock through the middle decades of the nineteenth century as likely more seriously to affect southern and eastern England.[2] The south-east was also remote from the best urban industrial markets. The higher proportion of small farmers in the north and west may also have been significant. The early 1870s saw rents reach their highest point in many areas, and for this and other reasons established tenants decided in some cases to quit;[3] to suggest that this may relate to the higher level of failure in the south-east, an area of large estates in close proximity to the expensive and fashionable delights of the capital, is speculation, but not unduly so. These are in fact hypotheses which await rigorous testing in the event of adequate sources being available.

The map of individual failures (Map II) provides a more detailed but less objective view of the early 1870s. It can take no account of variations in the number and size of farms and there is reason, therefore, to believe that in certain areas, Yorkshire and the west Midlands for example, the apparent frequency of failure is primarily a reflection of a more dense agricultural population of small farmers. Nevertheless the general impression is one which confirms that given by Map I. More particularly the relative absence of failure in the grazing counties of the east Midlands, on the Jurassic limestone from Dorset to Lincolnshire, on the chalk and on the lighter lands of counties where failure was relatively common, in Essex

---

[1] For example, Richard Jefferies, *Hodge and his Masters* (London, 1880) (and subsequent editions). This point of view is also strongly advanced by E. H. Hunt, 'Labour productivity in British agriculture, 1850–1914', *Economic History Review*, 2nd series, XXIX (2) (1967), pp. 280–92.

[2] For example, E. L. Jones, 'The changing basis of English agricultural prosperity, 1853–1873', *Agricultural History Review*, X (2) (1962), pp. 102–19.

[3] This phenomenon of the early 1870s is discussed by F. M. L. Thompson, 'The land market in the nineteenth century', *Oxford Economic Papers*, new series, IX (1957), pp. 285–308 and 'Agriculture since 1870', *Victoria County History of Wiltshire*, IV (1959), pp. 92–114; also J. Oxley Parker (ed.), *The Oxley Parker Papers* (Colchester, 1964), pp. 128–34, with reference to Essex. The high level of rents in the early 1870s was also frequently mentioned in evidence before the Royal Commission.

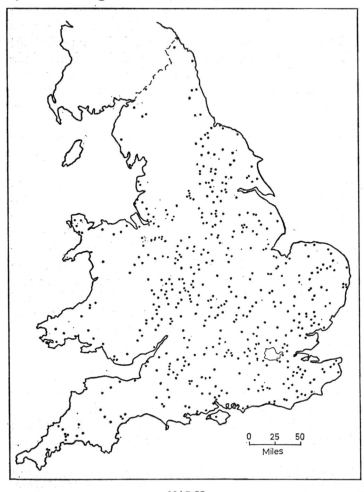

MAP II

Agricultural Failure (assignments and bankruptcies), 1871–3.

and Kent, for example, is apparent. The importance of the physical environment in this context is evident before the onset of depression.

By the early 1880s agricultural prosperity had ended, albeit temporarily in the opinion of most contemporary landowners and farmers. The heartland of the early depression

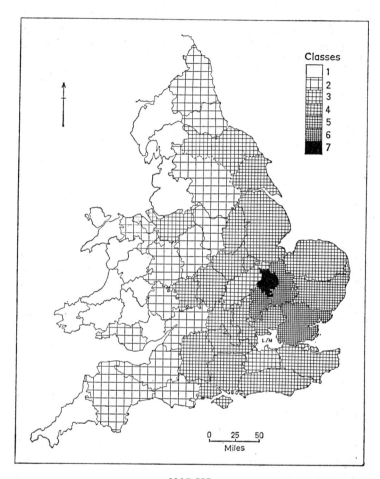

MAP III

Agricultural Failure (assignments and bankruptcies, annual average by counties), 1881–3, as a percentage of the farming population in 1881 : (1) less than 0·1 per cent; (2) 0·1 per cent to less than 0·2 per cent; (3) 0·2 per cent to less than 0·3 per cent; (4) 0·3 per cent to less than 0·4 per cent; (5) 0·4 per cent to less than 0·5 per cent; (6) 0·5 per cent to less than 0·6 per cent; (7) more than 0·6 per cent; L/M, London and Middlesex.

(Map III) was Huntingdonshire where on average, one farmer in 150 failed each year; locally (as Map IV suggests) the level may have approached one in say 20 or 30. In East Anglia as a whole, Norfolk marginally excepted, one farmer in 250 failed annually. The area where the annual average of failures exceeded 0·30 per cent extended from Hampshire in the south, north-eastward to the East Riding, with only Northampton-shire and marginally Surrey remaining, to some degree, islands of prosperity. The most obvious explanation of the Northamp-tonshire anomaly is its concentration on grazing and fattening, but this raises the problem why Leicestershire and Rutland, adjacent counties of similar reputation, were so differently affected. At the other extreme, failure remained rare in Wales and north-western England, for the most part below the 0·10 per cent level. This confirms recent work on the depression which has stressed that essentially, and especially in its early phases, arable agriculture on 'high farming' lines was most affected,[1] but if so why not Northumberland with its tradi-tion of expertise in this context? The relatively high level of failure in Cheshire by comparison with all but its eastern neighbours is also of interest, suggesting that livestock rearers had the edge on dairy farmers at this stage of the depression.

The map of individual failures (Map IV) for the early 1880s makes apparent the concentrated effects of the depression on the heavy land, and thus explains, at least in part, why some arable counties were not intensely depressed. Norfolk, Lin-colnshire and the East Riding are good examples, and within them western Norfolk contrasts sharply with the centre and east, the Lincolnshire Wolds with the Fens and Trent Valley, the Yorkshire Wolds with Holderness. That a series of un-usually cold and wet years exacerbated the situation on the heavy lands during this period must also be remembered, a climatic misfortune much more marked in the south and east than the north and west.[2] The deficiencies of such a dot map

---

[1] C. S. Orwin and E. H. Whetham, op. cit.

[2] The assistant commissioner for northern England to the Royal Commission of 1880–2 was able to report that in Cumberland and Westmorland only the autumn of 1879 and spring of 1880 had been unfavourable; Cameron of Lochiel, M.P., could claim that the seasons had not been bad for sheep in the Highlands (Q. 43444, 12 May 1881).

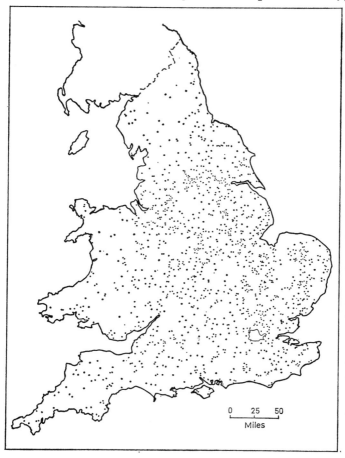

MAP IV

Agricultural Failure (assignments and bankruptcies), 1881–3.

must, however, also be considered; the large number of dots in Cheshire, east Lancashire and the West Riding more probably reflects the presence of a large number of small farmers rather than extremely intense depression.

By the early 1890s the number of agricultural failures had been considerably reduced, a consequence of the legislation of 1883 and of awareness that the depression and its causes were more than ephemeral. The depression (Map V) remained

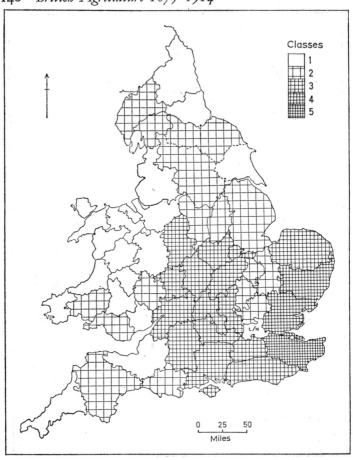

MAP V

Agricultural Failure (receiving orders – annual average by counties), 1891–3, as a percentage of the farming population in 1891: (1) less than 0·05 per cent; (2) 0·05 per cent to less than 0·10 per cent; (3) 0·10 per cent to less than 0·15 per cent; (4) 0·15 per cent to less than 0·20 per cent; (5) more than 0·20 per cent; L/M, London and Middlesex.

most intense in the south-east, Kent, Suffolk and Essex in particular, the degree of failure diminishing northward and westward. The most interesting anomaly is the comparative absence of depression in those counties extending from London to the Wash, including those most affected in the early 1880s. The intensity of the earlier depression in this area, proximity to London and opportunities for the development of market-gardening may all have contributed to the more favourable situation of the early 1890s. Most authorities have suggested that depression became more widespread and general in its later phases; it should then be noted that in both the early 1890s and the early 1880s there were about twenty times as many farming bankruptcies in the most affected as in the least affected counties. In the early 1870s the ratio was only ten times; throughout the depression all kinds of local advantages, of soil, skill, situation or specialization, were more rather than less important than in normal circumstances as far as survival and even prosperity were concerned.

The map of individual failures in the early 1890s (Map VI) presents once more a picture of which areas were at an advantage in their environment and position. Again chalk and limestone England contrasts favourably with the Essex clays and the Weald.

The discussion so far has taken a very objective view of the depression, and in the process a necessarily static one. This is to neglect the progress of the depression and the fact that those most affected by it, farmers in particular, were prone to take a subjective rather than strictly objective attitude to their experience of adversity. Most farmers, even in a period when changes of tenancy were frequent, could better compare past and present in the one place than take a broad, instantaneous and comparative geographical view of the situation, as the Royal Commissioners and their assistants tried to do in the early 1880s and mid-1890s. The evidence heard by these two bodies makes it clear that the depression was most intense in the arable east and south, but only a very small group of witnesses had almost no complaint. Most farmers, dairymen, graziers, even market-gardeners as well as 'high farmers' on traditional arable lines could find something to grumble at: labour costs, margins between store and fatstock prices, or railway rates. The last of the good years lay in the early 1870s.[1]

---

[1] For example, James Martin, a Lincolnshire land-agent, claimed that farming had been unproductive for four or five years (Q. 6868–6869, 20 May

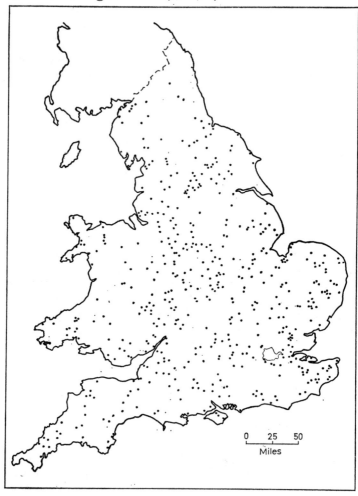

MAP VI

Agricultural Failures (receiving orders), 1891–3.

The farmer's view of the depression, and to some extent the landlord's, was then a complicated and dynamic one. A partial understanding of it in general terms can, however, be attained

1880); A. Doyle, the assistant commissioner for the western counties that arable farmers in the west Midlands had been losing money since 1874 (Q. 32514, 11 March 1881, but Doyle is a rather unconvincing witness in many respects).

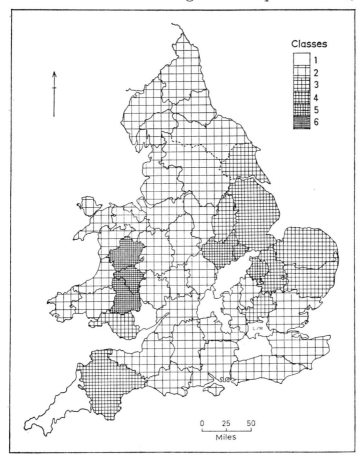

MAP VII

Agricultural Failures, 1881–3 (a) in relation to agricultural failures, 1871–3 (b), (a/b): (1) less than 1·5; (2) 1·5 to less than 3·0; (3) 3·0 to less than 4·5; (4) 4·5 to less than 6·0; (5) 6·0 to less than 7·5; (6) more than 7·5; L/M, London and Middlesex.

by comparison of the level of failure, county by county, between three-year periods. Comparison of the early 1880s with the early 1870s (Map VII) makes the counties around the Wash the focus of the 'subjective' depression, with a high degree of uniformity of experience in the rest of the country.

Northamptonshire and Leicestershire/Rutland remain the most striking anomalies, the more so because they are adjacent; a substantial element in this anomaly is perhaps the very low level of failure in Leicestershire/Rutland in the early 1870s. Even more striking is the high degree of depression in Brecon and Radnorshire, a breeding and hill sheep district exceptionally severely affected by disease in the early depression period;[1] Devonshire too was unfortunate in this respect.[2] These counties had been used to a very low level of failure in the early 1870s, and bearing in mind that adverse seasons and disease were commonly regarded as the basic cause of the depression in its early stages it is not difficult to understand why the depression was felt to be as disastrous here as elsewhere. It might also be noted that Huntingdonshire, Cambridgeshire and Lincolnshire, the areas most affected in subjective terms early in 1882, included much high-rented intensive arable land, particularly difficult to work and prone to flooding in wet seasons. Taking an objective view of the depression, on which Map III is based, the most depressed county of 1881–3 had a level of farmer bankruptcy twenty times that of the least depressed; by comparison, a subjective view of the depression, relating the situation in the early 1880s to the prosperity of ten years earlier, sees the most depressed county of the early 1880s no more than six times worse off than the least depressed. This begins to explain why farmers and landowners believed that the depression was general and extensive, despite objective evidence to the contrary.

Comparison of the early 1890s with the situation a decade earlier (Map VIII) suggests that by this date the depression was more keenly felt in Cumbria, North Wales, South Wales and Cornwall, than in most of the eastern counties. This is in part a reflection, and a confirmation, of the generally accepted view that the position of the pastoralist worsened in the later period of depression. On an objective view (Map V) the pastoral north and west remained less depressed; in subjective

---

[1] As noted by A. Doyle, assistant commissioner for the western counties.

[2] W. C. Little, assistant commissioner for the southern counties, noted that around Holsworthy the loss of sheep through disease on a group of more than 100 farms equalled half the annual rental or more than the average annual profit.

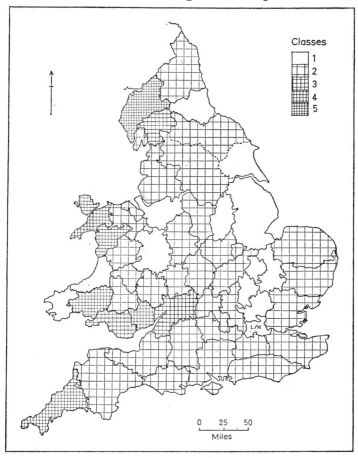

MAP VIII

Agricultural Failures, 1891–3 (a) in relation to agricultural failures, 1881–3 (b), (a/b): (1) less than 0·33; (2) 0·33 to less than 0·67; (3) 0·67 to less than 1·0; (4) 1·0 to less than 1·33; (5) more than 1·33; L/M, London and Middlesex.

terms the later depression was more keenly felt by reason of the absence of distress in earlier periods. This explanation is not, however, a wholly convincing one; this map is more complex and irregular than most in this series and raises such questions as why Pembrokeshire and Cardiganshire were so

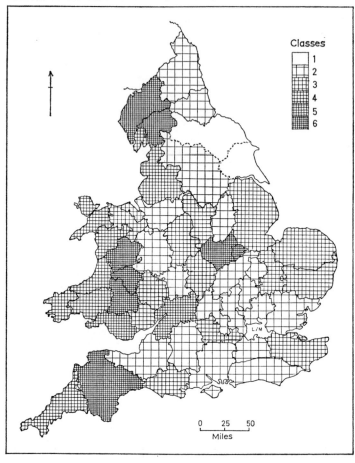

MAP IX

Agricultural Failure, 1891–3 (a) in relation to agricultural failures, 1871–3 (b), (a/b): (1) less than 0·5; (2) 0·5 to less than 1·0; (3) 1·0 to less than 1·5; (4) 1·5 to less than 2·0; (5) 2·0 to less than 2·5; (6) more than 2·5; L/M, London and Middlesex.

much more favourably placed than north-west Wales, Lancashire[1] than Cumbria, Devon than Cornwall. The matter

---

[1] Fletcher's excellent work on the Lancashire situation (op. cit.) certainly seems to deal with one extreme of the spectrum of depression, just as contemporary sources may appear unduly concerned with the other.

calls for further discussion and demonstrates the defects of visual analysis and verbal models, as well perhaps as the shortcomings and intractability of the material. It might, however, be added that construction of these maps may well justify the considerable effort required in their preparation by providing a series of eventually testable hypotheses.

To compare the early 1890s with the early 1870s is to venture on less certain ground. It raises the question of how far back the farmer looked in his judgement (and endurance) of the depression; twenty difficult years had seen new occupiers on many farms, but on the other hand was a sufficiently short period to be within the living memory of most of those concerned. Moreover, the early 1870s were the last, and thus best remembered, of the good years. The resultant map further emphasizes the late onset of the depression in the pastoral north and west (and also grazing Leicestershire), and presents fewer anomalies in this area than comparison over the shorter period. The dairying counties, Cheshire, Derbyshire, Staffordshire, Somerset, Dorset and Wiltshire, and the arable counties stand at the other extreme in such a longer term subjective view of the depression. This most probably reflects the stability if not great prosperity of milk production for urban markets, and in the arable counties the acceptance by landowners and farmers by the 1890s that the depression had brought about permanent changes, notably in rents. It also reflects the relatively high level of failure in these counties in the early 1870s.

What conclusions can be drawn from the use of this source material in the way outlined above? Firstly, the utility of the source itself is established in the patterns (and anomalies) which it generates, and the possibly testable hypotheses which emerge. (And this, after all, is the role ascribed to historical geography in some recent methodological writings!)[1] It also suggests potentially important county studies. Secondly, there appears to be a broad similarity between the geographical pattern of failure in the period immediately before the depression and that of the depression itself, its earlier phase in particular. This in turn provides partial explanation of why

[1] For example, N.A.S.–N.R.C. Committee on Geography, *The Science of Geography* (Washington D.C., 1965), p. 61.

farmers felt the depression to be widespread. Thirdly, the great importance of environmental factors, of the soil in particular, before, and to a greater extent during, the depression is evident, a feature of the depression which has often been suggested but never made explicit on a national scale. Finally, the widespread opinion of the farming community that it was experiencing some kind of depression, a view not everywhere substantiated by an objective view of the evidence, can be explained in part in subjective historical terms. These four observations neither explain nor explain away the depression; rather I would regard them as fingerposts for a more detailed, more complete and more sophisticated analysis of a critically formative period in the agricultural geography of Britain.[1]

[1] I wish to thank the staff of the General Assembly Library, Wellington, N.Z., the library of Canterbury University and the Canterbury Public Library, Christchurch, N.Z., for their unfailing courtesy, helpfulness and tolerance; also Miss C. Lynskey and Mrs S. M. Emanuel of Wellington, N.Z., who did most of the tedious work of extracting data from the *London Gazette*, assistance made possible through the generosity of the Research Assistants Fund of Canterbury University; also Mr J. K. Macdonald, B.Sc., Mrs C. McMichael and Mr G. Mitchell who prepared the maps; and, by no means least, my colleagues in the University of Canterbury for providing an academic environment both stimulating and relaxed.

8 Free Trade in 'Corn': A Statistical Study of the Prices and Production of Wheat in Great Britain from 1873 to 1914

MANCUR OLSON, JR. AND CURTIS C. HARRIS, JR.

This article was first published in the *Quarterly Journal of Economics*, LXIII (1959).

I THE PROBLEM

Some economists claim that economic historians have given too much of their attention to the development of economic policy, and neglected some other aspects of economic life, especially those requiring statistical analysis. The record of historians' efforts to explain British agriculture in Victorian times shows one instance where the criticism is justified. Much has been written about the Corn Laws – they are perhaps the most celebrated statutes in all of economic history – and about the controversy culminating in their repeal. This vast literature is, of course, quite significant, for the repeal of the Corn Laws must have had *something* to do with the obviously important fact that Britain, of all major nations, is the most overwhelmingly industrialized: it has the smallest proportion of its resources in the agricultural sector.

The quantitative and economic aspects of the decline of British wheat production have been much neglected, however, and it is the purpose of this paper to examine them, rather than the political controversies. The period from 1873–1914 will be studied for the reason that it was only after 1873 that the price of wheat (and other kinds of 'corn') fell below the level to which British farmers had been accustomed through most of the nineteenth century. Indeed, the beginning of the drop

G

in the production of this staple of British agriculture could hardly be set at an earlier date, for the acreage planted to wheat was at record or near record levels through the fifties, sixties and early seventies.

This paper will attempt to show how farmers reacted to the lower prices. The elasticity of supply will be studied, along with the factors affecting farmers' price expectations. The responses of British farmers to the lower prices in this period should be of more than historical interest now, when agricultural prices are stellar subjects of political debate. The period has value as a polar case in agricultural policy, in that there has been no other period or country in which the government has stuck steadfastly to a laissez faire policy in the face of a drastic drop in wheat prices and rapidly increasing imports.

Finally, there is a demonstration of a simple method which should in many cases be helpful in getting information about the elasticities of supply or demand functions from time series data.

II THE BACKGROUND

Almost everyone expected that the repeal of the Corn Laws in 1846 would bring lower prices immediately.[1] In fact prices stayed at about the usual level for most of the three decades following the repeal. The period from 1852–62 was called a 'golden age' for British agriculture; prices averaged over 50s. a quarter for most of the fifties and sixties, and reached 74s. 8d., the highest since 1818, during the Crimean War. There had been a price decline beginning in 1847, during the industrial financial panic, but this was neither deep nor long.[2]

The war with Russia, conflict on the Continent and in America during the sixties, the fact that most of the frontier lands of the new world had not yet been exploited, and rapidly

---

[1] 'I say, then, assuming, as I have given you reason to assume, that the price of wheat when this system is established ranges in England at 35s. per quarter, with other grains in proportion.' (The usual price before the repeal was 50 to 60s. per quarter. A quarter is equal to 8 bushels.) Benjamin Disraeli's speech of 15 May 1846, on the third reading of the Corn Importation Bill, *Hansards Debates*, quoted in the *Speeches of the Earl of Beaconsfield*, ed. T. E. Kebbel (London, 1882), I, 158.

[2] Lord Ernle, *English Farming Past and Present* (London, 1919), p. 441.

increasing domestic demand helped keep the price from falling
to the predicted levels. Another important fact was that
transportation costs had not been reduced enough to deprive
the British farmer of the 'natural protection of distance'.

The price decline began in 1873, though there was a temporary rise in 1876 and 1877 due to the Russo-Turkish War.
After 1877 there was no questioning the fact that farm prices
had collapsed. In 1879 the average annual price was only 43s.
10d. per quarter, well below the level common in the sixties.[1]
Prices fell inexorably until 1886, reaching 31s. in that year.
In 1885–6 the United Kingdom imported 147·1 million bushels
of wheat; the apparent domestic utilization (production plus
net imports) was 229·1 million bushels. Assuming no change in
stocks, 64 per cent of the country's needs were being met by
imports.[2] The price of wheat rose insignificantly for a time, but
dipped below 30s. in 1889. There was a measurable strengthen-
ing of the market from 1889–91.

After this respite came the final turn of the screw. Prices far
cheaper than any Disraeli had contemplated confronted the
British farmer. Wheat plunged first to 30s. 3d. in 1892, then
set a record for cheapness the next year at 26s. 2d.; this record
was broken in 1894, when wheat prices reached the nadir at

---

[1] It is one of the greatest ironies of British economic history that nothing
significant was done about the agricultural depression in the late seventies, for
Disraeli, by this time Lord Beaconsfield, was Prime Minister. Disraeli had been,
of course, the most famous and eloquent opponent of the repeal of the Corn
Laws. He made the following lugubrious prediction in the debate on the repeal:

> It may be vain now, in the midnight of their intoxication, to tell them that
> there will be an awakening of bitterness; it may be idle now, in the springtide
> of their economic frenzy, to warn them that there may be an ebb of trouble. But
> the dark and inevitable hour will arrive. Then, when their spirit is softened by
> misfortune, they will recur to those principles that made England great, and
> which in our belief, can alone keep England great. (Disraeli, *Speeches* . . ., I,
> 172.)

But in 1879, when the Marquis of Huntly used quotations from Disraeli's old
speeches to advocate *aid* for agriculture, Disraeli (now Beaconsfield) begrudgingly
acknowledged his 'rusty words' '. . . in "another place" and another generation',
but he was not willing to act upon his erstwhile recommendations: 'I cannot for
a moment doubt that the repeal of the Corn Laws has materially affected the
condition of those who are interested in land. . . . But that is no reason why we
should retrace our steps (*sic*) and authorize and sanction any violent changes.'
(Speech in House of Lords, 28 April 1879, *Speeches* . . ., I, 340.)

[2] Helen Farnsworth, *Wheat Studies*, X, Nos. 8 and 9 (1934), pp. 348–9.

22s. 10d. This was roughly a third of the price that had ordinarily prevailed three decades earlier. By this time most British farmers were on the verge of ruin. Many indeed had been driven past that verge into bankruptcy in the two decades of price collapse before 1894. While wheat production in Britain had been cut drastically, this had no significant effect on the British price (which with free trade was the same as the world price), since British output was almost minute in relation to the world supply. Foreign competition was by now at the root of the British farmer's difficulty, for in 1895–6 the United Kingdom imported three-quarters of its grain.

The improvements in transportation and the settling of the new lands in the United States and other frontier countries were the main causes of the increase in imports and the lower prices beginning in the seventies. The steam-powered, metal ship made ocean freight less expensive at the same time that the railroads and immigration made wheat growing important in the American Great Plains and other frontier lands. British wheat growers had many competitive disadvantages; Marshall even claimed that many farmers in the newly settled lands thought of wheat as a by-product, and the prospective increase in land values as the main source of gain.[1] The difficulties confronting the British farmer were aggravated by what was then called the 'Great Depression', which lasted from 1873 until almost the end of the century.

In 1894 prices reached bottom and a slight resurgence was soon experienced. The movement of prices was in general slowly upward at first, then the year to year fluctuations continued without any distinct, persistent tendency to move either upward or downward until World War I.

III THE EFFECTS ON ACREAGE

Between 1873 and 1894[2] the acreage planted to wheat fell from 3·63 million acres to 1·42 million acres.[3] The fact that both

[1] Alfred Marshall, *Principles of Economics* (8th ed.), pp. 429–30.

[2] The reference is to the harvest years beginning in calendar years 1873 and 1894. Harvest years begin 1 September and end 31 August. All subsequent references will be to harvest years.

[3] See Table I, for the sources of all acreage statistics.

TABLE I *Table of Variables*

Harvest[1] year	Acres[2] of wheat	Acres[3] T-1 minus T	Price[4] T-1	Price[5] T-2 minus T-1	Price[6] T-2	Average[7] price	Barley[8] wheat price ratio	Time[9]
	Y	y	X_1	X_2	X_3	X_4	X_5	X_T
1873–74	3·63	−0·14	688	−9	679	678	0·68	0
1874–75	3·42	0·21	735	−47	688	662	0·70	1
1875–76	2·99	0·43	535	200	735	630	0·90	2
1876–77	3·17	−0·18	551	−16	535	626	0·73	3
1877–78	3·22	−0·05	655	−104	551	644	0·70	4
1878–79	2·89	0·33	610	45	655	626	0·81	5
1879–80	2·91	−0·02	499	111	610	604	0·83	6
1880–81	2·81	0·10	553	−54	499	580	0·76	7
1881–82	3·00	−0·19	527	26	553	562	0·73	8
1882–83	2·61	0·39	565	−38	527	562	0·66	9
1883–84	2·68	−0·07	504	61	565	554	0·77	10
1884–85	2·48	0·20	462	42	504	518	0·81	11
1885–86	2·29	0·19	398	64	462	494	0·92	12
1886–87	2·32	−0·03	371	27	398	472	0·89	13
1887–88	2·56	−0·24	396	−25	371	452	0·75	14
1888–89	2·45	0·11	369	27	396	428	0·91	15
1889–90	2·39	0·06	372	−3	369	402	0·83	16
1890–91	2·31	0·08	374	−2	372	386	0·94	17
1891–92	2·22	0·09	420	−46	374	388	0·80	18
1892–93	1·90	0·32	401	−19	420	384	0·82	19
1893–94	1·93	−0·03	324	77	401	376	0·92	20
1894–95	1·42	0·51	309	15	324	360	1·03	21
1895–96	1·69	−0·27	256	53	309	344	1·00	22
1896–97	1·89	−0·20	300	−44	256	338	0·90	23
1897–98	2·10	−0·21	345	−48	300	334	0·83	24
1898–99	2·00	0·10	432	−87	345	330	0·75	25
1899–00	1·85	0·15	312	120	432	322	0·98	26
1900–01	1·70	0·15	313	−1	312	322	0·96	27
1901–02	1·73	−0·03	327	−14	313	330	0·91	28
1902–03	1·58	0·15	336	−9	327	338	0·92	29
1903–04	1·38	0·20	319	17	336	340	0·88	30
1904–05	1·80	−0·42	327	−8	319	336	0·80	31
1905–06	1·76	0·04	367	−40	327	328	0·80	32
1906–07	1·63	0·13	345	22	367	334	0·84	33
1907–08	1·63	0	336	9	345	340	0·87	34
1908–09	1·82	−0·19	393	−57	336	348	0·79	35
1909–10	1·81	0·01	437	−44	393	364	0·74	36
1910–11	1·91	−0·10	390	47	437	372	0·73	37
1911–12	1·93	−0·02	371	19	390	378	0·80	38
1912–13	1·76	0·17	419	−48	371	386	0·89	39
1913–14	1·87	−0·11	385	34	419	392	0·87	40

See footnotes on the following page.

price and acreage fell and the most venerable assumptions of economics, suggest that the decisions to plant less were in response to the lower prices. This explanation can be tested by measuring the effect of the average price in the harvest year before sowing (X_1)[1] on the acreage (Y), that is by finding the correlation of prices in harvest year T-1 with acreage in year T.[2]

This correlation, r_{Y1}, was 0·89 for the years 1873–1913. It is strong prima facie evidence that the price in the year before

[1] The calendar year price would be inappropriate because most of the wheat in Great Britain is planted in the autumn shortly after the end of the preceding harvest year. The harvest year average price was obtained by taking a simple, i.e. unweighted average of the monthly average prices in *Agricultural Statistics*.

[2] The wheat acreage figures give the acres standing in June of each year. For explanation of official agricultural statistics for Britain see J. A. Venn, *The Foundations of Agricultural Economics* (Cambridge, 1933), p. 432.

---

[1] The harvest year is from 1 September to 31 August. Wheat is planted in the autumn and usually harvested in August.

[2] Wheat acreages are in millions of acres. The figures relate to the acres standing in June. (Board of Agriculture and Fisheries, *Agricultural Statistics*, tables of acreages in the Report for each year, with the exception of the years from 1897–1903, which were taken from p. 124 of the Report for 1903.)

[3] The rate of change in acres. The acres in year T-1 minus the acres in year T. A decrease in acres shows as a plus.

[4] Prices are the average for the previous harvest year expressed in pence per quarter. The price in T-1 is in the same row as acreage in T. (From the Board of Agriculture and Fisheries, *Agricultural Statistics*.)

[5] The rate of change in price. The price in year T-2 minus the price in time T-1. A decrease in price shows as a plus.

[6] Prices are the average for the harvest year two years previous to planting, and are expressed in pence per quarter. The price in T-2 is in the same row as acreage in T.

[7] The average price is a seven-year average, expressed in pence per quarter. It is the average of the calendar year in which the harvest year listed in the same row began, and the preceding six calendar years. The seven-year period price plotted against the 1873–4 harvest year is the average from 1 January 1867 through 31 December 1873. (Board of Agriculture and Fisheries, *Agricultural Statistics*.) The septennial average price was computed and recorded in the official statistics for the determination of the tithe rent charge.

[8] The barley price in time T-1 divided by the wheat price in time T-1. The ratio is in the same row as the harvest year T and the acreage in harvest year T. (Barley prices are from the Board of Agriculture and Fisheries, *Agricultural Statistics*. The harvest year price is a simple average of the monthly prices, except for the 1872 and 1873 harvest years, which were estimated by linear interpolation from the annual totals. The monthly figures were not available for those years.)

[9] Time is used as an independent variable. The origin is taken as the 1873–4 harvest year.

planting was a most important determinant of acreage. It seems that the problem under study is already largely solved. Prices fell, acreage declined: the average price in the harvest year preceding the planting apparently influenced the decisions of most wheat farmers.

The statistics have revealed a convincing correlation, but what have they concealed? Correlation *seems* to point convincingly to cause, though perhaps a third variable dictates both price and acreage, or perhaps the trend of prices *per se* is responsible for the reduction in acreage.

IV THE TREND

Figure I indicates that prices fell drastically and rather persistently from 1873 through 1894, but after 1894 this trend

Figure I

ended and there were fairly large fluctuations from year to year around an average that was constant or perhaps rising slightly. If prices in year T-1 are intrinsically the cause of the acreage changes, and if the 0·89 correlation for r_{Y1} really does explain most of what happened, the correlation of the previous year's price (X_1) with acreage (Y) should be high both in the years before and after 1894, that is X_1 should explain the two distinct parts of the period. But most assuredly it does not. The correlation of X_1 and Y is only 0·37 – not enough to explain more than 14 per cent of the acreage variation – in the years from 1895–1913. There appears to be something misleading about the high correlation between price (X_1) and acreage for the whole period. For the years before 1895 r_{Y1} is 0·88. (The correlation for the last nineteen years is only 0·37, even though the correlations for the first twenty-two years and for the period as a whole are both about 0·9; this is due to the greater variance involved in the steep reduction of prices before 1895.)

Another method of testing the meaningfulness of the r_{Y1} correlation is by taking the correlation of the first differences of the harvest year average prices and acreage. If the price in year T-1 is subtracted from the average price in year T-2, and if the difference is correlated with the change in acreage between year T-1 and year T, the result will be another measure of the influence of the price before planting on acreage. If the direction and magnitude of the price changes in the two years preceding planting help determine whether the farmer plants more or less, it should be reflected in this correlation between first differences in price (X_2) and acreage (y).

Remarkably, the r_{y2} correlation is only 0·22: while prices in year T-1 had a 0·89 correlation with acreage, first differences of price and acreage show a correlation so small as to be trivial.

The incongruity of these results is increased by the fact that when the average prices in harvest year T-2 (X_3) are compared with acreage, the result is a 0·86 correlation. This is further evidence that the impressive r_{Y1} result is deceptive; prices two years before sowing, in isolation from prices in other years, could hardly be the basis for a farmer's decisions about acreage. Moreover, the relationship of the price difference between years T-1 and T-2 and first differences in acreage shows that both r_{Y1} and r_{Y2} do not reflect genuine causal relationships.

An additional reason for doubting the validity of the r_{Y1}

correlation for the part of the period before 1895 is that both the T-1 price (X_1) and acreage (Y) are more highly correlated with time than they are with each other. Time (T) and X_1 show a -0.91 correlation, and acreage and time a -0.94 correlation. The mere passage of time is more closely correlated with acreage than is the price in the previous year, and time *per se* certainly could not have been a cause of the changes in wheat acreage. The partial correlations involving price in year T-1, acreage, and time are also significant. Previous to 1895, r_{Y1} is 0.88 and $r_{Y1.T}$ is only 0.21. After 1894 r_{Y1} is only 0.37, but $r_{Y1.T}$ rises to 0.51. Wheat prices in year T-1 account for less than 5 per cent of the variance in acreage in the early part of the period when the effect of time is accounted for, yet in the latter part of the period when the small correlation between X_T and Y indicates there is no marked trend, the importance of X_1 is enhanced remarkably. All of the relevant partials tell the same tale. (See Table II.)

The parallel movements of Y, X_1, and X_3 then are due to the

TABLE II *Correlations*

	1873–1913	*1873–1894*	*1895–1913*
Simple Correlations			
r_{Y1}	0.89	0.88	0.37
r_{y2}	0.22	0.24	0.03
r_{Y3}	0.86	0.81	0.14
r_{Y4}	0.94	0.91	0.21
r_{Y5}	-0.59	-0.70	-0.47
r_{YT}	-0.88	-0.94	-0.04
r_{14}	0.91	0.92	0.55
r_{15}	1	1	-0.69
r_{1T}	-0.72	-0.91	0.64
r_{45}	-0.53	-0.63	-0.35
Partial Correlations			
$r_{Y1 \cdot T}$	0.71	0.21	0.51
$r_{Y4 \cdot 1}$	0.69	0.53	0.01
$r_{Y4 \cdot 5}$	0.92	0.85	0.05
$r_{Y5 \cdot 1}$	1	1	-0.32
$r_{Y5 \cdot 4}$	-0.30	-0.40	-0.43
Multiple Correlations			
$R_{Y \cdot 45}$	0.95	0.93	1
$R_{Y \cdot 145}$	1	1	0.47

[1] Not computed.

time trend common to all of them. From this one might infer that some other variable was the cause of the variation in these three variables. But study of the period reveals no such variable (imports are the main cause of the lower prices and smaller acreages, of course, but imports affect acreage only through their effect on price).

The lack of some other variable which could explain the movements of acreage and price prompts consideration of the possibility that the price trend *itself* helped to determine acreage. Farmers' decisions were perhaps influenced not so much by the absolute level of price in year T-1 as by the persistent direction of the price movement.

The hypothesis that the trend of prices has intrinsic importance can be studied by correlating a moving average of the prices in some number of years before each planting with the acres planted. (See Figure I.)[1] A fairly long series of years must be chosen or else the two or three year fluctuations will obscure the trend. A seven-year average seems most appropriate.[2] The correlation of the seven-year average price (X_4) with acreage for the years before 1895 is 0·91. In the second part of the period the correlation is only 0·21. The seven-year average

[1] Another way of determining trend values would involve taking the regression of price on time: $P_T = a + bX_T$. The value of P_T for each year would be correlated with acreage. But this is not ideal either, for the values of P_T depend upon which particular series of years is chosen. This means nothing more than that the linear time trend will be different for each time period selected: the trend values which are correlated with acreage will be changed whenever the researcher chooses a different year as the starting point for the trend. The seven-year average method does to some extent avoid the complications that arise from the fact that the historian using a linear trend can select a series of years to suit his argument.

Perhaps the best method of getting the trend values to correlate with acreage would entail taking a separate linear regression of price on time for the series of seven years preceding each planting. That is, the $P_T = a + bX_T$ equation that would be relevant to the year 1885 is that from 1877 to 1884, while that suitable for the farmers' 1886 planting would involve the years 1878–85. Obviously this method is too costly. Though the seven year average does not give a linear trend it does decline in all but two years between 1873 and 1895, and shows a high correlation with acreage during this time of rapidly falling prices. This is evidence for the importance of trend.

[2] The choice of seven years for the moving average is partly for convenience. The seven-year average was computed by the government to assess tithes. The seven-year average has the further advantage that it was published and made known to many British farmers in that day.

is very important when the trend is sharply downward, but accounts for less than 5 per cent of the variation in acreage when the trend is horizontal or rising slightly. This high correlation between X_4 and Y supports the thesis that the trend of prices was itself a factor affecting acreage in the years before 1895.

It would sometimes be rational for a farmer to decide what wheat acreage to plant on the basis of his knowledge of the trend of prices. It is the price at harvest time which determines the farmer's income, so he must, if rational, project *some* price ten months ahead when he decides how much to plant. What would be more natural to expect than that the farmer, in some rough and ready way, would project the trend? Or weight last year's price less heavily than the trend in his estimate of next year's price? If a farmer does in fact consider what has been happening to prices – the trend – when he decides how much to plant, it follows that he would plant less at any given T-1 price if prices had been falling for a long time, than he would have planted at that same T-1 price if prices had been at about a constant level for some time.[1]

V BARLEY–WHEAT PRICE RATIO

The ratio of the barley price to the wheat price in harvest year T-1 is an important variable, as barley is the producer's closest substitute for wheat. The farmer can change from wheat to barley with little or no outlay for new equipment. Oats would also be a good substitute, except that they are used mainly as a feed, and to make the growing of oats profitable many farmers would have felt they needed to invest in livestock. Since the ratio here expresses the barley price divided by the wheat price, when the ratio gets larger there is an incentive for the farmer to change to barley.[2] The ratio varies significantly, the extremes being 0·66 and 1·03.

[1] This, of course, assumes that the farmers do not expect quick and sizeable changes in costs. Since costs were very stable *by comparison* with prices, this is a reasonable assumption.

[2] The ratio of the two prices was used instead of the difference between them because at high prices a particular difference might make it profitable to plant wheat, but at low prices the same absolute difference might be consistent with barley being the better alternative: the absolute difference between the two prices has meaning only in relation to the absolute level of the two prices.

The correlations of the barley–wheat price ratio and wheat acreage are quite significant: -0.59 for the whole period, -0.70 in the first part, and -0.47 in the last part. These correlations are what should have been expected. When the wheat price fell relative to the barley price, the ratio became larger, and wheat acreage decreased.

Again the correlation is highest for the period before 1895. This is largely due to the fact that in the earlier part of the period wheat prices fell more precipitously than barley prices, and the ratio became greater during the years of the most striking reductions in wheat acreage. As a measure of the causal relationships the r_{Y5} correlation before 1895 is somewhat misleading. When a partial correlation is taken holding the trend factor 'constant', that is when the effect of the moving average (X_4) is taken out, the importance of X_5 is much reduced; the partial correlation $r_{Y5.4}$ is -0.40 before 1895. After 1894, on the other hand, the correlation between X_5 and Y is not significantly reduced when X_4's effects are excluded; $r_{Y5.4}$ is -0.43 in the later years.

These partials, in combination with other results, strengthen somewhat the argument that the trend has special importance. The best measure of factors other than trend influencing price is X_5; its correlation with acreage in the first part of the period is much reduced when trend is held 'constant', but this is not the case for the second part of the period, i.e. the roughly horizontal movement of the seven-year average price does not reduce the importance of X_5 significantly after 1894.

It will be remembered that the r_{Y5} correlation was -0.47 after 1894. This is distinctly higher than any of the other correlations that were tried for this part of the period; X_1 is a poor second with a 0.37 correlation, and X_4, which in other years explained almost all of the variance in Y, is only 0.21. Moreover, X_5 is not reduced materially by holding other factors constant in the years after 1894, as was explained above. These facts point to the conclusion that the price ratio is an important variable. It seems that, but for the severity of the downward trend before 1895, which made farmers abandon wheat in favour of grass (or letting the land 'tumble down' to weeds) and other crops as well as barley, the price ratio would have been the most important variable for all of the years between 1873 and 1913. The importance of X_5 after 1894, and the fact that it is often easy for farmers to switch from one crop to another, suggest that it is by no means always helpful to use Marshallian analysis in its simplest, most 'partial' sense in studying supply responses and prices for particular grain crops. It is often only by using price ratios, or other methods which allow simultaneous consideration of more than two variables, that realistic analysis is possible. Yet it is often the case that the supply of wheat is considered without explicit consideration of the prices of any substitute crops.

VI THE MODELS

The multiple regression equation that appears to be best for the period as a whole includes only the seven-year average price (X_4) and the ratio of barley and wheat prices (X_5); between these two variables almost all of the variance in acreage is explained. The collinearity between X_4 and X_5 is by no means intolerable.

Wheat prices in year T-1 will not be included in the model for the entire period because the r_{Y1} correlation is misleading, and because X_4 has a higher correlation with Y than does X_1, and the r_{14} collinearity is too great for the two to be used together. It would obviously be inappropriate to include X_3 and X_2 in the multiple regression equation.

The regression equation using X_4 and X_5 is:

$$Y = 0.97 + 0.0043X_4 - 0.77X_5.[1]$$

[1] This equation, involving a time series, is of course strictly correct only on the assumption that the error terms in the regression equation are uncorrelated, i.e. that the residuals in $Y^i = a + bX^i + u^i$ are not serially correlated. Several of the regressions in this paper have been tested using Von Neuman's ratio and the Durbin and Watson tables (*Biometrika*, June 1951, p. 175) at the 1 per cent significance level. It was found that the ratio was slightly below the lower limit for the simple regressions (for the whole period and the first part of the period) involving X_4, and in the range of indeterminacy using X_5. However, the highest serial correlation in any of the three equations was only 0.52. The accuracy of the test used to assess the seriousness of the serial correlation is debatable, and there is no indication of the true relationship of the residuals (e.g. no basis for assuming that $u_T = u_{T-1} + v_T$ where v_T is not correlated), so it is doubtful that there is any serious error here due to serial correlation or that there is any better method that could have been used. In any event the estimates are not biased.

The multiple correlation coefficient is 0·95: about 89 per cent of the variance in acreage is explained by these two variables. The simple correlation between X_4 and Y is 0·94, almost as high. The standard error of estimate is essentially the same for the simple as for the multiple correlation. This means that as a model for estimating Y the simple regression model was about as good as the model using both X_4 and X_5. The simple regression equation is:

$$Y = 0·19 + 0·0047X_4.$$

It would have been possible to have removed the linear trend from the b coefficients in all of these regression equations by using either of the following methods: (1) $y' = a' + b_4x'_4 + b'_5x'_5$ where x'_4, x'_5 and y' are deviations from the linear trend, that is $x_i' = X_i - a - b_TX_T$ and $y' = Y - a - b_TX_T$, or (2) $Y = a + b_TX_T + b_4X_4 + b_5X_5$. The value of the b coefficients are the same in both methods, i.e., $b_4 = b'_4$ and $b_5 = b'_5$.[1] But neither method would have been of much use here; the 'time element' should be included in the b coefficients. Any b values determined for this period after elimination of the trend will not be appropriate in other periods.

The same model which was used for the whole period seems best for the earlier part. The correlations for the earlier years of the period are usually much the same as those for the period as a whole because the largest variances are in the early years, and they are the dominant influence on the results for the whole period. The multiple regression model for the years before 1895 is:

$$Y = 1·59 + 0·0038X_4 - 1·15X_5.$$

The multiple correlation coefficient is 0·93, while the correlation of X_4 alone with Y is practically the same, 0·91. The standard error of estimate for the multiple regression is 0·21, while for the simple regression equation it is 0·22. The model using only X_4 is:

$$Y = 0·31 + 0·0045X_4.$$

[1] For proof see R. Frisch and F. V. Waugh, 'Partial time regressions as compared with individual time trends', *Econometrica*, I (1933), 387 ff.

For the latter part of the period it seems wise to include the variable X_1, wheat prices in year T-1. The problem of collinearity is not so great. Here X_1 can be in the equation without excluding X_4; their correlation for this part of the period is 0·55 – uncomfortably high, but far better than the figure of 0·91 for the whole period. Moreover, the partial correlations indicate that X_1 may here have some of the genuine influence that prices before planting are usually presumed to have. The correlation r_{Y1} is only 0·37, though when time (T) is 'held constant' the correlation rises: $r_{Y1 \cdot T}$ is 0·51. On the other hand, the correlation between first differences of (X_2 and y) was even smaller in the latter part of the period than it was when all the years studied were considered together.

The normal equations were solved by the Fisher–Doolittle method. The resulting equation is:

$$Y = 2·35 + 0·0028X_1 + 0·00017X_4 - 0·86X_5.$$

This multiple correlation, R_{Y145}, is 0·471. It is no improvement over the highest simple correlation, r_{Y5}, which is −0·465. The simple regression equation for X_5 is:

$$Y = 2·62 - 0·99X_5.$$

There is no significant difference between the standard errors of the two regressions.

It is interesting if not surprising to note that while a high proportion of the variance was explained in the first part of the period and only a small percentage was accounted for in the second part, the regression analysis in the second part gives a greater accuracy of estimate. The multiple regression equation for the years before 1895 had a standard error of estimate of 0·21, but in the latter part of the period the standard error was 0·17. Of course, different Y's are being compared; there is less variance in the later years.

VII THE RELATIONSHIP OF REGRESSION LINES AND FUNCTION ELASTICITIES

The next problem is to determine what information the regression lines give about the economic history of the period.

While the foregoing regressions relate prices and quantities (acreage is a tolerable indication of the quantity of wheat farmers intend to supply), it would be wrong to think of them as supply functions. A supply function shows the relation between price and the intentions to sell when all other things are held constant, but these regression lines, covering as many as forty-one years, reflect the effects of factors like technical change and movements in factor costs.

In a very interesting article[1] Professor W. W. Cochrane contends that the idea of the 'response relation' is often more useful than the supply function concept. The 'response relation' is the *actual* relationship between price and quantity during a particular period: unlike the supply function it does not require the heroic *ceteris paribus* assumption. It is based on the recognition that the units in the functions are often the largest part of the story. It does seem to be true that the response relation would generally be the most useful for historical research: it tells us (in Ranke's words about the purpose of the history) 'what really happened'.

Cochrane then offers the thesis that the response relation is more elastic in periods of rising prices than in periods of falling prices. His rationale is that during a period of rising prices farmers will have the capital and confidence to invest in new equipment, thus increasing output, but when prices are falling they will treat the expense that has been incurred on this equipment as a fixed cost, and continue to use the new production function. The data, already divided into a phase of declining prices and a series of years in which prices (though showing no distinct trend) rose slightly, can easily be used to test this contention. The regression lines of X and Y reveal that for the first part of the period the elasticity was 1·6 while for the latter part it was 1·9.[2] The thesis seems to be confirmed.

In fact, the question is much more complicated. Price–quantity regression lines are derived from the points of intersection of the different supply and demand functions during a

---

[1] 'Conceptualizing the supply relation in agriculture', *Journal of Farm Economics*, XXVII (December 1955), 1161.

[2] The elasticity was computed at the point of means. $E = dY/dX_1 \cdot \bar{X}_1/\bar{Y}$ where dY/dX_1 is the reciprocal of the b coefficient in the regression $X_1 = a + bY$.

particular period. The price–quantity regression lines could not be computed but for the fact that the true demand and supply functions were shifting. Only if the true supply function were constant during the whole period, while the demand function shifted, could an ordinary regression line represent a supply function. If the demand schedule shifts farther than the supply function, the regression line is likely to have a positive slope; conversely, larger shifts in the supply function will tend to create a regression line with a negative slope.[1] It follows that generalizations about the elasticity of the regression lines (i.e. statistically derived response relations) are usually meaningless.[2]

The elasticity of a supply function can be determined if the size and direction of the shifts in the supply schedule can be specified. That this is sometimes acutely difficult is evidenced by the paucity of reliable estimates of the supply function. Statistical virtuosity can succeed in solving the 'identification problem', but only by using additional data or making further assumptions. It seems impossible to determine the elasticity of supply with precision in the case at hand, for there is not sufficiently accurate data on the factors which would cause the supply curve to shift. The shifts in the supply schedule depend on several factors, like changes in factor costs, the prices of other commodities the farmer might produce and the extent of technical change.

The data clearly do not allow any reliable estimates of the exact size of the movements in the supply function; the most that can be done is to determine the direction of the shifts.

[1] An example of a study which neglects to draw an adequate distinction between a price-quantity regression line and a supply function is provided by B. J. Bowlen, 'The wheat supply function', *Journal of Farm Economics*, XXXVII (December 1955), 1177.

[2] Cochrane's emphasis on the response relation is still in order. The point here concerns the pitfalls of statistical measurement of the elasticity of the response relation. It can still be most useful to study a response relation in a particular situation as a source of information about the price-quantity points themselves. The thought that in some sense the supply response will usually be more elastic in times of rising prices is still plausible, though it is best stated in terms of a tendency for the supply function to shift to the right when prices rise. Finally, Cochrane's application of his concepts to the case of aggregate food supply is not affected, for his assumption is that in the years chosen the supply function for food did not shift significantly.

It is, for example, impossible to say at exactly what rate technical change proceeded on British farms.

Nihilism might seem to be the only justifiable attitude about the elasticity of the supply curve. *But in fact, extremely useful conclusions can be drawn from the logic of the relationship between the supply functions and the regression line.* Examine the representation of the regression line of X and Y for the years from 1873 through 1894 (Figure IIA). The earlier years of the period, when price and acreage were highest, are represented by the

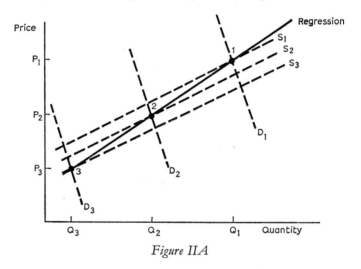

Figure IIA

upper portion of the regression line, while the years just before 1895 take up that part of the regression line nearest the origin. Assume that the intersection of the demand and supply functions for the very earliest years of the period is represented by point 1, while points 2 and 3 are examples of the points of intersection of demand and supply functions in the eighties and early nineties respectively. It is clear (for reasons discussed below) that the supply schedule shifted to the right. *But with the supply schedule shifting to the right, it is impossible to have the supply functions cutting the regression line from the bottom. The supply functions must be more elastic than the regression line, which has an elasticity of 1·6.* This is obvious from the fact that any supply function through point 3 which has a steeper slope

than the regression line must be to the left of any supply
function drawn through points 1 or 2: only if all three of the
supply functions have elasticities greater than the regression
line could they have shifted to the right. It is obvious, too,
that the demand curve shifted to the left, for prices fell.

The same logic could be used whatever the slope of the regression line. If the regression line had the negative slope of a
demand curve (as in Figure IIB) and prices had been falling,

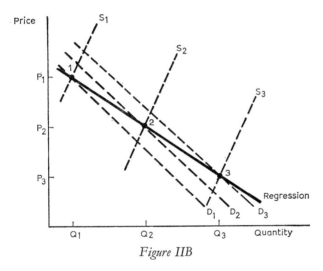

Figure IIB

it would follow that the supply function had shifted to the
right. Moreover, in almost any practical case the direction of
the demand shift would be evident, so it would be simple to
describe the relationship between the regression lines and the
demand functions: if demand had shifted to the left, it would
have to be more elastic than the regression line, while the demand curve would have to be less elastic than the regression
line if there had been an increase in the amount demanded at
every price. If price had risen the converse would follow. The
argument just developed holds whether the supply functions
are curved or straight, so long as each curve does not have
more than one point of intersection with the regression line.[1]

[1] This is possible, but unlikely, in the present case. But even if the supply
functions do intersect the regression line more than once, it still follows that the

The conclusion from the logic of the function–regression relationship, then, is that it is overwhelmingly likely that the supply function had in general an elasticity greater than 1·6.

This conclusion is based on the vital, but unexceptionable, premise that the supply curve shifted to the right. One thing causing the rightward shifts was technological advance. The twenty-two years considered were roughly the ones in which the reaper and binder came into fairly general use in Great Britain. There were improvements in the methods of seeding and threshing wheat, and chemical fertilizers were beginning to be used. The old-fashioned Norfolk four course rotation was being abandoned.[1] Several writers give evidence which implies that the rate of technological advance was, however, less than it had been in the preceding decades,[2] and this seems reasonable, for the price collapse must have reduced the marginal efficiency of investment, and left farmers without the capital or confidence necessary to rapid progress.

Colin Clark's index (in 'international units') of output per man hour in agriculture in the United Kingdom indicates that between 1870–6 and 1886–93, output increased by about 13 per cent. E. M. Ojala finds that product per worker increased by 8 per cent.[3] It seems that Ojala's index shows the smaller gain in productivity largely because his figures are net of the

---

supply function is quite elastic for some distance near the regression line, for a curve obviously could not intersect the regression line twice without having a flatter slope than the regression line somewhere between the two intersections.

Another minor exception is that supply-demand intersections are not on the regression line, but clustered around it, so every supply function need not be more elastic than the regression line. Any statistical estimate of a supply function is subject to criticism on the ground that there are some observations which are a distance away from the line. Any such criticism against the results here is weakened by the high correlation. It should still be true with but infrequent exceptions that the supply functions had an elasticity greater than the regression line.

[1] Two contemporary French writers testified to a considerable technological improvement in British agriculture. See A. Dulac, *L'Agriculture et le libre-echange dans le Royaume Uni* (Paris, 1903); and Pierre Besse, *La Crise et l'évolution de l'agriculture en Angleterre de 1875 à nos jours* (Paris, 1910), pp. 173–91.

[2] W. B. Wall, 'The agriculture of Pembrokeshire', *Journal of the Royal Agricultural Society* (1887), pp. 83, 86; C. Whitehead, 'A sketch of the agriculture of Kent', ibid., 1899, p. 456; A. D. Hall, *Agriculture After the War* (1916); and J. H. Clapham, *An Economic History of Modern Britain*, III, Book IV, chapter 2.

[3] Clark, *Conditions of Economic Progress* (London, 1957), p. 269. Ojala, *Agriculture and Economic Progress* (London: Oxford, 1952), p. 153.

effects of increased purchases of non-farm inputs like fertilizer and machinery, and because he assumed no change in the number of hours worked per person. Presumably the increases in the efficiency of wheat production were not radically different from those in the rest of agriculture, and so technological improvement must have been tending to make the wheat supply function shift to the right.[1]

Moreover, factor costs decreased somewhat between 1873 and 1895, and this meant (*ceteris paribus*) that farmers would have wanted to plant more wheat at any given price. It was the time of the 'Great Depression', and the costs of the things farmers had to buy were decreasing; the Sauerbeck–Statist index of commodity prices shows that the general level of commodity prices declined from 121 in 1870–6 to 84 in 1886–93.[2] It is likely that the cost of most of the things farmers needed for their business decreased with the general price level, though probably not in the same proportion. Rents, a large item in costs, were lower in 1894 than they had been in 1873. (While rents would be considered a fixed cost to the tenant in the short run, and a change in rent would accordingly have no influence on the optimum output, a change in rents would affect a farmer's 'long-run' decisions, e.g. his decisions about whether or not to continue farming. Because most rental contracts were for periods of up to twenty-one years, land rents, in the popular sense of the word, were not determined by price in the short run.) Between 1870–6 and 1886–93, rents in England and Wales decreased by 24 per cent, according to Rhee's index of rents.[3] *The Report of the Royal Commission on Land in Wales* holds that English and Welsh rents dropped

[1] The data on yields give no unambiguous information on changes in the production function for wheat. While yields increased from 24·7 bushels per acre during the harvest years 1873–9 to an average yield of 29·3 bushels from 1885–94, the inclement weather of the late seventies must have been an important factor. From 1853–73 the yield was 28·2 bushels per acre, only a little less than the figure for 1885–94. Any changes in yields must be explained partly by the tendency for the poorer land to be abandoned when acreage is reduced. From 1894 until World War I yields rose considerably. (The data for the years after 1885 are from *Agricultural Statistics*, while figures for before 1880 come from the estimates of J. B. Lawes and J. H. Gilbert, 'On the home produce, imports and consumption, and price of wheat', *Journal of the Statistical Society*, June, 1880, pp. 313–40.)

[2] Ojala, op. cit., p. 146.   [3] Ojala, op. cit., p. 216.

22·6 per cent between 1878 and 1893, while Scotch rents were said to fall 18·5 per cent.[1] Though the exact amount of the fall in rents cannot be determined, there can be no question that they were reduced somewhat. In that day of Henry George and Joseph Chamberlain people were sensitive to the advantages of the landlord's position, and there was much criticism of the rent takers.

A possible exception to the generalization that factor costs fell seems to be the case of labour, but again the data do not allow precise measurement. An index computed by Ojala shows a very slight but steady increase in farm wages in the years before 1894.[2] Other evidence makes it seem that farm labourer's wages sank in the late seventies and early eighties, but had risen again by 1891.[3] Though wages probably rose measurably, it is patent that this could not have negated the several other factors pushing the supply curve in the other direction.

The price of other commodities the farmer might have produced declined, though not by as much as wheat prices. Agricultural prices in general fell by about a third between 1873 and 1894.[4] As the previous discussion of the wheat–barley price ratio indicates, the price of the closest substitute to wheat decreased considerably. Even though the price of wheat fell more precipitously than the prices of other products, it still paid the farmers to plant more wheat, in response to any particular wheat price, than if the prices of other commodities had remained constant or risen slightly. So there was in the prices of alternatives yet another influence causing the supply functions to move to the right.

[1] King's College, Cambridge, has in its 'Mundum book' figures showing that the net receipts from the college lands in thirteen counties (with an above average proportion of land in corn) dropped by 38·9 per cent between 1878 and 1893. (J. H. Clapham, op. cit., II, 283.) Paradoxically, the assets of King's College were later to be much augmented by the speculation of a famous Bursar noted as an advocate of 'euthanasia of the rentier'.

[2] Op. cit., p. 138. His index is constructed from data in the *Nineteenth Abstract of Labour Statistics for the United Kingdom* and J. J. Macgregor, 'Labour costs in British forestry since 1824', *Forestry*, XX (1946).

[3] W. C. Little's report to the Royal Commission on Labour (1893–4), XXVII, Part 2, p. 44.

[4] Ojala shows three separate indices, all of which show a drop of about this amount. Op. cit., p. 146.

Accordingly, the conclusion that in general the supply functions between 1873 and 1894 had an elasticity greater than 1·6 seems almost as inescapable as it is surprising. (The elasticity of supply for wheat in the United States during recent times is widely, and probably justifiably, thought to be extremely inelastic.)[1]

The fact that the elasticity of supply, at least before 1895, was startlingly high, is only part of the story of the supply relationship. In conditions of uncertainty there are two elements in the farmer's reaction to a change in price: one is the way a price change affects his estimate of the harvest price, the other is the extent of his response to the estimated price. Since different price changes affect estimates of the harvest price differently, the response of quantity to prices is affected by whether, and in what way, the farmer thinks a particular price change gives a guide to the harvest price. The conclusions in this paper about the importance of the trend in farmers' decisions before 1895, the relative unimportance of year to year changes in price, and the causal importance of the wheat–barley price ratio tell more about the relation of price and quantity than the elasticity of supply does. There were conclusions about which price changes caused most of the movement in acreage, and about when and how British farmers responded to price changes before a supply function was mentioned, and before any regression lines had been determined. This shows that the correlation coefficient can often be as useful as the regression line in the study of the supply relationship.

---

[1] It was probably also the case that the supply functions shifted to the right in the years after 1894. If this is true, and the elasticity of 1·9 for the X and Y regression line is correct, it would follow that the elasticity of supply is even greater, and probably above 2, in the later years of the period. But with the much less impressive correlations for the years after 1894, this conclusion seems incautious; there is not enough correlation behind the regression line to justify confidence in the measure of its elasticity.

The elasticities of the regression lines relate the percentage change in price in the year before planting (X_1) to the percentage change in acreage. Earlier in this paper it was shown that the average annual prices were not the most important influence on acreage. This illustrates a problem in the concept of price elasticity: if the distribution of prices over time – the direction in which prices have been moving – also affects supply decisions, it is not altogether correct to speak of the elasticity of supply as a measure of the change in quantity prompted by the price before planting.

VIII CONCLUSIONS

It was not until 1873 that British farmers were faced with sharply falling prices. Contrary to the expectations of 1846, the free trade policy did not bring an immediate collapse of prices. But from 1873 until 1894 prices dropped precipitously, and British wheat production fell by about 60 per cent.

The principle of the relationship between regression lines and supply functions indicates that the elasticity of the supply functions in the years from 1873 through 1894 must have been generally greater than 1·6. This surprisingly high elasticity suggests that the substitution between wheat and other products the farmer might raise was fairly rapid. That the substitution between wheat and barley was particularly important is suggested by the close correlation between the wheat–barley price ratio and the acreage of wheat. This was also the case after 1894 when the ratio of wheat to barley prices appeared to be the most important causal variable. It is probable that the substitution between wheat and other products was easier in Great Britain than it is in many other wheat growing areas, such as the American Great Plains. With relatively ample rainfall and nearness to large markets, the British wheat grower had a larger range of alternatives than wheat farmers in most semi-arid areas. In many countries wheat is grown on land which is too dry for barley, but this is not the case in Great Britain. Another factor making for the surprisingly high elasticity of supply was the fact that in those days farmers had very little expensive, specialized equipment, and could probably switch from one product to another without great cost.

The main substantive conclusions of this paper concern the way farmers formed their estimates of the harvest price. In the first part of the period it seems clear that farmers did not expect that the price at harvest time would be the same as the price before planting. Among the evidences in support of this claim is the absence of any correlation between year to year changes in prices and year to year changes in acreage (that is, first differences in average annual prices and acreages). Farmers seemed to have thought instead that the downward trend of prices would continue. One of the arrows pointing to this conclusion (see Section IV) is the very high correlation between the average price in the seven years before planting, and acreage.[1] Farmers must have concentrated their attention on whether or not prices had on the average been falling over the last several years, and given scant attention to the smaller movements affecting the price at the time of planting. The average price in the seven years before planting was not thought of as the expected price, but when the average of past prices fell, as it almost always did from 1873 to 1895, the farmer extrapolated generally poor prospects for wheat production.

Thus price expectations, and the factors that affect them, are often vital to an understanding of a market. And sometimes expectations about prices several years hence may be important. Wheat is often planted on fallow only, and a decision about wheat acreage may require an adjustment in the rotation that must be planned two or more years in advance. Similarly when a farmer buys machinery, or decides whether or not to switch from wheat to livestock, it is the price expectations for future years that are relevant.

After 1894 the effect of price on acreage was much less distinct: the best correlation explained only one-quarter of the variation in acreage. Farmers must have felt, when prices were fluctuating considerably and there was no discernible trend, that past prices did not give a reliable basis for predicting the price that would prevail at the time of the next harvest. When the harvest price is more difficult to predict, it is natural that non-price factors, like the difficulty of changing rotations, the habits of the entrepreneur and institutional rigidities (e.g. leases which dictated the maximum or minimum acreage that could be planted to wheat) should be more important.[2]

[1] Costs, in comparison with prices, were quite stable, and so prices give a good indication of the profit margin.

[2] The statistical orientation of this paper is not meant to imply that only quantitative factors were significant. The nature of the leasing arrangements, for example, was a crucial factor. When the price collapse began many tenants had contracts which bound them to pay a fixed money rent each year for the duration of the contract, which was at times as long as twenty-one years. Rents were reduced by some landlords before the expiration of the lease, but the burden of fixed charges, assumed when prices were high, bore heavily on many tenants.

The differences among regions are also concealed in a study of the statistical aggregates. On the whole the adaptation to the price collapse was faster in the

The contrast between the two parts of the period indicates the need for the study of an aspect of the supply relationship which is generally overlooked: the manner in which price
changes affect the farmer's estimate of the price at harvest time.
The elasticity of supply seems to have been greater after 1894
than it was before, yet it would not be correct to say that the
effect of price on acreage was greater, or that price was causally
more important, in the latter part of the period. Since farmers
did not feel that past prices gave an adequate basis for predicting harvest prices in the years after 1894, they did not
respond in any regular manner. It can be very misleading to
think of the elasticity of supply without making a distinction
between the way a particular price change affects the estimate
of the harvest price and the response of quantity to price when
the harvest price is known. Thus another dimension of the
supply relationship comes into view. A different reaction should
be expected when there is a change in the price support level
than when there is a change in free market prices.

Here the analysis is directly relevant to the arguments among
economists about 'forward prices' for agriculture; if prices at
planting time, or in the years before, do not provide an adequate indication of the price at harvest time, presumably prices
are not functioning properly as guides for resource allocation,
and some system of guaranteed prices would be useful. On
the other hand, when harvest prices are predicted from the
trend with a fair degree of accuracy, then forward prices (that
is, estimates of the equilibrium price guaranteed for a year or
two in advance of the harvest) could not bring much improvement in resource allocation.[1]

---

west of England than in the east. In the west the land was poorer for grain, and
farmers turned to livestock more quickly. The growing demand for garden
products made the adaptation more rapid near larger cities. Observers in those
days often suggested that the Scots moving to English farms were an important
factor in the adjustment of the lower prices. The claim was that the Scots,
parsimonious and accustomed to raising oats and livestock rather than wheat,
were able to prosper when most of the English farmers could not.

These and other qualitative factors are discussed, albeit with some misinter-
pretation, by Pierre Besse, op. cit., and by Raymond Phineas Stearns, 'Agricultural adaptation in England, 1875–1900', *Agricultural History*, VI, Nos. 2 and 3
(1932).

[1] See D. Gale Johnson's *Forward Prices for Agriculture* (University of Chicago
Press, 1947), chapter 6. Johnson lists several bases on which a farmer might

The adaptation to the lower prices was fundamental and far-reaching. The reduction in the amount of wheat produced was a major factor in the decline of the whole agricultural sector. France and Germany imposed tariffs which gave their farmers some protection against the collapse in world agricultural prices. Britain is now the most urban or industrialized of all countries, partly because of her agricultural policy in the late nineteenth century. The ramifications of these *laissez faire* policies extended even to the political and social structure. The anciently important landed gentry and the country clergy lost a measure of their power and prestige.[1]

Britain's persistence in *laissez faire* policies at the price of a devastated agriculture is unique in the history of nations. Yet the problems discussed here have been at most cursorily treated by historians. From the attention lavished on the repeal of the Corn Laws one might assume that all that was important in

---

predict prices: (1) he may project the current price into the future, (2) he may project the price trend, (3) he may assume that the future price will be the same as the 'normal' price, which is the long-term average price, (4) or that the future price will be somewhere between the present price and the 'normal' price, (5) he may choose some particular past price (say a war or drought year price) and use it to predict the future price, (6) he may use complex statistical techniques, or follow the advice of those who do. Model number 1 on Johnson's list – the one so often taken for granted by economists – does not fit the facts of British agricultural history in the period covered by this paper; the continuation-of-trend hypothesis appears to be best for the years before 1895, and in the later part of the period no one hypothesis describes the facts adequately. Johnson finds that in the United States between 1910 and 1943 a mechanical projection of trend (model 2) gave less reliable forecasts of prices than models 1, 3 or 4. There is no conflict with the results in this paper, however, for Johnson's trend model was the assumption that 'the price next year will bear the same relationship to this year's price as this year's price did to last year's' (p. 81, footnote to Table 7). A trend over two years is naturally much less reliable than one which has continued over, say, seven years. Moreover, it is not the contention in this paper that farmers always project the trend of prices; it is obvious that they did not do this after 1894. The point is that when the trend is 'distinct', i.e. whenever there is an easily discernible direction to the movement of prices, farmers are apt to project the trend. Finally, Johnson compared the accuracy of the models for prediction; nothing definite can be deduced from his figures about what model(s) American farmers actually did use.

[1] Another aspect of the repeal of the Corn Laws which needs study is the hardship imposed on those who had to bear the burden of the adjustments, but this is beyond the scope of this paper. Some farmers, though lacking the facile mobility assumed in economic models, had to change occupation and domicile in the interests of the rest of the economy. The policies which were adopted to ameliorate the difficulties arising from the adjustment were only placebos.

British agriculture ended in 1846. But it would be more appropriate to say that the downfall of British agriculture began, not in 1846, but in 1873. The common concern of economic historians with the politics of the repeal of the Corn Laws has brought neglect of the economic developments themselves. The goal of this paper, aside from the purely statistical development, is to redress the balance and explain this most crucial part of the story of the decline of British agriculture.

Glossary of Technical Terms

Bimetallism: A monetary system in which gold and silver are on precisely the same footing in their role as legal tender. This system, putting silver in the same position as gold, was sometimes suggested as a remedy for the depression in agriculture and also for economic depression generally.

Covenants: Clauses – in the lease under which a tenant farmer occupied his land – which restricted his freedom of choice of farming system, for example how often cereal crops might be grown.

Distress (distraint): The seizure of goods for debt. In the case of rent the landlord had, during the period of the depression, a preferential claim over other creditors.

Fatstock: Sheep, cattle or pigs, sold in a condition suitable for immediate slaughter by the butcher.

High farming: Any system of farming based on high levels of investment as the basis for high returns. More specifically the intensive and highly integrated arable and livestock husbandry which was regarded as the best and the most typical farming of lowland Britain in the 1850s and 1860s.

Primogeniture: Inheritance, usually with respect to land, by the eldest son, as opposed to the practice, common in parts of Europe, of equal division among heirs. (See also settled lands.)

Settled lands: Real property (most commonly land) subject to a family settlement whereby the owner possesses only the rights of a tenant in order that the succession of the property within the family (usually through eldest male heirs) may be ensured. The subject is one of extreme complexity.

Store stock: Sheep, cattle or pigs, sold in a condition requiring fattening before they become suitable for slaughter.

Tenant right: The right of the tenant farmer to compensation for certain classes of improvement of a lasting (but not usually permanent) kind which he has made, and which still exist at the time of his giving up the tenancy. Drains and the unexhausted effects of artificial fertilizers are examples of matters where tenant right may exist. Until 1883 tenant right had little legal (but in some cases considerable customary) protection; from 1883 it was defined by Acts of Parliament.

Tithe rent charge: The manner of payment of tithe, the taxation of one tenth of all agricultural produce in support of the church, after the Tithe Commutation Acts of 1836–60. The amount payable was related to the seven-yearly average of corn prices and thus fluctuated, but less markedly than corn prices; until 1891 the responsibility for payment lay with the occupier of the land, thereafter it was the responsibility of the landowner.

Unexhausted improvements: Lasting (but not usually permanent) improvements made by a tenant farmer and still effective at the end of the tenancy. (See tenant right.)

Select Bibliography

This bibliography lists firstly important scholarly writings on the problems of British agriculture in the last quarter of the nineteenth century which have not been included in this volume; and secondly a small number of contemporary books and essays (the *British Parliamentary Papers* excepted) on these same problems. The first selection – it can be no more – is made necessary by the limited compass of this book; the second is made in the hope that at least a few readers will be stimulated to further exploration, and by the fact that, at least in Britain, apparently obscure items are in fact often readily obtainable in public libraries.

(i) *Recent Scholarship*

ASTOR, VISCOUNT, and ROWNTREE, B.S., *British Agriculture: the Principles of Future Policy* (London, Pelican, 1939), chapter 3.

Socialist League (Norwich Branch)   March 23 1889

On Saturday last Mrs Schack and H. Banner arrived from
London and spent an enjoyable evening with the members at
Gordon Hall. Songs - recitations. Sunday morning Mrs Schack,
Banner and Sutton attended a Demonstration in Yarmouth which was
very successful. In the afternoon a large meeting commemorative
of the commune held in Norwich Market. Comrade Poynts moved
the resolution of sympathy to the workmen of Paris
In the evening another large open-air meeting addressed by
Poynts at Dereham. The Gordon Hall Meeting opened by singing the
Marst. Dereham. Mrs Schack and Adams spoke in the evening
After singing revolutionary songs, sat a late hour they sung
the Marseillaise.

BEASTALL, T. W., 'A south Yorkshire estate in the late nineteenth century', *Agricultural History Review*, XIV(1) (1966), pp. 40–4.

FUSSELL, G. E., *The English Dairy Farmer 1500–1900* (London, Cass, 1966).

GAVIN, SIR W., *Ninety Years of Family Farming* (London, Huchinson, 1967). A history of a famous group of farms in northern Essex, chapters 5–7.

ORWIN, C. S. and WHETHAM, E. H., *History of British Agriculture 1846–1914* (London, Longmans, 1964), chapters 9–13.

OXLEY PARKER, J. (Ed.), *The Oxley Parker Papers* (Colchester, Benham, 1964).

PERRY, P. J. and JOHNSTON, R. J., 'The temporal and spatial incidence of agricultural depression in Dorset 1868–1902', *Journal of Interdisciplinary History*, III (1972), pp. 297–311.

RUSSELL, SIR, E. J., *A History of Agricultural Science in Great Britain* (London, Allen and Unwin, 1966), chapter 6.

SMITH, E. LORRAIN, *Go East for a Farm: A Study of Rural Migration* (Oxford, Agricultural Economics Research Institute, 1932).

SYMON, J. A., *Scottish Farming Past and Present* (Edinburgh, Oliver and Boyd, 1959), chapter 12.

THOMPSON, F. M. L., 'Agriculture since 1870', *Victoria History of the County of Wiltshire*, IV (London, 1959), pp. 92–114.

THOMPSON, F. M. L., *English Landed Society in the Nineteenth Century* (London, Routledge, 1963), chapter 11.

TROW-SMITH, R., *A History of British Livestock Husbandry 1700–1900* (London, Routledge, 1959), chapters 8–10.

WHETHAM, E. H., 'The London milk trade 1860–1900', *Economic History Review*, XVII (1964–5), pp. 369–80.

WHETHAM, E. H., 'The changing cattle enterprise of England and Wales 1870–1910', *Geographical Journal*, CXXIX (1963), pp. 379–80.

(ii) *Contemporary Comment*

BEAR, W., 'The agricultural problem', *Economic Journal*, III (1893), pp. 391–407 and 569–83.

BEDFORD, DUKE OF, *The Story of a Great Agricultural Estate* (London, Murray, 1897).

CAIRD, SIR J., 'Fifty years progress of British agriculture', *Journal of the Royal Agricultural Society of England* (Series 3), I (1890), pp. 20–37.

CHANNING, F. A., *The Truth about the Agricultural Depression* (London, Longmans, 1897).

GRAHAM, P. A., *The Revival of English Agriculture* (London, Jarrold, 1899).

HAGGARD, SIR H. RIDER. *Rural England* (London, Longmans, 1902).

HALL, SIR A. D., *A Pilgrimage of British Farming* (London, John Murray, 1913).

HUTCHESON, A. 'The past and future of Scottish agriculture', *Transactions of the Highland and Agricultural Society* (5th series), XI (1899), pp. 121–35.

JEFFERIES, R., *Hodge and His Masters* (London, Smith Elder, 1880).

MCCONNELL, P., 'Experiences of a Scotsman on the Essex clays', *Journal of the Royal Agricultural Society of England* (Series 3), II (1891), pp. 311–25.

SCOTT, J. 'British farming and foreign competition', *Transactions of the Highland and Agricultural Society* (5th series), III (1893), pp. 112–29.